Awakening Within the System
Evolution, Not Revolution

Nathan Z Townley

COPYRIGHT© 2016
A Global Band of Light Book
(The Global Band of Light Project)
Seattle, WA

Copyright© 2016 by Nathan Z Townley

Published in the United States by *Global Band of Light, Inc.*

Important Note: This book is not intended as a substitute for the medical recommendations of physicians and other health-care providers. Rather, it is offered as a supplementary guide that may be used to assist a balanced lifestyle and optimum wellness. The publisher and author assume no responsibility for any adverse effects or consequences resulting from the use of any of the suggestions discussed in this book. This information has not been evaluated by the Food and Drug Administration. Various modalities are listed in this book because many people have found them helpful. These listings are in no way advertisements and no one has paid to be listed in this book. The author has included alternative wellness modalities and products that may help in your quest for optimum health and happiness.

All rights reserved. No part of this publication may be reproduced or transmitted in any form or by any means, electronic or mechanical, including photocopying, recording, or any information storage and retrieval system now known or to be invented for public or private use, without prior written permission from the publisher and/or author.

Printed in the United States of America

Front and Rear Cover Art: Indigo Dog Design/Rhonda Dicksion (www.indigodog.com)
Interior Design: Norma McReynolds
Edited by: Julie Cooper
Illustrator: Chris Basumatary

Website: www.NathanZTownley.com

Library of Congress Cataloging-in-Publication Data
Townley, Nathan Z
  Awakening within the system: evolution, not revolution / Nathan Z Townley.
    p. cm
  ISBN 978-0-9862658-0-8
    1. New spirituality 2. Global change 3. Personal growth (psychology) 4. New consciousness
    I. Title

2015900841

"This is without doubt the best book to come along on this subject for a very long time. I read it cover to cover and have underlined 80% of it. That's unheard of for me! Nathan has absolutely nailed what it means to fully awaken from the dream we have been living for thousands of years. He shows how we have created a false 3D world based upon separation, duality, shortage, fear and suffering, aided and abetted by those who have found it convenient to keep us in locked into that dream. But even while he explains how they have kept us asleep, there is no blame implied. Aligning with my concept of *Radical Forgiveness*, he shows that the only way to break free from the chains that bind us is to see the perfection in our having created these institutions for a purpose, (which is to awaken), love ourselves for having created them and then, with awareness, disengage energetically from them. I highly recommend this book. For my students, it will required reading from now on."

~ **Colin Tipping**, Author of the ***Radical Forgiveness Series*** and ***Spiritual Intelligence at Work***

"A wonderful book written by an excellent author—everyone should buy this book!"

~ **Margaret Mcelroy**, Channel for the Divine Soul known as Maitreya, Author of ***Stories Along the Way, The Energy of Life*** and ***Intuition and You***

"*Awakening Within the System* can help you understand the deep changes going on in the world today, where you fit into the picture, and how you can more easily and joyfully navigate the energies. Nathan Z Townley brilliantly describes our current 3D Octopus world that keeps us in bondage. He dares to pull back the curtain on the true drama being played out, offering concrete ways to rise above and move into the higher energetic world we are meant to inhabit. More than a good book to read, it is a soul-calling to be attained. Read it. Absorb it. Live it."

~ **Krysta Gibson**, Publisher of ***New Spirit Journal*** and Author of ***Anything is Possible***

"As our world becomes more complex and more polarized around multiple issues, it is important to remember that we are all interconnected. This is particularly true when it serves the needs of the systems around us to promote greater polarization and individuality that keeps us from hearing what our hearts tell us—we are here to work together and care for one another.

Nathan Townley helps us see the world in a new way. He provides important food for thought and challenges us to listen to our own inner understanding and to honor our own knowing.

Whether you agree or disagree is not important. That you take time to think about the ideas and concepts in this book is highly important, allowing yourself to reach new understandings in your life. Nathan challenges us to remember the many facets of our connection—as well as our disconnection when things go awry. This book helps provide a deep, inner peace that comes from broader connections with others and is well worth your time.

~ **Teresa Rafael**, MSW, President
Teresa Rafael Consulting, Inc.—Facilitating Growth and Change

"The idea around awakening is to recognize your power and live fully within it. This book provides very practical information to the person embarking on their self-journey of awakening in a world that has been run by the 'powers that be' for so very long. I highly recommend this well-written and thought provoking book. You may not agree with everything, but there are core truths here that give you a perspective and direction that will sustain you as you move through your 'Odyssey.' Warning: If you want to keep living with your senses being numbed out and giving away your power, don't read this book."

~ **Valeria Moore**, Author of *Healer Wisdom*

"*Awakening Within the System* reveals our current global environmental construct for what it is. We are offered a brilliant opportunity to become responsible for our future experiences and fulfill our personal contribution to society's evolution."

~ **Moneca Jardey**, Founder
World Leadership Training Academy

"*Awakening Within the System: Evolution, Not Revolution*, is a clear and passionate read about the vibrational shift and spiritual awakening that is presently occurring across our planet. Nathan Townley offers an encouraging view of the long process of evolution that humanity has been experiencing since the beginning of our existence on Earth. Many authors speak of the shifting frequencies as threatening, perhaps even the 'end of the world.' Nathan's take on this is a positive one: that we are once again becoming one with our highest selves; we are reclaiming our original selves with the added perspective of having worked through many difficult energy frequencies. Coming out the other side of a very long evolutionary process, we are emerging as unique beings who are experts at manifestation and at moving through lower frequencies."

~ **Kriss Erickson**, Author of *Before There Were Words*,
Sky Eyes, *Brownbird's Luck* and *Journey to Brodantia*

CONTENTS

ACKNOWLEDGEMENTS ix
INTRODUCTION xi
CHAPTER 1:   Shifting Foundations 1
CHAPTER 2:   Salamander at My Door 5
CHAPTER 3:   The Vista Point 15
CHAPTER 4:   Creating the Uncreated 25
CHAPTER 5:   The Illusion of Separation 33
CHAPTER 6:   The 3D Octopus 41
CHAPTER 7:   The Systems of the Octopus 53
CHAPTER 8:   Traps Within the 3D Matrix 85
CHAPTER 9:   The Global Band of Light Project 103
CHAPTER 10: 5D Systems in Action 117
CHAPTER 11: The Universal Laws 127
CHAPTER 12: Unplugging from the Matrix 135
CHAPTER 13: Mastering Yourself 147
CHAPTER 14: Awakening the Giant Within 165
CHAPTER 15: Foundations for Healing:
             Bridging the 3D World to the 5D World 179
CHAPTER 16: Tools for Transformation 205
CHAPTER 17: The Return to Cosmic Consciousness 223
AFTERWORD 235
RESOURCES 245
GLOSSARY 249
ABOUT THE AUTHOR 261

ACKNOWLEDGEMENTS

Thank you to the many teachers and helpers along my path, both here and beyond the veil. A very special note of thanks to Z—I am in deep gratitude for your loving presence, constantly nudging me to remember who I am. What an amazing journey you have commenced with me—I can't wait for more.

I respectfully acknowledge and express appreciation to the Masters of Light for showing us the path to walk and walking it beside us. I also thank the Angelic Order for Lighting our way.

I am deeply grateful to my amazing wife and twin flame, Ruth, for her unwavering love, faith and support and allowing me the time to write this book; my beautiful mom, who has always been there for me and is my real-life Angel; my sister Teresa for her love, humor, never-ending encouragement and wisdom throughout my life; and my father, who agreed to provide such vivid experiential teachings in my life—it took great love to play such a challenging role.

Thanks also to my many soul-family friends and Tribe: Julie C., Vicki Lynn S., Meisha R., Valeria M., Larry S., Tawn H., Pam C., Marion H., Dianne D., Collen M., Moneca J., Michelle D., Kathy I., Monty B., Carol B., Chris J., and Kriss & Michael E.—thank you for your friendship and support. I love you all.

Otis, thank you my dear friend for choosing to stay.

Last, but not least, I honor the Cherokee Nation Elders and all of my Cherokee ancestors. Your guidance, teachings and presence is heartfelt and sacred to me. Running Wind, we did it—together.

INTRODUCTION

A truth's initial commotion is directly proportional to how deeply the lie was believed. It wasn't the world being round that agitated people, but that the world wasn't flat. When a well-packaged web of lies has been sold gradually to the masses over generations, the truth will seem utterly preposterous and its speaker a raving lunatic.

~ Dresden James

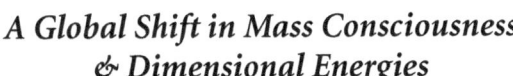

A Global Shift in Mass Consciousness & Dimensional Energies

We collectively stand at a large precipice on our planet. A passageway is before us and our challenge is not only to recognize that this passageway exists, but to navigate through it. What is this passageway? It is a dimensional doorway that represents the end of a very long journey. It is a bridge by which we can return to far higher states of consciousness as compared to our current state. It is a portal to the next expansion of our collective evolution; one that no longer involves living in duality, where we feel separate from each other, our Source and mother Earth. Our planet is going through a profound transformation (unbeknownst to many people) and is wrapping up the end of a very long cycle at a cosmic level. Gaia (the soul essence of our planet) is entering a higher vibration, as are we, if we open ourselves to this evolution.

What does this mean at an individual level? We are being given a tremendous opportunity to heal from our vast and varied experiences and begin a brand new adventure upon a new Earth. Throughout the upcoming pages, I speak of a 3D (3rd dimension), 4D (4th dimension) and 5D (5th dimension) Earth. These dimensional comparisons are energetic and vibrational in nature, but they are also multidimensional and interdimensional.

The 3rd dimension exists upon a platform of duality, whereas a 5th dimensional reality does not—it is free of polarity between low vibrational and high vibrational energies. Brought down to the final denominator, the transformation occurring is simple: it's a choice of *fear versus love*. If we were to deduce all human emotions down to a final sum equation, we are left with only these two emotions. Fear is an illusion outside of a 3rd dimensional construct, so in essence, there is nothing *but* love.

The 4th dimension, as it stands for us currently, is acting as a bridge between the 3rd and 5th dimensional energies. As we venture higher in our individual and collective consciousness levels we literally vibrate faster and higher in octave. As we morph and transition to new vibratory levels, we also shift into a higher dimension. At an experiential level, it is as if we have lived in a goldfish bowl (3D perspective) and then graduate to a swimming pool (4D perspective). There, we experience a much broader perception of life as we learn and remember more about ourselves and each other. We continue to vibrate even higher as we raise our levels of awareness and consciousness until we find ourselves within a vast ocean. We begin to notice ourselves within each other and we remember our connectivity. We find ourselves in a huge sea where we finally realize that we are an inherent part of it as well (5D perspective). This process of self actualization is not a destination, but rather an ongoing infinite experience in the evolvement of our soul-level consciousness.

We have lived within these third dimensional energies for a very long time. Currently, many are experiencing within a 4D reality as we continue our ascension to Earth's 5D destination. Each dimensional level requires far greater conscious awareness, growth, evolution and the remembrance of ourselves as the divine Beings that we all are. Many of us are quite literally straddling dimensions as we learn to navigate the intense new energies and allow them (or not) to settle within us. When we are not in alignment with these frequencies and we resist major changes in our lives, we cannot grow and evolve. Life can, and usually does, become very challenging for us. The more we awaken to the unlimited potential that we are, the faster we realize that we have outgrown the fish bowl and are ready to embrace the new paradigm.

There is a much larger vista from which to launch our inner journey towards the truth of who we really are. This platform allows us to break the chains and free ourselves. It allows us to unplug from the 3D matrix and instead plug into the magic and wonder of the newly arriving higher energies. Once we do this, we begin to live authentically and as the divine Beings of Light that we have always been.

The Powers That Were

Our various societies and civilizations have existed within systems that were, over time, architected by those who desired to have power over humanity. They (and their lineages) designed and implemented the systems and institutions in which we have historically lived in a way that greatly benefitted them.

The origin and history of the powers that were is a topic for a different book. The intent of this book is to provide a greater perspective for the experiences that we ourselves have chosen to experience within this unique matrix. We have been taught to divide the world into "good or evil," but this simplistic view limits our understanding of our experiences and our capabilities as co-creators. We have arrived at an intersection in consciousness where the critical question has become how we will define the energy in which we collectively move forward. Will we choose the same worn-out path of separation, violence, conflict and conformity of thought? Or, will we take responsibility for our evolution so that we elevate our frequency and consciousness enough to bridge the gap into a new way of Being? The lower vibratory systems are winding down very rapidly, and even in the midst of what appears on the surface to be greater chaos. Energetically, chaos is required to redefine order at a higher frequency level.

Humanity is quickly evolving into a higher octave of itself as the newly arriving energies are no longer supporting agendas that harm humanity in any way. Only that which is energetically capable of vibrating at a much higher level will remain in this new world that is upon us.

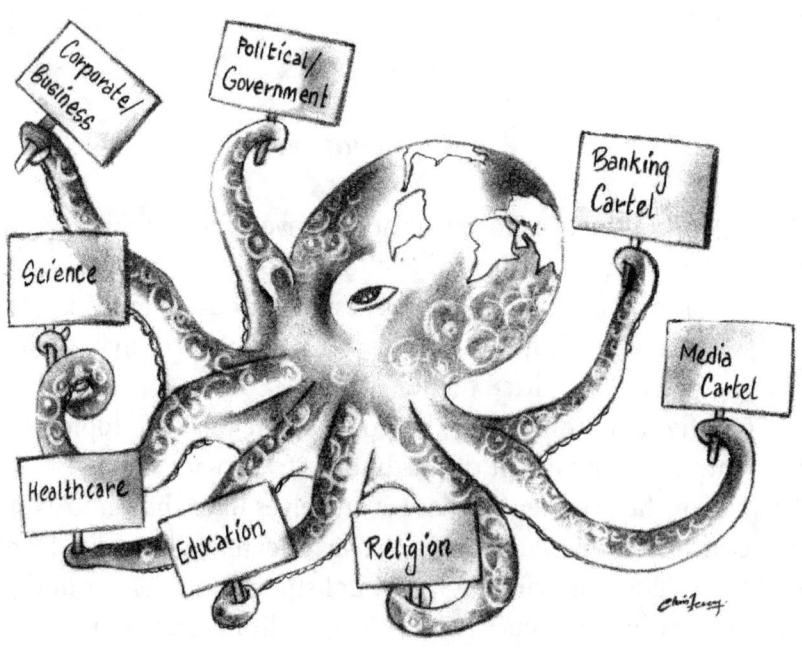

The 3D Octopus

Throughout this book, I refer to a "3D octopus" as a synonym for the powers that were. These individuals that function out of mainstream attention are playing a crucial role as humanity is awakening, and their roots are extremely deep. They have greatly shaped the way that we view and experience "reality." They have been an integral part of our experience on this planet over many, many decades. We cannot truly understand our past, nor the excitement of our future, until we are willing to understand what has occurred beyond our awareness.

I had a very profound dream many years ago about a giant octopus that ran around my house trying to hide from me. It even climbed on top of my kitchen table and tried to become invisible underneath a large, but empty, sea turtle shell. Even though it tried to hide and appear dormant, it was easy for me to still see and readily examine it. This is exactly what is happening in the larger picture. We are now waking up enough to be able to see we have allowed ourselves to be sound asleep and unaware at a conscious level. As our awakening continues and accelerates, our task is to awaken within the systems that have been put into place. We are to examine and understand how and most importantly, why, we have collectively allowed ourselves to live within such deep slumber. *The willingness to examine our past is the key to releasing it and moving forward into the 5D world.*

The more I read about the octopus as a totem animal and sea creature the more I realized how appropriate it was to this book: "The octopus is primarily a bottom-dweller, does not have a spine, is quite mobile and can move very fast. It is a master of camouflage and disguises. The octopus pulls a secondary veil over reality by injecting a thick, black ink into the waters as a method of escape, creating chaos and leaving those near it lost and confused. It is able to shape-shift to match any surrounding so that it blends in un-noticed."[1] The octopus reminds us that nothing is as it seems, behind the veil of this reality. When we have the courage to peek beyond this now very thin veil, it creates an opening in our consciousness and our awareness that allows truth to rush in.

The 3D octopus has given humanity a spiritual opportunity to further evolve via a global stage. For those of you familiar with animal totems and what they symbolize, both the octopus and the sea turtle have enormous meanings attached to them. After really pondering this dream, I understood that the intended meaning for me was about examining the octopus and understanding that there is a higher reality to which we can anchor, breaking the spell under which we have lived for so long.

The sea turtle in my dream is symbolic of cosmic order. The shell represents the heavens and the body signifies the Earth. Mother Earth (Gaia) has greatly suffered under the systems created by this octopus. It is time for Gaia to be restored and healed and time for us to reclaim our rightful place as stewards of this amazing planet, not destroyers of it. The octopus and its tentacles (systems) appear to be the perfect representation of the large, intricate web of contradictions and illusions that are common-place within the current systems that are in place. We are finding out that so much of what we have firmly believed to be absolute truth—is not, and we are realizing that the only real measure of truth is found within.

These systems encompass every branch of our society and include governments and their political systems, dogmatic religions, corporate conglomerates, the banking/financial systems, housing, education, healthcare, mainstream science, recorded history, our food supply, ecology and the mainstream media that is quite literally currently owned and controlled by the octopus. These are the front lines used to hold the illusion in place, but the foundations are falling apart and fading into the Light of exposure.

---

1 What's Your Sign: www.whats-your-sign.com (2014)

The systems that we see failing are doing so because they are no longer a vibrational match for the new consciousness in our world. Our outer world always reflects our inner worlds and this is where the true change is happening. As we grow and remember who we are (our expansion of consciousness) the outer realities that we experience expand as well and mirrors our new state of beingness as a collective.

One may not easily see the large, well-hidden facade created by the octopus. What is real is underneath *what appears to be real* and it requires our analysis from a different perspective than we are accustomed to. When we place the 3D octopus upon the stage and take a close look at it we reveal how we have arrived where we currently are.

Our enmeshment with the octopus has happened because the octopus is simply a metaphor and a manifested reality for the experiences that humanity has chosen to create for itself at a spiritual level. Everything we experience is a creation of our internal state and how much or little we remember about who we really are. Our internal states are expanding and our "memories" are becoming clearer every day. The primary drama that has played itself out throughout history has been one of a deep analysis of how we intermingle with all types of power—the perceived power over us and how that reflects the level of empowerment and worthiness we each feel. The octopus has provided a perfect platform that has allowed humanity to experience every angle of power play.

As mass consciousness continues to rise, our sense of internal power is returning, but in a far different way than we have ever defined power in our past. We speak of our rights being dwindled down to nothing these days, and that is very accurate, but it has been a direct reflection of our inner worlds. It has expressed as apathy, feelings of powerlessness and the resulting acquiescence.

As we play the game of reality on the stage of life, energy often continues into the "absurd" until we are finally able to see the drama we have created for ourselves collectively. Once we can "see" it, the hologram collapses and we then move on to the next chosen collective examination of a different type of reality.

This is exactly what has happened in the US 2016 presidential elections—we are now into the absurd, which is the escalation and grand finale of this experience. The absurd hastens the awakening because it often forces people to sit up and take far greater notice of their reality so that it can be altered collectively.

The octopus is to be looked at, acknowledged with love and acceptance and then released, allowing our emotions around it and the systems to be felt, processed and healed. This is transmutation in action as we then move forward, not in anger or revenge, but in our collective Love and Light. Part of our reclaiming our Divine Power is taking full responsibility for our collective manifestations. It is the journey away from victimhood and embracing and remembering just how powerful we are as co-creators. When humanity remembers its own level of creational ability, shifting paradigms will seem like child's play. Anger and revenge only serve to manifest more of the same—it will *never* truly help move us forward as so many believe. The revolution that must occur is the revolution of consciousness, not a revolution that involves yet more war and bloodshed. The Universe is asking loudly if we as the collective have grown tired enough of the 3D matrix to move past it? Have we sufficiently evolved enough to grasp that violence of any kind is counter-intuitive to peace of any kind? This process is an important part of our recall. We have never been victims on this planet, as much as it might seem so from our limited 3D perspectives.

> *One can be awake within the systems of the octopus and see through its charades and yet still not grasp the higher spiritual reality that is unfolding all around them.*

Many people are living in anger and victimhood and have become stuck in their fight against the systems that they see as corrupt. The following chapters can help unravel a much larger picture of the true transformation that is occurring. We are powerful and intentional co-creators who deliberately chose to incarnate here for the opportunity of this unprecedented and extraordinary evolutionary experience.

> *The dark is inherent within the Light. When all colors are added together, there is black. Although we can no longer visually see the individual colors that we originally added to the palette, they are there in vibration. So it is, living in a dualic world, where we have learned to shun and ostracize the so-called "darkness" instead of remembering that the darkness is an amalgamated potion of All That Is—just as we each are. When we embrace and love that which we consider to be "dark" we are in essence, loving All That Is and ourselves in **totality** as we transmute the dark energies into Love. Fighting or hating the darkness is called resistance and when we are in resistance to any form of energy, we are simply creating more of that which we do not want. It is time to remember how energy works and how it plays out in the material, manifest world. We are each here to transform the lower frequencies into love, at every level of our Being.*

The Gift of the Octopus

As you journey through this book, you may realize that the octopus has actually been a large gift to humanity, acting as a catalyst for our awakening. It has played its part very well, providing contrast for the Light and soul-level growth upon a stage designed for evolution. The old adage that "everything is always in divine and perfect order" applies to the duality in which we have lived. It is through the contrast between the low and high vibrations that we have learned so much and are now defining what our priorities are in our lives. Contrast "highlights" vibrational differences and provides greater possibilities through freewill choice. It is the see-saw on the playground of life that ensures a 3D reality offers the rich and priceless experiences that it does. Contrast offers us the vastness of *perception* through the vastness of *perspective*. The narrowing of our consciousness within 3D has served to allow tremendous growth that is invaluable to us all. The great influx of advanced energies is gifting us with a brand new focal point—our spiritual growth and the remembrance of why we are here.

As we awaken from our slumber, we awaken to and within the systems of the octopus. At a soul level, we agreed to play within them for a limited time. As we awaken, it is common that we want to alter our participation in the current systems because our vibration is no longer in alignment with them at their foundational level. We begin to see them for what they are and realize that we are *far* more powerful than we have been led to believe. Our consciousness shifts from the false belief that we are all separate, to the desire that new systems be put into place that serve everyone at a core level. The shift in systems that is occurring is not in any way connected to a political cause or party. You cannot embrace 5D consciousness through the old 3D model of experience. The awakening is very simply put, a soul/heart level remembrance that we were never separate to begin with.

I invite you to journey through the following pages with an open heart and mind, discovering what an important, special part you play in creating the new matrix for our amazing planet. The new foundational energies of 5D are ushering in our next grander experience *together*. May we remember our oneness of heart and Spirit as we continue along this transformational journey.

~ *Nathan Z Townley**

---

* Author's Note: I have capitalized a few words in this book that have not traditionally been capitalized and may not follow what is typically considered proper spelling. This was intentional, because my use of these particular words is intended as a sacred energy. My use of the word "Universal" and "Universal Laws" denotes (to me) a divine part of our cosmos, therefore, capitalization felt appropriate to me. I also capitalize the word "Light" because our divine essence consists of Light. The English language (and all languages in general) are quite limiting when trying to describe or share a broader energetic concept, especially when referring to our divine, spiritual nature. I have taken a bit of "creative liberty" in the hopes that the ideas are received with their fullness of intention.

CHAPTER 1

Shifting Foundations

*Illusion meanders over the senses,
like fog caressing the moonlight.*

Reality is holographic. That which appears to be so very real and fixed to us is actually quite fluid energetically. Our reality changes with the slightest shift of our perception and observation. It is an interactive canvas in constant motion and we each hold a brush in our hand. Just as one might walk around a third-dimensional object such as a piece of sculpture and observe how it looks different at various angles, so does our reality shift and look different from multidimensional perspectives. This is the basis of the truth that no "true or false", "right or wrong", "good or bad" really exists—there are only individual interpretations of one's infinite choices, opinions, perspectives and observations. Reality then, is a *highly personal* interactive journey and a deep inner experience that offers the opportunity for the pure expression of each soul and a collective expression of mass consciousness. A hologram is a medium that allows a reality to be observed as form.

A crucial part of the inner change that we are all experiencing is a process that asks us to let go of the many fixed, false beliefs about our reality that we have been conditioned with throughout our lives. We are being asked to replace them with new, Universal Truths based upon our divine nature and oneness. We are building a new beginning, but we cannot build it on top of an old paradigm that is no longer applicable to humanity as a solid, sustainable foundation. We cannot stack two vibrations that are incongruent on top of each other and expect a new and grander paradigm to emerge. A more apt description of this colossal change is a *transmutation* of energies—meaning, the new world will not have the old as its foundation.

The old dualic paradigm is being transmuted and transformed into new higher energies and what does not desire to transmute through freewill choice will not be a part of the new world that is upon us. Energetically, through the Universal Law of "like energies attract like energies," it will not be possible. Remember, we are graduating out of the world of duality into a new framework that is architected through harmony, collaboration and oneness. The foundation is simple—*unconditional love* and respect for all other life forms.

If you doubt that the powers that were will just go away, it will not work like that. You would be correct in thinking that those who have designed these broken systems for their own gain aren't going to suddenly wake up and change their ways (although, some definitely will as the frequencies continue to rise). Instead, the vibrational essence that makes up the very foundation of the 3D systems is crumbling because the *energies* that supported it are quickly fading from this reality. They are incongruent with what is now arriving. All that we need do is to consciously embrace these higher frequencies and as we do, we assist in releasing the old energies from our planet. It is not about waiting for the powers that were to step down or change their ways (that will likely never happen)—it is about *our awareness* and understanding of the new frequencies and our enmeshment with them that will do the work.

Our own deeply personal inner processes and inner healing affect the global shift underway. Everything and everyone is intricately connected in a web of existence and we are all creating it as we go. In this way, every single soul upon this planet is crucial in importance to the greater outcome. We are all important pieces in this universal puzzle and no person's contributions are any less important or meaningful than another. It would be like saying that the apples are more important than the crust in an apple pie. Each one of us contributes a highly unique and critical ingredient to the outcome—all 7 plus billion of us.

Over time, we have became immersed in many agendas, designed by the powers that were, that were not in the best interest of humanity or Gaia. We were led to believe that life, and our worthiness of it, revolved around doing, doing, doing and in the process we forgot that it is in our *beingness* state that we feel our innate divine connection. We forgot that *we* are the creators of our lives, not the dictates of the octopus and all of its unenlightened systems in place to keep us in slumber. We have forgotten so much, at the expense of our connectedness with our fellow brothers and sisters on this journey.

> *Beingness is the space between Spirit and matter. It is a state of oneness with our highest Selves and our natural state if we allow it. Beingness is the space that allows all matter to be highlighted as we observe it, and Spirit to be felt through matter. It is the bridge that connects us to all dimensions at once within our consciousness. It is in reality, the state of no state. If you wish to observe beingness, nature is the grandest example of all. Observe a tree or a flower—there is nothing but pure creational energy residing in beingness.*

Recall

You will not find external "proof" of who you truly are. There is (so far, but that is rapidly changing and it does exist as sacred geometry, cutting-edge neuroscience and new DNA mapping tools) no science, no academia or mathematical formula that will prove the contents within this book. If you need empirical evidence, you will only find it when you open yourself to the sacredness of your very nature. Your validity and greatness lies within you, not within test scores, awards or 3D successes. It is a solo journey that only you can take, as all truth and remembrance is within.

One only needs to begin asking the questions to receive the answers. Get quiet, go within and ask the questions that reveal what is truly behind your individual perception of reality. Ask for the ability to decode the illusion. The magic is in the asking.

We all have internal "truth meters" but we have been tremendously cut off from this awareness. It has been deeply suppressed, but as we awaken, so does our ability to decode what's truth and what is not.

However, the perception of "truth" is highly subjective, and easily distorted when we allow others to define our truths for us. Your truth *is* your reality. It is your truth through your perspective only. Someone might have a reality that consists of poverty or disease—but do you want that to be your truth? Reality is flexible, malleable and conforms to consciousness, thought and intention. Truth does not follow or conform to manufactured facts or lab tests, as the octopus has ingrained in humanity's consciousness.

One thing is certain: the large shift in consciousness that is underway is manifesting itself as a major recalibration of the global systems. Most of the players that are currently upon center stage have a soul-level choice to make—to continue resisting the new paradigm and new foundations being built all around them, or to join the rest of humanity as we come together to clean-up our planet and advance to new levels of conscious awareness. We each hold the seeds of change. The seeds themselves are being transformed into an amazing new reality that so many of us deeply seek.

CHAPTER 2

Salamander at My Door

The Changing of the Guard

A few years ago, I awoke in the middle of the night and remembered that I had left something in my car and needed to bring it in out of the cold. I put my robe on, opened the front door and noticed a cute little orange salamander sitting right in the middle of my threshold. I thought it very strange that a salamander would even be awake at 2:00 am on such a cold night and right in the middle of a brightly lit threshold, but then I remembered that salamanders are nocturnal. I gently stepped over it, making a mental note in my half-asleep brain to contemplate this more when I was fully awake. As I re-entered my house, the salamander hadn't moved an inch. I said goodnight to it and made my way back to the warmth of my bed.

Having already had many experiences with totem animals appearing to me with messages, I decided the next morning to research what the salamander represented and why it appeared to me in such a way. This little messenger in Native American tradition is all about *change* arriving at our doors as well as renewal, transformation, enlightenment, rebirth and growth. The salamander asks us to evolve in our own lives. As we navigate through the tremendous change occurring on this planet, the salamander asks us to adapt to the changes and embrace them. I instantly knew that this little messenger represented our evolution and was going to be part of this very book because *we all have a salamander at our door* right now, beckoning us towards a new way of life.

Humans can be so very resistant to change and we often see any change as frightening or bad. Many of us avoid change at all cost because it disturbs our comfort zones. Our resistance causes us great pain, worry and unnecessary stress. Going with the flow has never been so important. It is when we feel disconnected from our Source and each other (as the systems have taught us to do) that we find change so frightening and threatening. The history books are riddled with examples of humans acting out their fears and the ensuing wars and confrontations around impending change, even when they greatly disliked their current state of affairs! Many are quick to resist or discredit something new just because it is unfamiliar to them. Change is the vehicle for our metamorphosis. We cannot get from point A to point B without, in our case, *large* movement.

Why do we resist change so much? There is the obvious answer around fear of the unknown, but I sense that at a deeper level it is because we have lost touch with our inner voice and intuition. Within the 3D systems, we have lost the ability to accurately judge what is in resonance with our inner truth and what is not. We are numbed out by the incongruity that is inherent within the current systems and we have depended upon others to define many of our truths for us. We have handed over our freedom to make higher vibrational choices for ourselves and our planet. This disconnect is apparent at every turn. Apathy and depression follow when we shut ourselves down from the inside out. Our health and happiness depends upon a strong connection to the highest aspect of who we really are.

The concept of our lives remaining static is just a facet of the grand illusion we live in. Every single atom and molecule is in constant transformation in every second. There has never been anything or anyone that is *not* in a constant state of change. Furthermore, out of this constant change (which can appear to be very chaotic while it is happening) comes evolution—ours and the Universe at large. The true message of my little salamander friend was that we are sitting upon the threshold of a huge leap in our evolution and to be ready for it. Indeed, to embrace it with an open heart and with great anticipation and positive intention.

Awakened Judgment

We are all *feeling* the call of urgent change in the air and it is part of our awakening process. This change is not one of mass destruction or the end of the world. There is no "judgment day" upon us, only the *awakened judgment* to stop resisting the changes at hand and welcome in a new paradigm of oneness and unity. It doesn't matter what the powers that were are "trying to do" in the world once we recognize that our collective positive intent is *far* more powerful. This is why it is so critical that we stop giving our "consent" energetically and unite as the higher frequency force we are capable of being. This cohesion can be achieved through pure intention (or prayer, as some prefer to label the energy of manifestation and co-creation) but it will also be achieved as like minds and like vibrations come together to build new common visions, through their awakened judgment. This collective restructuring will be the basis for all new and/or transformed global systems.

The new direction in which we are rapidly traveling is towards global harmony, but what does that really look like? It's the expansion of our peripheral vision, metaphorically speaking, to remember that we are all intricately connected as individual parts of the whole. We are inseparable parts of each other, of Gaia and all of her kingdoms, our Universe and our Source. We are here as an expression and expansion of Source energy. We each possess every particle of the Universe within us and we have direct access to all of the mysteries held within it.

When we observe things that cause us to feel pain and sorrow, the sadness that we feel is the incongruence between our inner core-level knowledge and what we are witnessing around us. Beyond this time and space experience in this 3D vibration of duality, we are totally aware of our oneness and how deeply and intricately we all dance with each other. We are greatly affected by all others, not just in our personal lives, but even by a stranger who lives across the globe. When one person (or animal) feels and experiences pain (or joy) it reverberates through the whole and we are all affected at levels we are not currently aware of.

Thoughts, beliefs and feelings are very powerful, as they set a course of action into play that affects all of us at an energetic level. Many people are completely unaware that this is happening because they can't visually see it. We feel it subconsciously though and are affected by it, whether the thoughts are positive or negative. That is why you cannot do anything to another that you do not also do to yourself—it is impossible, as there is no such truth as our being divided or separate from each other energetically. We may each have our own letter in the alphabet soup, but we are all in the same soup bowl together. Our arguments that one race, color, religion, ethnicity, sexual orientation or gender is better or more valid than another is no more based upon truth or reality than arguing that a "B" is better than a "Z" in our bowl of alphabet soup. There's no such thing as *better or superior*, there are only *different* letters with countless expressions and every one of them was created from the exact same recipe with the exact same core ingredients.

The 3D octopus thrives upon the disharmony and discord among us, and that is why the systems were designed around separation, power, ego dominance, scarcity, violence and competition. Based upon the current state of the world, we have obviously bought into these falsehoods over and over throughout our history until they became the new norm for "civilized" societies.

You Are a Key Shifter

We sense and feel impending changes before they actually manifest, and so many are feeling the tremendous energetic and spiritual "nudge" into the new paradigm. How we perceive change and how in-tune we are with our core determines how we experience the planetary shift. So many of us are trained from childhood to go into fear and as long as we remain in fear, we are immobile and feel powerless. Fear actually shuts down all of our intuitive gifts that we each have. Our intuition is our GPS system that can be relied upon to always give us correct, truthful information from our Higher Selves. Most people do not know how to use this gift and this lack of awareness has been intentional. Fear puts us in "lock down" mode and we go into a survival state, which is not conducive to hearing, seeing, or feeling our internal sense of direction. Fear prevents us from connecting to the wisdom of the Universe to obtain valid, truthful information.

We tend to think that true change happens outside of our control and we question how we can achieve large change at a local or global level. Remember that no pyramid exists without the foundational stones holding it up. The octopus has convinced many people that only governments, politicians and leaders can effect great change and we have allowed them this level of empowerment. This has supported the subconscious idea that citizens are powerless unless we go through the octopus' systems, which are designed to remain as they are. The truth is that change begins in our hearts, minds, homes, communities and *most importantly, through our intentions and visions of a better way for all.*

Many people fear letting go of the old paradigm because it's all that they know. It is quite comfortable and familiar, even if it is horrid compared to the new 5D paradigm now arriving. When we become rigid in our beliefs and seated in this illusionary reality, it can be challenging to expand our minds and consciousness in regards to change. Mass consciousness has been deeply programmed to be resigned to a life built upon fear, struggle and lack. We resign ourselves to "this is just the way it is and it isn't going to change."

When we change the programs within our minds, we change our capacity for an alternative reality. If you have thoughts such as "That never worked in the past, why would it work now?" The answer is, because there has *never* been a time such as this, in these exact energies. We are here to successfully shift paradigms and you are a *key shifter*. Know that what is happening is rendering a world that we have only dreamed about, but deep inside, we have not believed it was possible. It is more than possible, it is here—right now. The complete hologram has already manifested energetically, but the evidence of these manifestations is just now coming forth. Failing is no longer even a probable reality, even though we can't see the entire picture yet.

We have all heard that knowledge is power. This is quite true, but in this case, *awareness* is the key to navigating the many changes at hand. As you become able to view the old systems for what they are and understand why they are failing, not only are you able to remain calm and in positive expectation, but you assist all of humanity by holding space for the new to arrive. Greater awareness about this process will allow you to live in a state of deep and genuine inner peace and calm. You will feel great excitement as you realize and understand that just past this brief feeling of chaos is a new world that is far different from the old one. This higher dimension is palpable and it makes everything now occurring just a small blip we are all going through to actualize a new reality that works far better for all souls upon this Earth, not just a few.

There truly is *magnificence* on the horizon. Embrace it and trust the larger picture of our evolution. It is returning us to the sovereign, peaceful Beings that we inherently are, without the influences and overlay of the 3D matrix.

Our Metamorphosis

Many people find themselves searching for a deeper meaning and purpose in their life. Their lives may feel like an empty shell during this transmutation process and they have no clue why or how to change it. Suddenly, material possessions and pleasures, careers, houses and fat bank accounts that used to be the sought after goal and blueprint for success, no longer bring the happiness and contentment they once did. It feels like something big is missing, but you can't pinpoint exactly what it is. The closest description might be "a longing for something that has no language."

Our world is shifting so fast we can barely keep up. Lives are turning upside down overnight in many cases, yet the turmoil is providing the perfect bridge to reach what we are seeking in the deepest parts of ourselves. It is causing great fear and unrest in those who are not yet awakened to the underlying cause and effect of the much larger picture being painted. At the cosmic level, we are also experiencing greatly accelerated energies. You may have felt that time has sped up and your day might seem *much* shorter for no apparent reason. This is because our entire Universe is involved in this great shift and our sense of time as we have known it will continue to morph. Our planet and our Universe is traveling into vastly different frequencies than it ever has before and this is the major catalyst for the planetary changes we are experiencing. These energies are providing an extremely powerful catalyst for our transformation into the higher dimensional energies, where time, and many other aspects of our reality as we have known it, does not exist in the same way.

Opening Up

As we move into the higher dimensions, we will find that the way we have learned to interpret and navigate our world has significantly changed and the defining lines no longer exist. We will learn to navigate our new reality through our internal guidance systems that have evolved and synched into perfect alignment with our greater Selves.

The external framework by which we interpret and judge what is normal is evolving into far greater individual acceptance for each other as we feel safer in expressing our own "normal." The constructs of the 3D reality are collapsing to allow our perspectives to greatly expand. The methods by which we judge normalcy must now shift dramatically if we are to grasp this new paradigm and become a conscious, active part of it.

As the global changes continue and intensify, we are able to experience a deep cleansing of ourselves and our planet at a very sacred level. This cleansing is clearing out all that no longer serves us or our world. It has nothing to do with judgment, condemnation, right or wrong, good or evil. It has everything to do with embracing and calling forth our divine nature and how we treat each other, as well as Gaia.

Many people are still understandably looking outside of themselves for answers around the current global shift. This is what has been taught within the systems of the octopus. They look to their countries, their unenlightened leaders and the old structures that no longer make sense to them at their core level. They feel stifled inside what seems like an indefinable "mess," especially when there are no satisfying answers from the powers that were. They feel as if their country has fallen apart and is broken with no cure in sight. Their soul level *knowing* no longer matches what they are witnessing in the world around them. For so many, this awakening has not yet reached their conscious minds. As trained to do, they point their fingers at what seems like the obvious causes of their ills, including their government leaders, politicians, laws, courts, statutes, the economy, their jobs or the banking system.

They don't understand that all of the above are simply manifestations of the octopus and these manifestations no longer serve the new consciousness being downloaded. They are also not grasping the complex 3D game in which they have agreed to play at their soul level and that their experience in duality is wrapping up to allow a new experience to begin. This is a spiritual journey of transformation—one that we have chosen to go through, both individually and collectively. As we open ourselves to greater possibilities, that in and of itself allows these new possibilities to anchor within us.

The Fish Bowl Effect

Imagine a small goldfish bowl with many fish within it and an entire world outside of its confines. This analogy is a great portrayal of our limited reality in which we have based our beliefs upon. We have only been able to grasp a small percentage of the true nature of our greater reality, yet we think we have a broad perspective upon which to base our beliefs, judgments and societal norms.

Many will not be able to see or believe what is right in front of them. They can only see as far as the edges of the goldfish bowl and cannot see *anything* outside of the glass. When confronted with the truth they ask, "How can that be? There's no way, it's not logical. And off they go for another lap around the bowl.

What is not in energetic alignment with truth, love, unity consciousness and oneness, must transform if it is to travel with Earth to her 5D destination. This process involves conscious change and the willingness and courage to look outside the confines of the bowl.

Change is a Choice

Which reality you reside within is one-hundred percent up to you. You get to decide as the Master Co-Creator that you are. You decide with your very next thought and your very next belief about this world and those in it, followed by your next actions based upon those thoughts and beliefs. You create your own reality in every moment and you have the ability to alter it as you choose. You accomplish this through your beliefs about this matrix and your determination of your worthiness while experiencing within it.

You also possess the divine gift of freewill and may choose to create your world as threatening, frightening, angry, depressing, hard, ego-driven, dangerous, poor, or any number of adjectives that might describe aspects of the 3D world. Or, you can at any point make different choices and decisions about your reality and embrace peace, love, oneness, ease, joy, abundance, freedom and sovereignty as you connect with the higher aspect of your Self.

Ask and you shall receive—always. This is Universal Law. This is an inward journey that only you can take and it requires effort, focus and a heart-felt desire to expand YOU. Many people have no idea that they are surrounded by a non-physical Light Team of guides and angels that they have access to for immediate help and guidance, if they only *ask*. Our respective Light teams cannot interfere with our freewill. Part of giving your permission for help is in directly asking them for it. They love you deeply and are eager to assist you with this journey.

At a core level, everyone is making the choice of which reality they wish to continue experiencing. It is a soul level choice, whether we align with one dimensional world or another. This choice is not right or wrong, nor good or bad. It is simply a decision for each soul to determine, based upon what type of experiences are desired for their continuing soul evolvement.

CHAPTER 3

The Vista Point

Our lives are like holographic green screens[2] and we each create the inserted background. We project the images and backgrounds that best depict the platform we desire for our experiences and growth.

There is a roof top vista that offers a very expansive, revealing view of life. It is available to each of us and it allows us to observe life on planet Earth from a very different perspective. This higher perspective can shed much light upon who we really are and how we actually got to this current place of experiencing.

Perspectives

Webster's Dictionary defines the energy of the word *perspective* as: a) "a specific point of view in understanding things or events" and b) "the ability to see things in a true relationship." I particularly like the later as it defines the type of perspective relayed through the Vista

---

2 A "green screen" is found in a filming room in which the entire background is green and the producer then inserts any computerized background that they choose as the scenery drop. Your local news station utilizes green room technology for their weather forecasts.

Point. The true relationship that we are all seeking to understand is the relationship with and to our Highest Selves and how that soul connection inter-relates with our concept of our Source, whatever name we might attribute to this infinite, creational energy. It is our Highest Self, that sacred essence of us, that transcends the personality and ego. It extracts and encapsulates the greater meanings from our daily experiences and interactions with others. Feeling enmeshed with our Higher aspect allows us to feel integrated with our Creator and the cosmos at large.

If we feel disconnected from our Higher Self, we feel disconnected from that which we call God, Higher Power, Prime Creator, Source Energy, All that Is, etc… Our most important relationship on this journey is the alignment with our Highest Self. All else falls into place when this relationship is consciously nourished. In reality, there is no such thing as a true disconnection from your Source or your Higher Self, but when we move through life only partially awake, our predominant perspectives circle around aloneness, pain, isolation, depression, suffering, separateness, disconnection and the resultant fear energy. These energies lead us to believe that we are separate from our Source.

Many people feel a sense of disconnection because they hold the false perception that their soul Self is located somewhere outside of them; somewhere up in the ethers and someday, upon their death, they will be reunited with their soul if they are somehow "good enough." This is octopus propaganda and until we remember that our soul is housed within us (and in many dimensions and realities simultaneously and concurrently, far beyond any Earthly constraints) we will continue to feel separate, isolated and alone in this world.

To gain greater perspectives we must literally choose to mute the entire drama of the outside world. We must create quietness in our lives and psyches so that we can hear the whispers of our soul. Our Higher Self exists at a higher level of vibration than we currently do (this shift underway will re-unite us with our Highest Selves at the same vibrational level) so to feel truly connected we must do our part to raise our vibration so that we can experience that connection within. We can't be on a constant hurried run from one 3D deadline to the next and expect to feel a soul-level connection within ourselves.

Many things in our lives do not make much greater sense until and unless we are able to view them away from a non-linear, third dimensional framework. When we ponder the meaning of life solely from a linear, logical mind seated in 3D, life within this Universe and our place in it doesn't make much sense in a larger capacity. The current systems have gone to extravagant means to ensure that this is so.

This game within the matrix is a web of consciousness expressing through all of us, both individually and collectively. Although you may not recall that you are a multidimensional Being, this does not stop your other aspects from carrying on with their chosen experiences that factor into the totality of who you are. Your soul Self is ecstatic about the participatory opportunities in each and every dimension with a total understanding of the intricate connection between all of your other aspects also experiencing consciousness in a variety of ways.

When you fully realize how very indestructible you are, and that death is a tremendous illusion, you will instantly understand how magnanimous you are as pure creational energy. The greatest gift from our Source is the unrestricted use of our freewill to go forth into various space and time realities to create and experience whatever we choose to create. *We are the unfolding of Light into matter.* If that doesn't send fire racing through your veins with almost intolerable excitement and awe, I don't know what will! Just remember that to dance each dance of experience, we had to agree to some amnesia. If we fully remembered the totality of our Being, we could not play this particular 3D game within duality to the extent that we desired to from our non-physical Selves. We could not suck the nectar out of the 3D experiences that we ourselves chose to have. If we didn't fully immerse ourselves in the play happening on stage and the drama of our roles, our performances would seem empty and pointless. The energies and outcomes that we wanted to create from our Highest

Selves' perspective would be lost. It would be like *watching* a movie or play instead of actually writing and starring in it.

The life experiences we believe to be so real are truly just performances within the game of amnesia as we go about the grand productions of ourselves. In this way, there is nothing about our lives that is haphazard. We are masters at turning energy into form. It is our freewill choice whether or not to do it accidently (by default) within the amnesia or to wake up and do it with great intention and deliberation instead. When you remember how it works, your stage self allows your Higher Self to be in charge and write the script. So how do we do this? With our intention to do so—it really is that simplistic and that powerful. *Intention is freewill in action. Visualization is the spark to the fire. The emotions of gratitude and appreciation are the lighter fluid.*

Elevators of Consciousness

Imagine an elevator within a very large skyscraper. This skyscraper has a dimly lit underground parking garage and each floor has many windows that offer a particular view or perspective of the outside world, depending upon what floor you are on. Human consciousness is much like an elevator in a tall building. Over the centuries, our consciousness levels have been rising from the very low vibratory levels akin to the parking garage, where there was very little light and no outside windows. It was cold, musty and difficult to see in the dim light. The energetic vibration there was very low and it felt limited and confining.

Gradually, over centuries of linear time, we as a mass consciousness have gone up the elevator, floor by floor. With each escalation, we explored a new floor and realized that there are more windows and greater light the higher up we travel. If we choose to look outside, we notice that our perspective greatly changes with each floor. We are more aware of what is around us and inside of us. Each floor up offers a larger, broader and more expanded version of reality as more light is allowed in through our collective windows. We begin to unfurl and remember more about ourselves and our world in a grander capacity. It's part of our enlightenment and our evolution to carry us through and beyond this cycle of experience.

Things that looked so real while at the basement level are not how we believed them to be now that we are on a higher floor. Things that seemed so large to us on the first floor now look really small as we move to higher levels. And so it is with our consciousness. As we travel up each floor of the elevator, our consciousness levels grow and allow us to feel stronger connections to our Source in far more expansive ways than we ever dreamed.

The building (matrix) has been our collective metaphoric platform in which to explore and expand our consciousness. It has been all about the ride to each floor and what we observed and witnessed as we looked out. It has been a foundation for us to gain perspective about our reality from our own individual springboards. In fact, at the top level, we are able to see things in the distance that we had no idea even *existed* while we were down in the parking garage. We would have labeled them crazy and *impossible* through the lens of our very limited vision at that time. The varying frequencies inherent on each floor allowed everyone in the building to have their own highly unique ride and to choose their own escalation as they were ready to see more.

You have the power in every moment to move your perceptions up the elevator of consciousness and re-create your life from that new perspective.

You cannot think your way to the Vista Point—
you must feel and intuit your way there.

The higher we choose to go up the elevator of consciousness, the easier and faster it is to perceive ourselves more authentically. This process is never-ending, as we are infinite beings on infinite journeys and on infinite elevators. We are truly eternal beings of Light and that is our grandest blessing of all. Perception is *everything* in raising our consciousness levels. How we frame what we observe determines how we react to life and how well we understand this experience from the highest vistas of ourselves—or not. *The Vista Point* teaches us how to live from the perspective of "the Big Picture." When life is viewed from this context on a day by day basis, everything begins to make far more sense and the details simply fall into their proper place of importance. Your soul Self is *always* seeking the highest expression of **you** in every way possible, regardless of what that appears to look like and regardless of whether you label those experiences as good or bad.

Consciousness is the interface between the experience of matter and spirit. When you awaken to the 3D reality you have existed within and believed to be so real, your entire consciousness and perspective about life in this Universe greatly opens and the Vista Point becomes enormous.

Once you have experienced the vista from the rooftop deck, it's hard to go back and revel in the view from the basement; it's just not as appealing anymore. Especially since you weren't aware that there was a rooftop deck! Who knew? The real jewels to be found are outside of the illusion of this experience.

All of the Universe and cosmos is conscious. As we each go forth to create and experience our creations, we further the consciousness of All That Is, in all of existence. In essence, as we evolve from our chosen experiences, all of the cosmos evolves with us and from us in one massive stream of creational potential. It is as beautiful as is the Waltz, and we are always dancing with the Universe, either consciously or unconsciously. In our complexity as multidimensional and inter-dimensional Beings, our experiences are unlimited in all ways. Who you think you are right now is but a tiny fraction of your totality and your capabilities.

The Cage

Our awareness of the big cosmic picture has been very much like a little pet hamster that has spent its entire existence in a small cage in a child's bedroom. All that the hamster knows to be real is his little cage he calls home and the exercise wheel that spins round and round inside his cage. He can observe that his home rests upon a large piece of wood that feels safe, stable and protected. His food arrives at about the same time each day and he is happy and feels secure in his little world.

But if our little friend could climb out of his cage and jump onto the top shelf of the bookcase in the same room, but much higher up, he would quickly notice that his home sits on a large desk in a large room. What he could not see from his cage, but nevertheless remains true, is that the large room he observes is part of a very large house, which happens to be in a large neighborhood, in a large city, in a state, in a country, on planet Earth and within a Universe amongst hundreds of thousands of Universes (many with far more spiritually and technologically advanced civilizations than his own, and many that even share his DNA ancestry) and existing within many different dimensions of time and space. It could, in effect, blow his little hamster mind to take all of this in at once as he would have an explosion of consciousness that would take him into complete overwhelm, meltdown and possibly, denial and fear. But just maybe, he might also *remember* that his meager little existence within the hamster cage was an agreed upon experience so that he might extract some wonderful new understandings, teachings and perspectives from and about his little piece of home. The little hamster might now be able to recall the entire picture of his greater reality, not just a tiny piece of the puzzle that his prior limited view had offered. He might perhaps see that he is a part of something much larger than he ever thought. He might understand through his new perspective that he chose his tiny little hamster body as an appropriate vehicle so that he could fully delve into exactly what it was like to be a hamster on planet Earth, in this particular dimension of time and space reality.

Why is 3D reality often referred to as an illusion? It certainly feels real, doesn't it? As in our hamster analogy, the realities that Mr. Hamster experienced were indeed very much real to him. If he fell off his exercise wheel and broke his leg, it would really hurt and that would certainly not feel like an illusion to him. But he could not fathom that there could be more than his daily life in his little cage until he was able to gain a far greater perspective. Then, his consciousness was able to massively expand into what awaited him outside of the construct that he called normal. In this way, the belief that his cage, wheel and daily life was all that existed, was an *illusion*. He just couldn't see, feel or hear the rest of the vast picture. Our perspective of our world and life is but a tiny fraction of existence that we are able to perceive in any given moment from our current state of limited consciousness. As we move into 5th dimensional energies and return to *full consciousness and remembrance*, this veil of illusion will cease to exist.

When we begin to examine how the microcosm within us is projecting into the macrocosm outside of us (and vice-versa) then we can see the entire grand play going on. We understand how our individual and collective roles contribute to the formation of what we term "real" and how we all contribute to mass conscious beliefs about what is real. Mass consciousness is really the result of a *mass intention* sent forth to manifest into form. Mass consciousness sets the boundaries for how concepts such as oneness and unity or the very opposite of those energies such as hate, greed and separation play out.

> *Mass consciousness can be defined as "consensus thinking" at an energetic level. We manifest as a global citizenry through the sum consciousness of all involved. Imagine our world when we intentionally manifest from a collective belief in oneness, collaboration, love and unity.*

Many believe that they have no part in the direct creation of what they observe on the 6:00 p.m. news. This has served the octopus well, because it has kept humanity in a state of fear and not understanding how the outer world is manifested through us. Life never just happens to us. We are happening *as* life and *to* life, as we all create it as we go, minute by minute, day by day, century by century. How exciting it is to understand and embrace that we each have the power to create great change and build the world as we want it to be.

*We are the one's "giving reality" to all that we place
our focus, validation, acknowledgment,
energy and attention upon.*

CHAPTER 4

Creating the Uncreated

Vibrational Levels

So, how can an entire planet with 7 billion people create a large jump in their evolutionary abilities? It is helpful to remember that every particle of creation, including you, is simply made up of energy and varying levels of vibrating atoms. The denser an energy is, the slower it moves or vibrates at a sub-particle level and the more it appears to be solid and fixed to our eyes. The lighter the energy is, the faster it vibrates and moves at a subatomic particle level and the less solid it appears to our eyes. This is all basic physics of course, but crucial to understanding the subtle, yet very powerful, changes happening right now in this shift of dimensions.

At the Vista Point, consciousness is an inherent tool that our soul uses for experiencing within many various dimensions and realities, both physical and non-physical. Our consciousness remains whether we are embodied or not and we can raise our consciousness by expanding our awareness, redefining our subconscious thoughts and beliefs and healing our traumas and wounds. As we clear the debris from our chosen experiences, we make far more room for Light to enter our energetic field, which serves to raise our vibration and facilitate our evolution into the higher realms. Truly grasping and living in *unconditional love for all* is the motherload goal for all of us as we become citizens of our new Earth. It is indeed a *prerequisite* and there is no other way to move into this higher dimension without actualizing unconditional love for self and all of humanity.

We are shifting into higher vibrational expressions of ourselves. Our thoughts, feelings, emotions and beliefs are catalysts that actually determine whether or not our energy is dense, heavy and vibrating at a low frequency or whether it is light and vibrating at a higher frequency. How do you know? By observing how you *feel*. If you feel depressed, angry, competitive, greedy, jealous, etc., it is likely that you are currently playing upon a low frequency, dense energetic playground. And that is part of your experience here, to experience these types of low vibratory feelings and learn how to transmute them. They are simply an experiential choice within this dimension. The good news is that with *conscious intention* and tools, you can easily learn to shift yourself out of the low densities and into far higher vibrations of joy, peace, love and contentment—if you so desire.

Consciousness Hacking

Your mind is not your consciousness, it is only a tool through which you *interpret consciousness* and propel it forward via your thoughts, beliefs, emotions and perspectives. As you observe each moment of your life (and other's lives) and make determinations about it, you are propelling your consciousness into a manifest reality for you to then experience.

Mind and consciousness hacking is not unlike computer hacking. The octopus has inserted many viruses into the program of humanity's experience. It has created confusing and contradictory messages that cloud our perceptions and resulting beliefs. Just like a computer that has been hacked and has a virus affecting its ability to fully function, we are surrounded by non-truths and information that lead us astray from our intuitive knowledge.

We have *allowed* everything that we protest against because we have downloaded and believed the stories of the octopus, time and time again. Our consciousness was indeed hacked and the inserted "programs" of belief replicated throughout mass consciousness, effectively changing the rules by which we interpret reality. Over time, we have accepted the octopus' rules of the game, which are far different than the Universal rules designed to guide our spiritual development and advancement.

Our Non-Physical Selves

From our non-physical states, we loosely decide what our next adventure will be. We plan with whom we will be dancing, what family best serves us (and them) for our next level of experiencing and where we will land geographically. We choose what soul-level experiences we want to have for our next level of growth and new understandings and what karmic balancing we need to do from our previous lifetimes here. We also choose what astrological sign we wish to be born under because we know how very influenced we will be by the energies of certain planetary alignments. We know that a particular blueprint of the sky at the moment of our birth can greatly assist us with our missions and goals while here.

We then began this particular journey as a aspect of our Highest soul Self—our descent into what we call reality in a 3D world. We squeezed our energetic Selves into these physical vehicles, ready for and *excited* about our next level of experiencing on this planet.

You were also fully aware that you were choosing to enter a planetary energy currently operating in duality, and you knew the challenges would be many. You thoroughly understood that the rewards were going to be huge in spite of the descent into a lower vibratory energetic field. At your birth, you entered into the reality of this planet with full awareness of who you really were. You had awareness that you just came from non-physical as a pure, high vibrating Being of Light and you had full memory of your magnitude, your abilities, your divine empowerment, birthrights and your connection to All That Is. You understood your nature as part of Source energy and that you would never be alone on this journey, because your chosen Guides would be right beside you, gently nudging you along your own chosen path. But the dimensional veil does exist and we quickly forget all of the above as we integrate into the systems and institutions designed to assist in our slumber.

Every single experience here has contributed to who we now are and who we are becoming. Whether we label those experiences as "good" or "bad" is truly of little consequence from the Vista Point, because all served to provide something valuable to us at a higher level (or else we would not have created the experience for ourselves in the first place). It is not uncommon to look back at what we remember to be some of the worst moments in a lifetime and marvel at how significant the experience was to further something else along that was important in our lives. That hindsight is the golden nugget that your Higher Self intended you to garner. If you look back and can see no meaning whatsoever in those highlighted experiences, take a closer look. How did that incident or person affect you long-term? What role might they have agreed to play for you (at a soul level) to help you realize something or change and heal something within or outside of you? Did you get the intended message? What role might you have played for them?

Remembering Your Own Plan

So, let's look at this once again:

As the powerful and amazing Being that you are, you agreed from your non-physical state to step down in vibration to enable you to live within this 3D existence on Earth. You eagerly grabbed the opportunity to **experience** this planet because of the ability to learn more about yourself and to overcome duality through the expression of your Light. You came here to create balance and to master *yourself*, while operating in this specific paradigm of vibrational energies. You understood that the word *life* is omnipotent and infinite and that you, no matter what you chose to experience on this planet or any other, could never cease to exist. You might elect to change form or put on a different outfit entirely or none at all, but the eternalness of all life is sacred and a never-ending adventure as a multidimensional Being. I will repeat throughout this book—you *cannot* get it wrong!

From your non-physical state you understood that you are a magnificent creator and that even whilst visiting in 3D, you were responsible for every manifestation that occurred along your path. In fact, you would prefer it no other way, because your co-creative powers were of divine grace. They were given freely to you from your Source, which you are inseparable from, and part of. What an empowering feeling to know that, through your gift of freewill, you are the one pulling the strings of your life and in doing so, you and all others are furthering All That Is. You knew that your Source was cheering you on throughout every experience, delighting in your examination of life and form.

You chose your life path and purpose before you became physical. You also chose who you would rendezvous with on this great stage called life. You loosely planned how you would intertwine and influence each other in your life plans, healing objectives, and greater outcomes while on Earth.

Many of your connections have continued from prior lifetimes. You might sense a deep connectedness with these people now. You might feel a deep familiarity with certain people for no apparent reason. You might notice lately that more and more often you seem to meet new people with whom you feel a keen déjà vu or like you've known them forever. This is no accident—there are no accidents. You might not understand why, they feel so very familiar to you, because you have never actually met them before in this lifetime.

And perhaps you sometimes feel this sense of urgency about your life, like you are supposed to be doing *something* important now, but you can't figure out what it is. It is always running in the background like a low-burning flame as you strive to figure it out.

You raised your hand very high to be here at this particular time of great change. You knew, along with many others from all over our Universe and other Universes, this particular incarnation would be an unprecedented, historical time and a period in Earth's history that has been talked about for eons. A time of incredible importance and great change that is to herald and usher in an entire new global structure and age. You knew that it was to be the grandest of grand moments and the talk of the cosmos. You knew that it would mean the end of the powers that were and all of the very outdated systems. And to think that you might have a shot at actually being there to witness the changes and help them along! *And here you are, doing just that, in your own unique way.*

You knew that as the planet and all life upon her went through such massive change, that the Earth would warm up, in general, because of the increase in vibrational frequency. This was normal and to be expected, creating more usable land masses on the planet in which to inhabit. You didn't know exactly how this end game would play out because of the gift of freewill of all souls, but you knew that it would be all in divine timing and trusted it to be exactly as it should as the final act occurred and the curtain came down. This curtain represents an ending to life as it has been for so many eons and that supported wars, suffering, hunger, lack and poverty. You also understood that even the souls labeled "dark" or "evil" have, by playing their roles in duality, helped humanity further define themselves and what they really wanted instead. And it was all simply "OK" because you knew that it was just an experience. From your expanded Higher Self, you could see the entire drama playing out on Earth as simply that—a single drama within unending experiences for humanity's evolution and growth.

The fact that you are reading these words means that you are very blessed to be here. Even if your life is currently in shambles by your own definition, you are so incredibly fortunate to be here and there is a part of you that fully knows that. And, my friend, please also remember that you came here fully equipped to handle *anything* and *everything* that this journey might bring your way, even if it often does not feel that way.

The intent of this story is to help you remember the truth of who you really are. There truly is nothing to *learn* from this book because it is all stored within you; in your heart, your consciousness and your billions of cells and DNA. You know it all, but you may need some help to recall it because of our deep indoctrination into the 3D systems. There is nothing that you need to *do* to remember. In fact, all that is required is that you remember how to *be*. So relax, enjoy the recall of who you really are and let's get down to why and how we all ended up feeling so separate from what we absolutely knew at one time. How, over centuries of time, did we forget so much? It is important to revisit how we got to where we are now. The Universe, like a loving parent, is gently tapping all of us on the shoulder to wake up from our long slumber *and remember*. It is an invitation, not a requirement, and there is not one ounce of judgment involved either way.

You have a life plan but in addition, you are here to observe and witness the shift and in that process contribute to your soul-level toolbox. If you choose to make it mean far more than that, that's ok—it's all part of your experience here. And if you choose to make it meaningless and believe that there is nothing beyond this one physical lifetime that's ok too. See, you truly cannot get it wrong! It is impossible. It is *your* experience.

This 3D reality can be very hypnotic from the day of your birth. You are immediately taught things that are totally incongruent with your higher knowingness. You are socialized by the systems to accept without question that what you are told is "real." Your greater perspective is all but lost in the shuffle. You might be told by well-meaning loved ones and others that all of the knowingness and gifts that you entered with are really not useful here. You are taught that your truths are actually distractions to becoming a fully "functional" and "normal" Earth Being and these discrepancies must be corrected until you mostly or entirely forget who you are and why you are here.

Our Higher Self orchestrates situations and experiences, sometimes repeatedly, until we get the intended message at our *conscious* level. From there, we are able to then heal our issues or acknowledge what we need to acknowledge. Your Highest Self seeks the accumulated knowledge from your experiences. When we stop labeling our adventures as good or bad, and positive or negative and allow them to just be experiences, we achieve a huge leap in our evolution and growth. Our experiences, individually and collectively might land us at the point where we say "Enough, I can't live like this anymore and things must change now!" Often, our level of exasperation is the needed catalyst to shift us to the next steps on our journey. This energy of transformation leads us to new spiritual opportunities if we are able to reclaim our divine power and chart our next steps from the Vista Point.

If you feel a familiarity in these words, that's the part of you that has retained your expanded memory, regardless of how vague it might be. Your challenge now is to further explore that greater remembrance and open yourself to the full expression of it.

As your memory returns to you in varying stages and degrees, congratulations are in order, for you are returning to who you always were outside of this 3D reality! You are unveiling the masterpiece that is **you**.

And the day came when the risk it took to remain tight in a bud was more painful than the risk it took to blossom.

~ Anais Nin

CHAPTER 5

The Illusion of Separation

In Sanscrit, the word Samsara means "the world of illusion." That which is not real is called Samsaric in Buddhism. Our entire third dimensional construct has been built upon illusion. The current vast majority of so-called truths of the 3D world are not truly real in any greater context except upon this fading platform of duality. We have all agreed to participate within a tremendous dream world that we believe to be real. We experience emotional pain within the illusion until the moment we are able to see through the agreed upon construct and realize that pain does not exist outside of the illusion. The awakening that is upon us is the exit from the illusion of separation in every way.

The greatest illusion that we entertain as real is that we are somehow energetically separate from our Source and from each other. Unbeknownst to the vast majority of the mainstream public is the fact that the spiritual texts (most all of them) were long ago highly edited to not only include, but to subtly *promote* the energies of duality, fear, isolation and separation *within the context* of the higher energetic messages of love and oneness. The insertions by the powers that were have pitted mankind against each other century after century, bloody war after bloody war. These wars have legitimized the self-righteous concept of killing others "in the name of God" or in more current times, in the name of national security, terrorism, economics and other opportunistic labels.

The misperceptions were set into motion eons ago to instill a firm sense of separation from our Source and each other, both individually and collectively. Once we felt separate from each other, it would be easy to convince us to mistrust, harm and kill others. The lies divided us into groups and we learned to fear and hate each other and to believe that our own Source was outside of us. We would even kill each other over whose representation of Source was most valid. For the octopus, it was a brilliant, self-sustaining tentacle to have people turn on each other and unwittingly, carry out its agendas.

Over many generations we have descended deeper and deeper into the rabbit hole until we stopped asking questions and submitted to the concept that we are independent and disconnected from the sacred, infinite energy stream we are from.

The false messages were intended to create such a magnitude of fear and sense of powerlessness among the people of Earth that they would never question the governing authorities. For centuries, those who dared to question the ruling authorities were imprisoned, tortured or murdered. It was simply too dangerous to have people remember who they were and speak the truth, for the masses might possibility wake up and the octopus could not continue.

These fabrications have firmly instilled a sense of subservience, guilt, worthlessness and powerlessness around a falsely-perceived angry and wrathful god, the very opposite essence of the truth. We were taught that we are born into this reality as "sinners" and must somehow atone for our supposed innate unworthiness. Over time, the octopus has successfully spread the myth of so-called original sin, unworthiness and subservience through religious institutions and into mass consciousness. This produced large groups of people who have accepted a vast amount of lies as deep truths. The powers that were historically altered truths from sacred texts and reframed them for their own agendas. They successfully injected fear and unworthiness into humanity's consciousness. For so many, these half-truths are the norm and the truth feels blasphemous and frightening to them because they have been indoctrinated by the system. Those who see through the octopus' charade and voice their knowingness have historically been murdered or banished by the ruling authorities.

See God in all or don't see God at all.

~ Yogi Bhajan

With this grand shift, *everything* is surfacing for our re-examination, including the revelations of all of the octopus' antics throughout history. The stones are rapidly and thoroughly being looked under and those that are ready for the truth will easily find it.

The story of separation created through fear is a predominate ingredient that is relied upon to sustain our sense of separation. Deep, core level fear keeps this story in motion, for if it is "against God" to even question these infiltrated and altered texts of supposed truth, then the octopus is assured of its ability to maintain a sense of separation within the hearts and minds of the believers.

As we awaken, we remember that we are, and have always been, inseparable aspects of that which we call God, and we are also inseparable from each other. The truth is that God/Source/All That Is, is pure *unconditional* Love and Light—nothing less. With this remembering, we can return to the birthrights that we have always had. It is time to love ourselves as much as Source unconditionally loves us and know that the instilled concepts of unworthiness and powerlessness have simply been a part of the 3D octopus-directed reality we have been living in.

Your non-physical Self is individualized Source energy. As a physical Being, you are Source energy within a body.

The Playground

This may at first sound contradictory, but one major element of our choice to be on this particular planet is the desire to experience what it actually *feels like* to be separate from our Source. Since it is 100% illusionary, the only way to have this experience is to incarnate upon a planet that offers not only the veil of forgetfulness, but also a construct that would support this illusion so that one could feel the full emotional, spiritual, mental and physical impact of the *experience* of separation. Remember that the soul is seeking to gain from all levels of experience; void of judgment and void of loss, as the soul knows that it is infinite. From a soul's perspective, the more that the persona is immersed within the illusion, the deeper the experience and the deeper the gain. The persona's mission then is to heal the trauma from the experience of separation once the persona's consciousness is able to see that the experience was not "real" in a greater context.

The journey for the persona (not the soul, for the soul is in full awareness that no separation could exist) back to the remembrance of oneness becomes the golden nugget of attained wisdom. It is the journey to remembrance that we are now completing as our holographic construct is ending.

From our 3D perspective living within a highly emotional body, it can be extremely challenging to view our traumatic events as "just an experience." Please know that I am not reducing or being flippant or disrespectful of anyone's pain and suffering. The horrors and wounds that humanity has endured are to be acknowledged, grieved and honored on every level. From the soul's perspective, they are meant to be experienced and healed, fully releasing the lower energies from our minds, bodies and spirits. We are not meant to replay these past experiences over and over in our psyches because when we live in the so-called "past" we cannot then embrace our now moments, as the newly arriving 4D–5D energies require of us.

Within the illusion of 3D, many people still desperately seek the love, approval and forgiveness of our Source, because of the illusion of separation. We have forgotten our immutable enmeshment with the infinite energy stream that we call God and that no judgment, punishment nor condemnation has ever existed. We consequently believe that love is outside of us and must be captured elsewhere for us to feel whole and fulfilled. We long for a deep divine love with each other, but we are ingrained with the false belief that we are energetically disconnected. The truth is that we **are love**—it is our composition.

Ego Integration

The energy and illusion of separation has provided a very fertile ground for our egos to flourish and create large imbalances. The extreme engagement of the ego has served to enhance our deep feelings of estrangement from each other and our Source. It has created a deep mass wound that is ready to be healed. At a deeper level, we *know* that it is not natural for us to feel that we are each an island and to live our lives in a state of me, myself and I.

We are evolving spiritually to a point where we have the capacity to integrate with our Highest Selves with even a little effort and determination to do so. When we do, we heal the schism of separation between us. If we truly desire to transform our world into oneness, peace and love, we must establish the enmeshment with our divine Selves and see that same Light and divine greatness in everyone we encounter. We must allow and command that our egos take soul-level direction and not the other way around. Our ego/personas are necessary for us to be able to experience this 3D construct. The ego/persona is the bridge that allows the soul to experience our reality as we each know it to be. It is not something to constrict, rather it is an important part of us that we simply want to reframe through our remembrance of the greater perspective.

Nothing challenges our ego more than the words, beliefs and actions of other actors upon our stage. When we live our lives in a state of egotism, defensiveness or judgment, we completely miss the gift being offered by those around us. Hold the space for your fellow humans to find their spiritual mastery. As you do this, they will reflect your own mastery back to you—the "**I am**" that we each are, as aspects of our Source. When we see other people in their *perfection* instead of their illusionary limitations, we hold a valuable space for them to reveal their spiritual mastery to themselves and to others.

Gandhi wisely said: "Be the change that you wish to see." The underlying energy of this truth is one of becoming that reflection for others. As we embody our highest visions for the planet and ourselves, we create it by its reflection back into the world *through* us. It's the law of "Like Attracts Like" in motion and actualization.

> *Source energy is streaming through all of us (including the powers that were) from our core outwards; it's who we are, expressed through our gifts, creativity and creations. Your full remembrance includes the fact that you are a powerful, magnificent, magnanimous Being of Light and Love. Everything else is just the coating upon your essence and the ingredients of your illusions.*

Incongruent Realities

Those who have awakened within the 3D systems of the octopus often feel very isolated. Many are ostracized when others find out they are no longer willing to conform within the systems and contribute to their own separation. As the matrix continues to shift into a higher expression, we escalate into the remembrance of our infinite beingness. The veil of separation ceases to exist as our full consciousness returns. We then find ourselves operating from a new set of energies and rules that underscore the higher versions of ourSelves. The new norm becomes peace, love, unity and harmony.

Once this new norm becomes a part of one's life, there is no desire to go back to the old paradigm. It is easy to feel alone and out of sorts because our new level of consciousness often does not yet match up with our external reality. We can feel and see the incongruence between our new evolvement and the outside world as it is appearing to be. Our consciousness and spiritual growth happens at a faster pace than our material world changes, even though the external construct is going through massive shifts as well. Eventually, the inner and the outer realities will match up and harmonize. It will be as if mankind has deeply synchronized in support of each other and our divine contributions to the whole. No longer will the lower energies over-power our intrinsic desire to love one another.

Truly, how fun or effective would the rabbit hole have been if we knew all along at a conscious level that this was just a playground of experience? We would have been pretty bored and like a child, homesick and wanting to go home! Embrace the rich experiences you have had and the amazing ones yet to come. They are tremendous gifts, every single one of them.

Can you imagine a world where the people in every country have fully realized that they are inseparable as one and that the borders created by duality no longer apply? We have the power and ability to take back the reins and reclaim our planet in a non-violent way and it is slowly happening across the globe. This huge tidal wave of freedom and new-found sovereignty will continue until every system has been transformed.

It is through intention and imagination that manifestation can actually occur. We must see and feel what we desire to create, for it is our visualization and heart-felt emotions that directly magnetize this new world to us.

> *"Imagination is the beginning of creation. You imagine what you desire, you **will** what you imagine and at last you create what you will."*
> *~ George Bernard Shaw*

CHAPTER 6

The 3D Octopus

*Reality in the 3rd dimension is an epic story, broken down into scenes of energy and expressions through our consciousness to bring about awakening and remembrance of the "**I am**" that we all are.*

Truth

Many people say that they do not want to know the truth because it is too frightening and they feel powerless to change anything. They avoid it because they perceive it as negative. The reality is, *the truth will set you free* when you realize that you can make a conscious choice not to be influenced by the old paradigm. When you make this personal choice and intention, you free yourself from the matrix of the 3D world. Awareness brings change. If you have no clue what is really going on beyond what you are told by all of the systems, you are not empowered to make choices about your future, or even understand how to create change.

The critical question that we must begin asking and answering is: "What do I want instead of this for myself and everyone else?"

This question is immensely important and is the new, critical launch point in these times of change. If we have no idea where we currently are, how can we determine where we wish to go?

> *When a system intentionally gives citizens only bits and pieces of the larger vista, it is very hard to see the entire picture—and from the perspective of the octopus, you were never meant to. Just about everything you have been taught within this system is the **opposite** of the truth. We have been indoctrinated into the systems of the powers that were since our birth and it is now time to reverse-engineer all that we think we know.*

Products of a Program?

It is certainly not a new concept that we are programmed with thoughts and beliefs that dramatically shape our lives. However, let's take a closer look at what this actually means. The octopus has gone to great lengths to program our hard-drives/brains with beliefs about our reality and we have, over time, accepted these beliefs as truth. In fact, the powers that were are masters at shaping reality via human perception. I would venture to estimate that well over 80% of what we hold as sacred "truths" did not originate from within our core Selves. We were *taught* the vast majority of our beliefs and truths by the systems. What this means is that so much of what you teach your children and grandchildren and firmly believe yourself is most likely not your "own" thought or belief, or based upon what your Higher Self knows to be true about this world and the Universe at large.

How many of us have ever really stopped somewhere along the road of our lives and seriously questioned what we have been raised and educated to think and believe? The construct you may hold firm to may not be exactly as you believe it is. It is intended that there are such large platforms of accepted reality that you do not question them to be anything other than "how the world is and has always been." What humanity is now discovering is how very far from the truth this is.

Where do your personal beliefs come from? Do you dislike or lack tolerance for those who are different from you? Why? Do you have a sense of superiority or "rightness" about your race, social or financial status, gender, sex, religion or education? If so, how did you arrive at those conclusions? Why did you arrive at those conclusions? How worthy or empowered do you feel? Do you feel safe and if not, why not? What causes you fear? Who do you believe yourself to be beyond your body?

Most of us are products of large, systematic programs of thought and because they are so deeply rooted within us, our beliefs can be set in stone. Where else did your beliefs come from? Your church? Your educational system? Your television? Hollywood? Your unenlightened government and leaders? Your Parents? (Where did their beliefs come from?) Did they stop to ponder whether or not these teachings were in full resonance with their divine Selves? I will go out on a limb here and say that I *highly* doubt it.

I encourage you to consider that a vast amount of information that you believe in and *vehemently* standby and defend was encoded to become your truth and your reality, occurring over a long period of time and in small increments. Our sovereignty has been whittled away over many centuries. Have you ever taken many small bites and nibbles from a cake over a few days and then all of a sudden wondered how you consumed the entire thing? It seemed as if you hardly ate any and yet—it is gone! The same has happened to our sovereign rights as human Beings.

The ways and means of the octopus (through its systems), has invaded our minds, hearts and consciousness, little by little, until we think that it is normal and we have little awareness of what has happened, because it began long before our births. We swallowed little bits at a time as did our parents, grandparents and our entire lineages.

So many people are trained to make most of their decisions out of fear and it's become so secondhand that they don't even recognize that they operate their lives from this foundational energy. As we awaken, we must re-establish our boundaries in a benevolent manner and reassert our power as sovereign Beings of Light.

We cannot know what we truly think and believe about our lives until we slow down, go within and take the time to do some deep sea diving. We cannot find that congruence without connecting firmly to our Higher Selves as we ponder these questions. If we are willing to question and even dump (or at the least allow for a large upgrade) a lot of the information and beliefs we currently have, we open ourselves up quite literally to miracles.

Those who freely embrace and welcome these changes and are willing to go within for their answers, will find that a very large percentage of their information is not true. Rather, it is part of the 3D systems and pertinent only to this 3D matrix. Further, they will likely uncover that the programming is seated within separation—not oneness, nor unity consciousness.

Pulling Back the Curtain

The discussion of the 3D octopus is not a political statement, a conspiracy theory, a theoretical or philosophical discussion or contemplation. Nor is it a religious statement. Instead, it is an unearthing of the large network that has been well hidden behind the systems put into place. *The octopus and its many factions have remained behind the scenes for a very long time. You cannot identify and change what you cannot see or find. Given that, you are then far more susceptible to believing in a reality architected by those who are shaping your perception of it.*

Remember, the octopus is operating at a level far above all governments and they have historically controlled these governments. This is where the seams are unraveling for them, because many of these governments are now reclaiming their sovereignty. As they do, the octopus is desperately trying to create wars in these countries to maintain their long-standing control.

At the top echelons of the 3D systems, one will find the global handful of elite families. The octopus goes back in our history of Earth much further than most people might think. These energies have been on this planet since the Mesopotamian times and even before then, off and on. Their bloodlines originate from some of the first visitors to Gaia.

Part of our awakening and rising consciousness is to recognize and begin to see that the powers that were exist on this planet. As the masses are rapidly experiencing this shift of realities, there are three likely choices: We can become enraged and angry as we discover the intentions of this group. If we choose this reaction, we become victims. Victims are energetically powerless and wounded, unable to move forward to create large change. Second, some people will go into fear and denial. These reactions are normal steps when processing grief and loss, but they become a problem if we get stuck there and do not move forward. The third choice is the willingness to understand how we, and all of our ancestors, have allowed this group of people and their systems to not only exist, but grow. In the Western world, many have bought into the programming that happiness equals money, control, power, status and gross runaway consumerism. We fell asleep at the wheel and became apathetic, and decided that as a mass consciousness, it was ok to turn our power over to the powers that were. We decided that once we cast our vote we were done and could relax because everything was "being handled" properly.

*When we are willing to take **full responsibility** for our reality, we completely empower ourselves to create large change, both internally and externally.*

Now that the 3D energies are rapidly fading, the bigger question becomes: what have we learned through these experiences? What wisdom have we gained? The answer is unequivocally that we can and are coming together on a global scale to heal our planet and build a new reality that is based upon a greater reverence for all of humanity and Gaia.

We have never been each other's enemies; we have only been *taught* that program of consciousness. We fear each other because we have been *taught* to fear each other.

Welcoming this planetary shift will unite us and serve to rectify and heal the damage created by the whole; damage that we have allowed and often participated in through our slumber, karmic balancing and chosen experiences.

3D System Manifestations

The Results of Forgetting Our Oneness

Below are examples of how our amnesia within the systems has manifested:
- Race/ethnicity divisions
- Religious divisions, intolerance and hatred
- Homophobia/Transphobia
- Gender identity discrimination
- Gender discrimination
- Cultural separation
- Class divisions based upon socio-economic or educational factors
- Separation between ourselves and our sacred connection to Gaia (notice all the corporate concrete?)
- Disrespect and cruelty for our animal and plant kingdoms. Dominance and widespread abuse, instead of gratitude for the unconditional love that animal's gift to humanity.
- Separation from Mother Earth and her healing energies. Dominance and destruction of Earth, versus being responsible, loving stewards of this planet as we were meant to be.
- Separation from, and denial of our cosmic, Universal star families.

The above examples are the foundational components of the illusion that feed our sense of separation and veil the truth of our innate oneness.

Thoughts and feelings broadcast powerful energies and when you buy into the above thoughts and beliefs that underscore these energies, you assist in manifesting them with your contribution to mass consciousness.

Thinking Like an Octopus…

*When you control the flow of truth and money,
you control the world.*

If you desire to fully understand the octopus and the systems it has created, you must briefly think like the octopus. If your ultimate goal was to provide direction to a very large group of people but there were only a handful of you in comparison, how would you achieve such a monumental task over time and over bloodlines? It would be a very wise move to create complex (but it's not so complex at all once you see through it) systems within systems. One would create the branches of each system as directly connected to the head of the octopus and each system would consist of a highly structured, "legally-controlled" segment of society.

These segments were designed in great detail to mold asleep citizens within the matrix of a 3D reality. These non-questioning, compliant world citizens would be born into a world where they are taught to live in much subconscious fear energy. They would fear losing their basic survival needs if they don't abide by the foundational set-up of your many systems and the rules governing those systems. The result and goal would be a population that is collectively unaware of their true divine nature, their tremendous abilities to co-create any and everything they desired independently and be unaware of their multidimensionality. In essence, they would feel powerless in every significant way that is threatening to the nature of your construct.

The octopus believed that most people would not remember their innate power and divine abilities as master co-creators.

However, the octopus is aware of the massive shift that is upon us. Behind the scenes it is very concerned that the masses might actually be waking up and it fears that its game of control is coming to an end. This is playing out on the global stage in a myriad of ways, with one false flag after another, both in the USA and abroad.

Most of all, the octopus is concerned that we will begin to put it all together and single them out for accountability. We will successfully shift paradigms only through benevolence, not through additional violence. And there will come a day when arrests will occur for crimes against humanity.

The octopus' greatest and most powerful weapon in preventing its worst fears from happening and to maintain the status quo is to keep *you* in great fear and within the illusion that you are not powerful. It wants you to "just keep shopping." The powers that were know and understand the Laws of the Universe and that fear plummets one's vibration and energy frequency.

As the structures and systems of 3D shift into a higher frequency expression, so do our beliefs around these systems change *within us* in a highly personal and tangible way. This transformation calls us to shift our beliefs around the old systems. If we try to explain the changes through the old 3D methods of graphs, statistics and formulas, we find ourselves spinning within a huge vortex of confusion, uncertainty and angst about our future. The old formulas just don't add up any longer. You will not be able to embrace the shift of the old paradigm by analyzing it through an old lens of reality, as the path to enlightenment is not through the old ways.

> *Understanding this shift involves trusting your wisdom, inner direction and knowledge. The time that we are now in is the long-awaited embrace of each other as a family of one. At some point, to move forward, you must let go of the old edicts.*

Saying "Yes!"

The vast majority of citizens across the globe, just like you, want deeply to live in peace and unity and see abundance for *all people* across the globe. We want it badly, but we are afraid to even think much about it, because we have been subconsciously programmed by the old systems to believe that it is simply not possible. For many, it feels overwhelming to entertain such a large dream and we then abandoned it, because we have no idea how to bring it about. We have felt powerless to bring about such tremendous change. Just know that there is a new day dawning in this moment, and there will no longer be anything that is usual or normal as compared to past energies. The Universe is enticing us to ride this wave to 5D. All we need do is step up to the plate and say, "Yes!"

The Messengers

The octopus does not operate under the same rules that most of humanity does and because of this, many have found it very hard to entertain that all of their reality is not spot-on.

Go within and use discernment with all messengers. There are many out there intentionally and unintentionally spreading misperceptions and giving out false information. There are in fact, misinformation specialists, especially on the web and on television.

The reality is that when we find the courage to acknowledge the truth it disempowers those who created the falsehoods. We are coming together and realizing that we can transform the 3D systems by saying, "no more, your time is now over." Many whistleblowers are coming forward at great risk to themselves and their families. We are seeing this energy in our demand for a cleaner environment; pure water and foods that do not poison us; the right to say "no" highly toxic vaccinations (there isn't a shred of non-octopus funded research that shows any vaccine to be preventative). We are seeing this energy in Iceland, Russia, Ireland, Egypt, Greece and Turkey. Recently, we see it also in the new BRICS nations, who are now turning their backs to the U.S. Federal Reserve dollar (and Euro) and creating new financial systems and alliances with other countries who are also dropping the worthless US Federal Reserve dollar.

As our awakening continues, we are finding like-minded friends through our travels or through the web where we can befriend someone across the globe from an entirely different culture and through this friendship deeply know that we are all one. Our hearts and minds are expanding as we allow sweeping changes to begin within us. We are beginning to question any doctrines that teach us to hate, judge, feel unworthy about ourSelves or cause us to feel separate from *any* of our brothers and sisters. We are realizing how we have allowed the antics of the octopus to come between us and how futile it has been. We are remembering to honor and appreciate every thread in the tapestry that creates the sum of us.

The Vista Point unfolding is stunning and this is our most pivotal journey of all journeys. This last leg of activity in duality is enticing us to remember and recall so much about ourselves. As we do, we find the inner knowingness that no matter how bad things may appear in the outside world, in truth, there is absolutely nothing that can or will stop this amazing, welcome transformation that is underway.

Aligning Ourselves with the Whole

It is time to deeply evaluate the octopus and all of its various systems and determine how we each support them and keep the status quo in place. Are the institutions that we hold so dear as a part of our society truly in service to *all of humanity*? It is also time for us to take a much closer look at each branch within the current

3D system and determine from our heart center—what still serves us as a human family and what does not.

We have a large responsibility to change what is no longer serving the greater good of all people. How can we possibly achieve such a tremendous undertaking as to create and implement all new systems within our many varying societies across the globe? We do it together—that's how. We recreate from the inside out. When any system is materialized from a high frequency, heart-centered consciousness, it will flourish and will benefit all people, because it was designed with "all" in mind.

What system in your country or in the world are you most passionate about changing? What sacred gifts and ideas will you contribute as we rebuild our world together? Remember, you (yes you!) are critically important to the whole. The days are over when humanity can just sit back, nominate others to be in charge and think that everything is wonderful. That's exactly how we arrived at our current fork in the road. We are each responsible for our collective outcome.

Our newly arriving paradigm requires each of us to step up to the plate, embrace each other as one human family and think on our own. We must examine everything and then actively contribute to our greatest vision. The responsibility is on each of us to require accountability and true transparency of our new leaders and governments. We do that by being true stewards of this planet and making our sovereign, divine rights as humans our largest priority.

What lies behind us and what lies before us
is tiny compared to what lies within us.
~ Oliver Wendall Holmes

CHAPTER 7

The Systems of the Octopus

PART I

- Religion
- Science
- History
- Educational System
- Government/Politics/Corporations
- The War Machine
- Banking System
- Healthcare
- The Media Conglomerates
- Our Environment
- Parenting

Over time, the many systems created by the octopus were designed to ensure that we believe in the reality that they constructed for us. As we awaken within the systems, transparency is becoming very common and more people are able to see through the design.

Some Religions

One of the greatest truths that we can embrace is that we are not broken and we have *never* been broken. It is impossible to ever be broken as a human Being. It is an 3D falsehood that we are "sinners" and that we need forgiveness from our Source to be a worthy human Being. As long as you believe in this misconception, you will feel in separation from your Source and from others. You were born into every lifetime a perfect divine Being, full of cosmic awareness. It has been life within these densely lit systems that has blurred our vision and created a massive disconnection from our Sacred Selves.

There are many original, profound and deep spiritual truths foundationally woven through all organized religions. And there are *many* paths to enlightenment and awakening and none are wrong or better than another. But it is very important to understand that there are also a lot of inserted half-truths, misconceptions and mis-interpretations (over centuries) by the octopus in order to shape consciousness. The dichotomy of these messages makes it difficult for many people to ascertain truth from fiction. Historically, the powers that were have successfully combined the true teachings of unconditional love for all, with their own agendas to instill the energies of fear, hatred, separation, punishment, judgment and unworthiness into mass consciousness. Many organized religions have unknowingly passed along and taught these half-truths that are rooted in fear. This was done long ago as a control mechanism. The true message of unconditional love for all and humanity's innate divine perfection has been very distorted.

Many people believe that "Armageddon" is upon us. This false information only serves to pump fear into mass consciousness, which then hinders the manifestation of love and peace that most of us desire. Instead of this being a great time of destruction and disaster, it is instead a time of a new and far higher consciousness replacing the old grid. In essence, it is a large vibrational ascension for our entire planet and Universe.

Dogma often teaches that we are separate from our Creator. It does not teach that you are a powerful divine co-creator aspect of

Source energy. Teachings that perpetuate disrespect or judgment of other Beings is not of truth. There are countless churches in the USA alone that condemn, judge and ridicule (or at the very least, promote self-righteousness) gay, lesbian and transgender people, African Americans and many other various groups. These teachings promote hate crimes, violence, murder, disrespect and denial of basic human rights. Theses teachings have nothing whatsoever to do with God. They promote the very opposite energies of love and oneness and only serve to further the agendas of the powers that were on this planet. No true freedom exists for anyone until we are *all* equal under the law, but even more importantly, equal in each other's eyes and hearts.

Many people dislike other countries (and their people) that supply products and services to the USA. They promote boycotts and petitions, never understanding the source of their grievances, or how they are energetically supporting the very issues that they protest against. Granted, the octopus has damaged this country with its severely failed global economic "systems." But pointing hostile fingers at other citizens is targeting the wrong party. The people of other countries have been just as hoodwinked as we have here in the USA. It is because of the powers that were global economic fraud, that this promotion exists.

When we champion that all of our purchases be "made in the USA" or "only buy American," we are participating in global separation that has been created by and for the octopus. The issue around Americans losing out on jobs is a *symptom* of a much larger issue—the octopus' (and their abc agencies) gross misuse and abuse of the funds they have been entrusted with by the people to effectively manage and run our economies for the good of all. They have wasted money and tremendous resources that were intended for all people, not just their .001 percent share of the global population.

When we realize that we are one upon this planet and take our power back, we shift into the larger understanding that the only borders that truly exist are in our minds. The people of all countries possess a rich, important and unique offering to the world.

As we unite together, we will all benefit tremendously in sharing our resources, talents, gifts and knowledge, in which to rebuild our world. Instead of enemies, we must become diplomats with each other—individually and collectively, and the first ingredient in this recipe is respect and kindness to all others across this planet.

Every single person currently experiencing upon the global stage is critical to the overall picture. We cannot continue to dislike others because they are not from our respective countries or able to fully speak our language and expect to ever attain peace, unity, oneness and love—it is impossible. The problem is not with import/exports, in-country jobs, or with immigrants—the problem is that *division* between us has been turned into a packaged system that we were sold and we think should somehow work.

Many organized, dogmatic religions were infiltrated by the 3D octopus long ago to control people's experience and perception of how they view "God." The octopus has taught that you must convert or reject anyone who does not believe in your particular model of God and your personal concept of reality. Throughout history, the octopus has attempted to control or delete anyone (or any group) who has awakened to the sacred energetic basis of who they really are.

We are Beings of pure divine Light with tremendous abilities to co-create our lives and our world. How effective of the octopus to create fear of our Source *and* of those people who see beyond the 3D systems and who embrace their innate gifts and birthrights. We threaten the existing version of reality as we awaken to these truths.

Manufactured Shame

The insertion by the octopus that God judges us, leads us to subconsciously assume that we are to judge ourSelves and each other too. It is *manufactured shame*. "We are all far from perfect," is a common 3D saying and concept that is not a sacred truth. You came in perfect and you will leave perfect and whole, regardless of what your chosen experiences are while you visit this planet. Over centuries, humanity has been shaped by the systems and has forgotten many core truths. Worthiness, divinity, joy, freewill and abundance are your birthrights. Your chosen experiences for soul growth or to satisfy karmic experiences are simply that. Every soul that exists is loved *equally* by Source and *is of Source*. There is no hierarchy of favorites, nor are there certain people or groups who are more worthy or divine than others. That belief is purely ego-based. We are of the same Source—regardless of how far a soul may have drifted from their memory of who they really are and their resultant actions while here.

The only judge of you will be *you* as you exit from this experience and reflect back upon whether or not you accomplished the teachings and understandings that you yourself chose to attain before you incarnated. You will then, along with your non-physical support team, decide upon your next best experience for your continued evolution, karmic balancing, understanding and growth.

Source wishes you to seek knowingness of who you are through your expression of the *I am*. As you reach new levels of knowingness, you provide the ability for your vehicle to hold more and more Light, which in turn automatically raises your energetic vibrational level higher. The higher your vibrational level goes, the more you experience full consciousness, leading you to Enlightenment. You literally expand the container that is you, as your consciousness expands. Your expansion expands All That Is, *simultaneously*.

> *All that exists is Light.*
> *Darkness is a factor of density and vibration*
> *and over many eons, Earth/Gaia, became a platform*
> *in which the Light experienced Itself.*

Acknowledging the truth of who we really are is to own that we are divine sparks of All That Is and that being separate from that truth is impossible, except through the 3D illusion.

> *Going outside of yourself for answers and solutions in your*
> *life is like searching for your toes on someone else's foot.*

How Dogma Creates Separation

When you identify yourself as "Mormon, Jewish, Catholic, Christian, Muslim", etc., you are stating that you align with a certain set of beliefs and traditions. There is nothing wrong with this at all, as *all* paths lead to the same Source.

I *greatly honor* and respect every person's journey and freewill choices. However, there is one unequivocal truth that supersedes all else: the one Source Energy from which we all originated runs through the veins of every soul upon this Earth and all other Beings in existence. It is because of this that we are irrevocably one in spirit and collective energy.

If you align yourself with an organized religious institution, I encourage you to deeply examine what components the octopus has inserted within its teachings and what is of the truest high vibrational essence.

All religions contain the spark of the true teachings of the Masters of Light about our Prime Creator/Source Energy/All That Is. However, many of the messages are very limited interpretations and have distorted the very premise of the Master teachings, which is **love**. Conditional love, judgment of others and violence have no place within *any true* spiritual teachings.

These distortions have served to dilute the truth of our divine nature. If you want to know what is of truth, it is extremely easy to find out: go deep within your core Self, connect to your heart and you will find that anything that is not of love is a manufactured teaching that is not of the Light.

Collectively, we have barely skimmed the surface of the true energy of the word "love." Until we remember how to deeply and unconditionally love ourselves and each other, without judgment or *in spite* of any judgments (if we can't let go of that illusion) we will not reach what we understand to be *the promised 5D land* and we will not experience what it is like to fully express our divine Selves.

The Science of God is this: **You** *are the Base Reference Point for the prime factor that is Source Energy. Source Energy is All*

That Is. You are Source Energy experiencing Itself through the evolution of consciousness in every life form, on every planet and in every Universe. You and your Source are inherently and ultimately inseparable.

The Scientific Tentacle

The scientific aspect of the 3D system has historically only validated what can be demonstrated by physical laws and testing methods. The quantum world has traditionally been omitted as "valid." There has been intentional suppression of advanced technologies because they would greatly reduce profits to the powers that were, as well as facilitate the evolution and consciousness of humanity.

Traditional science as it is known and practiced in our world has evolved within a vacuum of tight control. When humanity remembers how our Universe really functions within the cosmos, it leaves the door wide open for new free-energy technologies to spring forward that can no longer be capitalized upon, hidden or monopolized for profit by the old systems. Science has been treated as an authoritative formula by which to measure our lives and abilities. We have all heard the adage "facts don't lie." Yes, actually they do, when the "facts" are "tweaked" by those who go to great lengths to ensure a certain result is achieved on paper. It is always a good idea to trace scientific "fact" directly to the funding source and determine how and why they are involved in the research and how the results from the research are connected to their profits.

Countless scientific studies have been greatly altered by the corporate interests that fund them and appear valid. Examples include foods that the FDA deems safe, like aspartame (a proven, highly dangerous neurotoxin), prescription drugs that in reality have *not* gone through thorough testing to determine their safety on humans; "studies" stating that GMO-laden "foods" are safe for human consumption; vaccine research, fluoride in our drinking supply (there is no valid study outside of octopus-funded research that has ever shown fluoride to prevent a single cavity, and yet the American Dental Association insists upon continued support of this major carcinogen and neurotoxin) and the *extremely* long list goes on. Discernment is an invaluable tool in these times.

You have been taught to distrust anything that you cannot explain, especially anything that cannot be seen by your own two eyes. This model *invalidates the energetic 95% of your reality that cannot yet be seen or explained but nevertheless, exists.*

Huge scientific advancements actually have been made over the decades, but they have been used solely by the powers that were and the governments they control. The octopus has a far greater understanding of the Universe than we have been led to believe or encouraged to have ourselves through their systems. The beauty is that quantum science is now validating the unexplained energetic basis for so much that mainstream has labeled "woo-woo." This will be occurring much more frequently as the new paradigm unfolds.

The (awake) quantum scientists and physicists understand that traditional science models are flawed and full of half truths. As this shift continues, there will be a new understanding that quantum and galactic science has been suppressed from the public at all cost. Many brilliant mathematicians and engineers work in industries to create new advancements for the government, but they are not aware how or where their little piece of the puzzle is going to be used. Often, it is in weaponry, missiles, drones, vaccines (definitely used as a weapon upon unsuspecting third world countries and their citizens—many of these vaccine cocktails induce sterility), and other objects of war. The octopus and its highly enmeshed corporate partners cubby hole their project workers so that they are not aware of the larger picture being created.

Old science has controlled how we perceive our place in the cosmos and among other planets and Universes, teeming with their own societies and Beings. This area too is rapidly changing. Many people have *remembered* that we are far from alone and that we have advanced, benevolent, star families out there that are very much like us and tied to us in our ancestral lineage.

The science of who we really are is about 5% visible and 95% invisible in this reality. We get stuck in beliefs that are based upon only 5% of valid Universal information.

History and Linear Time

Time consists of non-linear periods or "flavors" of energy come forth to manifest group consciousness and group experience within a multidimensional framework. Time energy is a tool for soul growth and change. Time is comprised of many energy streams at once that create an illusion of a fixed, linear reality construct.

History as we have been taught is a fraction of what has actually taken place on this planet. Suffice it to say that this could be a book within itself and much is soon to be revealed about our true heritage, beginnings and human ancestry upon planet Earth. Why would the powers that were delete and hide huge periods of our history? Because the truth would reveal that we are far, far more than we think we are and also reveal the many ways they have covered those truths. Our true ancestry would connect our DNA in broader ways than we think and would explain that our true heritage is actually off-planet, not the Darwinian concepts so widely accepted or the story of humanity being descendants of apes. Our true capabilities are exceedingly more advanced than we have been led to believe.

Time also does not function in the way that you have been taught, as our "past lives" are actually *concurrent* as part of our interdimensionality and multidimensionality—they are not linear. We exist upon a landscape that involves many, many planes of existence occurring all at once, each with many probable outcomes and they too, are multidimensional. All that we consider to be in the past actually exists in the *now*. So does our concept of the future and our ability to manifest our "future" once we remember how energy truly manifests into form.

As we journey through this shift, our perception of time as we know it is greatly speeding up. Our planet has now traveled into what is termed the "galactic center" in outer space. As we experience this incredibly intense energy, it serves to further break down the illusion of linear time, as well as the old structures. We might notice that the days seem to race by at an unbelievable pace, or we might start losing track of time, feeling that we are living more in the now moment of each day. Our memories can also be affected as we begin to defocus upon the so-called past or our thoughts of the future and instead simply embrace each moment as it appears. It might even feel as if time is standing still or that we are not nearly as cognizant of time in general.

We could find it challenging to meet our daily 3D "to do" lists or keep up with life's demands around our jobs, families and other responsibilities. I assure you that this is all quite normal as we transition through this dimensional shift.

The Educational System

From kindergarten through graduate school we have been taught to believe in a reality that does not include our inner knowledge and spiritual nature. Rules are enforced that often stymie creativity, deny true individualism and create people who follow the guidelines of the systems to survive in this material-driven world.

Obviously, there are components of education that are desired, critical to functioning in the world and necessary, but they have been wrapped in a *greater package of conformity*.

Living in and understanding higher states of beingness, is not something we are taught in school. We are taught to fear authority from our youngest experiences instead of being supported in finding our own inner authority as a divine Being. Education is a system that is heavily influenced by the octopus as a *means of relaying* the vast historical, scientific and economic misinformation, generation after generation. The end result is that people grow up disconnected from who they are at a core level and have forgotten the deep spiritual connectedness and truths that they entered the world with. They leave college programmed with the coding of the systems as their axioms for truth, fully believing the non-truths about their reality. The existing educational system has made many non-truths seem very real.

Because of the design of the octopus' systems, our brains and neurological systems have atrophied in a energetic sense. Our brains are not only *receivers* of higher spiritual information through the crown chakra and pineal gland (third eye), but it is also a transmitter of frequencies and information.

We utilize a very tiny portion of our brain's true capacity. I am not referring to our intellectual capacity, although this is certainly factored in. I am speaking of our ability from birth to tap into our innate multidimensionality and gifts. In a 5D world, children are taught from their youngest years to develop and advance these birthrights and further their spiritual, mental, physical and emotional evolution. 5D children are taught how to use and develop their divine abilities such as *clairvoyance* ("seeing" through one's third eye/pineal gland), *clairaudience* ("hearing" the guidance given from our Higher Selves and our Guides/Angels) and *clairsentience* (our kinesthetic feeling/innate knowingness).

Consciousness has been "institutionalized" through academia to a certain extent. I highly admire all teachers and feel that the intent to serve and help others is why they are in their professions. Teachers bring so *much good* to the planet through their intentions to help others grow and learn. However, they have been educated and socialized within the 3D systems too, just like the rest of us. There is no blame or judgment here, and there are many who are now awake within the various systems that are *changing them from within*. My hat is off to them with much appreciation and admiration. We have all been ignorant to some extent of the greater truths and within those limitations we have done the best that we can to contribute to our world. It is as if we have traveled this entire path with one eye covered.

In the very near future, our entire concept of education at all levels is to be transformed into a far more encompassing reality that honors and greatly encourages the remembrance and expression of ourselves as Beings of Light and protective stewards of Gaia.

The Political/Governmental/Corporate Connection

Governments have functioned as large *fronts* for the octopus for two reasons: (1) so that citizens *believed* they had leaders who were making decisions with their best interests at heart and representing their voice and (2) as a buffer between the people and the powers that were, so they were not directly involved with the masses. The Governments have acted as a shield for the octopus to remain guarded behind the scenes. The large corporations that currently dominate our food supply, air, water, transportation and utilities are very much supported by the octopus if not actually owned by the powers that were.

No government agency or political party has jurisdiction over the truth, especially in these shifting times. They can deny, distort, or try to hide the truth, but truth always prevails. Your internal compass always recognizes the truth if you choose to listen and trust its solid direction.

The Political Game

If you want to understand this construct better, you will need to really think about the *illusion of freedom* and you will begin to see what has been our political history. In the USA particularly, the media spin doctors are busy at work to sell the agendas of the octopus to the public at large. They accomplish this primarily through fear energy and with the smoke screen that the public's best interest is a priority and at heart. Always, their main goal is to execute their agendas and still publicly look like the "good guys."

The USA began as a true Republic, by and for the People, and our constitution was divinely created through our Founding Fathers. When the octopus infiltrated it was then illegally made a private corporation (under the control and possession of the English Crown) and has operated as such (in secrecy) for well over 100 years. A "Corporation" with a legislature was established, with all the apparatus of a distinct government created (Incorporated) by (Presidential) Legislative Act, February 21, 1871 Forty-first Congress, Session III, Chapter 62, page 419.

This is the point in our history when the octopus took control of the Republic of the United States of America and completely shifted the intent of our Founding Fathers to create sovereign states that were united. This is the major insertion point in the USA that changed everything we think we know. We have not been operating under our original Constitution since 1871, when our country and human rights were, quite literally taken over by the powers that were.

You have been taught in octopus school that you live under a US Constitution and Bill of Rights—you do not. You live under a "Corporate Constitution" and once you understand the implications of this as a corporate citizen, everything from the federal government down to your city government will make far greater sense. You are in a legal (not lawful) sense, "property of the corporation" and you do not have the legal rights that you think you do. All courts of law are obedient to the octopus' corporate law. This has been well-hidden from your knowledge.

We are soon to return to a true Republic, but it will be an expanded version, because we are also returning to the remembrance of our cosmic, star family ancestry and connections as we become Galactic Citizens operating in full consciousness. We are moving into a position of being *part* of our greater Universe—not just sovereign global citizens, but *cosmic* citizens as well.

Those who cannot digest the truth of these systems will defend them and die for them, because it is too hard for them to change their ingrained belief structures that support them. We greatly want to believe in the construct or hologram depicting what we have thought to be real. We find our comfort zones there, and in many cases, we have dedicated our entire lives and careers to upholding and defending these systems. Truth can make people *very* angry and fearful, because it requires them to grow beyond what they know and deeply believe to be true. This is the very basis for being able (or not) to see through the matrix and allowing ourselves to awaken within it and then move forward.

Political parties were not "allowed" to be a part of the political system designed by the octopus to offer freedom of choice through the voting system. They have been utilized to create an *illusion of choice* and to quiet the masses through a false sense of empowerment. In this way, the octopus would not be seen as the one's pulling the strings behind the curtain. The multi-party system has served them well because it has divided the people into opposite corners, rallying for one tidbit over another, creating division instead of the very real possibility of coherence and cooperation between elected officials and humanity, working together for the good of all.

We label this "democracy," but because of the octopus, only candidates who agree to support their agendas (or are later forced to, i.e. John F. Kennedy and so many others) are allowed to be in office. John F. Kennedy's death was directly related to his efforts to buck the Federal Reserve and stop other octopus plans that were in the works that he did not agree with. With the party system in place and much disagreement between the two major parties, no cohesion is ever likely, especially that truly represents the best and highest good of the people. That level of consciousness is in direct opposition to the powers that were desired outcomes.

Many think that a world that honors and factors in all people is noble, but impractical, and is a Pollyanna form of thought. Remember that whether or not you understand the Law of Like Attracts Like (or the power of intention) it still works in perfection and our vibrational signature is the fuel for all creation in our Universe. Our current state of affairs was created through the Law of Like Attracts Like, and it will change for the better when we change the energy from which we are manifesting.

It is a natural part of our divine nature to trust others and that is a very good thing. It is part of our Sacred Self's remembrance of a dimension where people are not capable of manipulation or lying to each other. Your chosen 3D experience in duality has simply offered to you a different kind of playground where the energy of discernment is highly useful if it is well-developed. In the end, regardless of how much or how little you see through the illusion of this reality, you can rest assured that all of these varied experiences have served you well along your soul's journey.

The War Tentacle

The war machine creates massive money and power for the octopus. How have they managed to assemble such a large power base to carry out their agendas? They have achieved this through the energy of fear, hate, separation and instilling strong beliefs within the psyches of humanity that one country (or one group of people) is disposable and less important than another because the octopus has deemed them dangerous. The truth is that the octopus has large agendas within many country's borders and "danger" becomes the dominant card to play to justify their means.

Feelings of extreme loyalty to our own country and our own way of life have grown to epic proportions, not only in this country, but globally. We are taught in our childhood to be "good supporters" of our country. After all, it is the American way, right? This entire topic is a difficult one for many people and I hope you will stay with me as I share my concerns about the ultimate outcome of these loyalties and how they make us more willing to wage war and hurt those to whom we are so deeply connected. My hope is that you can see how this energy has been highly misused by the octopus to recruit humanity in the name of patriotism and pride.

There is a very definite formula and energy to the octopus' approach and it promotes separation from our Source and each other. Its foundational energy is pride and ego. This energy feeds upon one's healthy and deep desire to be a part of something greater, especially when we are led to believe it is for such a noble cause as freedom. But under the octopus, these impulses became a tool for enmeshing people into the low vibrations of violence and war. It has offered a misused and *misplaced sense of unity*, housed within fear, prejudice, revenge, domination, and destruction.

One of the grandest mis-perceptions of all is that as divine Beings on this planet, we must fear one another and kill each other to stay "safe." This is an oxymoron. There is absolutely nothing in your core divine blueprint that naturally supports taking another's life. The citizens of a country *do not* go to war without inflammation by a government with a clearly defined agenda and a created source of conflict that benefits no one but themselves and their political partners. Of course these agendas have been well-masked from the general public.

With all major media outlets now owned by just four powers that were-collaborative corporations, every manufactured event that is planned and executed is accompanied by carefully written media spin. This propaganda is designed to create fear and convince the public to agree to and support the latest round of profit-driven wars in the name of democracy, terrorism or even humanitarian acts. These are bankster wars, in congruence with the octopus because it is the octopus that designed the global financial system and all associated agencies that run their banking system. It's the same pattern: create the problem or crisis and enact the solution that best furthers the overall, long-term plans of the powers that were—always. Their "stories" are in alignment with their desire for greater power and control; not the reasons you have been given on their news channels.

Humanity is on the cusp of putting the blood-soaked swords down forever. Violence has no place in the higher 5th dimensional energies we are fast approaching. I do not mean this figuratively—this is very literal, as any energy that is not in congruence with love, peace, sovereignty, unity and oneness cannot move forward into the new paradigm.

Can humanity let go of the promotion of these agendas or will we continue to buy into the story that we must "defend" something? It has always been the octopus that has created the object of fear or distain and then also provided the means to correct it. The octopus cannot survive with peace on Earth. War sustains tyranny and it promotes agendas to keep humanity participating in the illusion of separation.

When we mindlessly accept the octopus' agendas for humanity without question, and out of fear, we give them the green light to continue. Our trust in authority has been grossly abused and manipulated. Those who are deeply asleep within the system cannot even see how they are led over the cliff. They cannot yet see, that their actions are harming humanity.

What happens in any given country affects every soul on this planet. If you feel proud of your country, great—then feel proud of all countries because there is not one that is better than another. It's like saying that the ocean is better than the desert or your hand is better than your foot. Each entity serves an *integral and divine purpose* in this world. We do not "own" our countries—Gaia does, and Gaia did not construct border lines and walls to keep us separated and in fear of each other. We are simply her guests for as long as we are here in physicality.

The emotion of pride is not, in and of itself, a bad thing. The *differentiation* here lies in the distinct energy of fear, arrogance, revenge, anger and ego that make up the energy of the war cry. Feeling proud of our accomplishments is great. It is when we then take that energy to promote superiority that causes us problems. These energies will not be a part of the new 5D paradigm—they are duality in action.

The media and Hollywood movies have created very romantic, idealized concepts of war. We've bought their story that war is a *necessary evil*, therefore it is accepted as inevitable and required to live safely. The carnage has been romanticized so much that the reality of global peace falls by the wayside as seemingly impossible or as some ideological attainment.

I deeply honor, respect and appreciate *every single veteran across the globe*, because each and every Being has had the same good intention and truly believed they were doing the right thing in service to their respective countries. Many enlisted personnel at every rank are now seeing through what they have been told and realizing the true "causes" of conflict and war, as well as the real outcome to be achieved.

Peace only appears to be impossible because we have been taught by the octopus to believe this. The message is that "unfortunately," we must kill others to live in freedom. Many will tell you that "we wouldn't be here today but for the (fill in the blank) war." How is it we wouldn't be here and *thriving* in a way that we have yet to experience *because of war*, tyranny and violence?

Is it because of war's deep scar upon our psyches and the resultant pain and loss that we must use romanticism and heroic validation to justify the deaths of those who were murdered in the war games of the octopus? Has becoming a hero become the consolation prize for returning home mangled and damaged from the carnage of war? There is no such thing as "winning a war." There are *no* winners—it is illusion within this 3D matrix.

As the truth about the octopus continues to unfold and the Light shines *brightly* upon its actions, it will be particularly difficult for those who have personally suffered and sacrificed greatly because of war. There is soon to come a time when people will fully realize (as consciousness continues to rise) that the justifiable reasons given by governments to create and staff wars have been non-truths created under false pretenses for a very long time.

Who are you *really* serving? If you want peace and unity on this planet you must first *be it* and *live it* in every way. An equation of rifles plus bombs will never equal peace, freedom and sovereignty.

Responsibility starts and ends with each one of us. We must heal ourselves from the inside out, for just stopping the war games does not, in and of itself, heal the energies within us that allowed them to begin in the first place. You cannot force something into ease. It must rise from a higher collective consciousness.

From the perspective of the octopus, democracy and peace were never meant to materialize on this planet. The concept that peace can be achieved *through* war and destruction is a powerful belief used by the octopus to assemble a force on its behalf.

When you are "fighting against" anything, you are in opposition to 5D energies and 5D consciousness. The low vibrations of war and aggression are at the opposite end of the spectrum of how evolved Beings solve their conflicts. If you enjoy feeling patriotic for your country, then *also* be a patriot for global peace and oneness. Be a patriot for unconditional love and acceptance for *all* people. The citizens across this planet deeply desire peace. But because we have not understood the foundational *cause* of the violence surrounding us, we have not been able to change anything. This was by design—one cannot alter what they cannot see and understand.

When we begin to channel the same passion we have for our respective countries into a passion for the freedom of *all* of humanity across this Earth from tyranny and manipulation, we will find *true* freedom.

The octopus still very much desires to create their "new world order," but what is rapidly transpiring instead is a "New Order of Higher Consciousness" across the entire globe. It is igniting even those who have been sound asleep and there is nothing that will extinguish this blaze. The only way that humanity will actualize true, real and lasting peace is through the deconstruction of the 3D systems. This enormous project has been happening for quite some time and the fruits of this labor will soon be apparent to all people.

The Banking System

The financial system that was designed by the octopus is the pitcher and the catcher in the octopus' ball game. As global citizens, we are now watching their game strategy crumble before our very eyes. People are viewing the impending financial collapse with great fear, but in reality it is the take down of the old corrupt system to allow implementation of the new system. If one is paying attention, the steps have been being put into place for many years now. The powers that were have been given many opportunities to become a part of the new consciousness, but have repeatedly refused, or made promises that are never kept. Humanity (nor Gaia) can no longer wait and it is time for the new systems to come on board.

The corruption within the global financial system alone is so deep it constitutes volumes of future books. The construct of the financial/banking cartel is one of the deepest rabbit holes of all when it comes to shaping humanity.

Our "economy" has not been a factor of any sort of natural order of economics as it should be and as you have been led to believe. Recessions, depressions and inflationary periods in history have been planned, staged and carried out through deliberate manipulation of the ebb and flow of fiat monies into the currency system, solely controlled by the octopus at the top level behind the mystical curtain.

This system has always been in alignment with the powers that were overall agenda for increased power, profits and control. The octopus has controlled *all* global banking systems (including the BIS, IMF, World Bank, and most other arms of the financial system). Because they have designed and controlled all facets of international banking and investments, they can and do also control our economies, pricing structures and lack versus abundance. We have not functioned in a natural, free-flowing economic reality as we have been taught by academia—it is a highly controlled system that supports the illusion of economic freedom for the vast majority of the world's population. However, the creation of the new BRICS alliance is the first tangible step we are seeing that other countries have had enough of the contrived banking system.

The banking system (in the United States) quite intentionally fed the housing boom with easy to get loans as they raked in trillions in contractual notes. Then, just as planned, they pulled the rug out and watched the housing market crumble. They then bailed themselves out (the government is intricately connected with the banking system so it's a non-truth to think that the bailouts are separate) and then proceeded to spank their own hands and promise never to do it again. In this way, they steered millions of homeowners directly into foreclosure as they raked in billions of dollars through the illegal foreclosure process that they used. This story is one for many solo books because it is directly tied to exactly how Wall Street and the banking system divided mortgage deeds from notes and illegally resold them in great numbers, making trillions in profit. They could no longer provide their "notes" for each mortgage, and as such, had no legal authority to foreclose on a property without the notes as instruments. But remember who designed the legal system, as part of the entire construct? No judge (historically) is going to buck the well-oiled system in place that supports the octopus at the highest levels. And in the vast majority of cases filed and heard in courts, they have not.

With the help of their media corporations and the Feds, they then painted a picture to the world of a housing bubble that caused deflated home values and a bad economy that then justified their illegal foreclosures.

The banking employees that you meet and greet at the local level of the systems have no clue who they are truly working for, nor of the agendas being played out at the top level. Employees within the lower levels of all of the systems of the octopus are not privy to this information. They are simply trying to earn a living and stay afloat like the rest of us. However, there are many that are now awakening and realizing that what they have been blindly doing is not right and is harming others. We each have a critical choice to make—to support the incoming frequencies of 5D, or to continue being instruments of the powers that were.

Remember, to clearly see the picture that the octopus has tried to create, you must climb that elevator to the rooftop Vista Point. It is from that clarity and transparency that you will be able to see and understand the entire puzzle all put together. Otherwise, the many compartmentalized *pieces* will not make sense to you. Seek the **big picture**.

The financial tentacle has always manipulated the economy, but the vast majority of citizens bought the 3D economic educational construct and through academia, believed that this is "how it all works." The credit scoring agencies have also served the octopus well by keeping people in fear of losing their financial stature and means to survive. Their scoring *awarded our good behavior* and willingness to acquiescence and play the game as dictated. The falsehood is that "good" people pay their debts and are to be respected and people who cannot or *no longer choose* to play the 3D games are treated as irresponsible, bad citizens or deviants who are to be penalized and shunned. It has been an effective way to keep the masses under tight control and playing the game.

The octopus has created the financial ruins we are finding ourselves in. The US Corporation is now completely bankrupt and broke, while other countries associated with and supporting their objectives are also in financial ruin. They are running from the dollar as fast as they can. As announcements are made about our Republic and the return to global metal/asset-backed currencies, we will collectively begin to see the Light at the end of the tunnel.

Future banking practices are to be Basel III compliant and transparent so that any further monetary manipulation will not be possible. This financial changing of the guard equals the death of the existing financial tentacle of the octopus and a new and better way of life for the people of Earth.

Healthcare

Allopathic (Western) medicine has a *very* valuable place in our world, and we are blessed to have the many advancements and care that is offered. Many healthcare workers devote their entire lives to helping other people and truly care about their patients. However, the entire system is highly controlled by big pharma and corporate insurance companies, as part of the system designed by the powers that were.

An ideal situation would be to combine the best of allopathic medicine with highly effective alternative medicine and allow them to work together. However, until the octopus is no longer a factor, this feat is not possible because the basis of the pharmaceutical and insurance companies is to support the agendas of the powers that were and vice-versa—it's all about the money and other goals, not the health of humanity. There is a distinct conflict of interest between the octopus-controlled allopathic tentacle and alternative medicine and self-healing tools. Humanity's needs have taken a major backseat to corporate power, profits and other agendas.

There are many amazing, alternative healing tools to discover if you choose, versus relying solely upon the allopathic community and drug companies. The only three healthcare solutions offered by the allopathic system are: surgery, various kinds of therapy and prescription drugs, which all have serious side effects that can often be worse than the ailment being addressed. Options such as homeopathy, herbal medicine, energy medicine, acupuncture, and DNA-level trauma release are all effective healing methods that have been tried and true for hundreds, if not thousands of years. They can safely release core level issues, not just offer a band-aid so that they are further suppressed into the body, later returning in an even larger way.

The octopus has gone to great lengths to ensure that centuries old, highly effective natural healing methods are mostly hidden or discredited and seen as inferior to allopathic options. The holistic medical community is rarely covered by insurance companies, although this is slightly better than it used to be.

I encourage you to remember yourself as a very powerful self-healer and research many avenues around your health and your family's health. Use your inner discernment regarding your health issues and how to solve them. Make your doctor(s) *part* of your team, not the end all. So many people hand all of their power over to their doctors without any core-connected input or thought as to their best course of treatment and most of their decisions are made out of pure fear. Every single illness or disease begins in the energetic emotional and/or spiritual field before it integrates into the body. Disease is the messenger for the soul, conveying what we need to address at a far deeper level. Physical manifestations are always energetically based. Thoughts and beliefs are energy, as are emotions and spiritual blockages.

Allopathic medicine certainly has a valuable and valid function in our world, but it offers no method to heal core-level issues, nor does it treat a person holistically, mind, body and spirit. *We simply do not exist as compartmentalized Beings, nor do we heal that way.* Your physical vehicle is purely energetic, existing at varying levels of density and frequency. Therefore it also heals energetically, first and foremost. The physical body always follows the energetic body's lead.

We literally "bring in" many of the illnesses we manifest, through our DNA and energetic bodies. Many are trauma-induced emotional patterns created from our ancestors' experiences that have materialized within our bodies. When a major emotional trauma anywhere in our lineage goes unreleased and unhealed, we inherit that unhealed energy through our DNA and psyches. The energy then plays itself out in our lives and in our physical bodies. The closest science has gotten to the above is epigenetics. Merriam-Webster

Dictionary (www.merriam-webster.com) defines epigenetics as "the study of heritable changes in gene function that do not involve changes in DNA sequence." Epigenetics is an exciting new frontier that is bridging many gaps and answering many questions. However, traditional science and medicine (mainly because of the compartmentalization of the mind, body and spirit) has yet to factor in or understand how our experiences and traumas also alter our DNA from a multidimensional perspective.

We have the ability to release these patterns of trauma if we know how and anyone can learn to do this if they desire. Once the emotional body is addressed, the cells will release the disease patterning exhibiting within the body, if the healing is in alignment with one's life plan for this to happen.

Traditional Western medicine has been primarily shaped by the octopus' corporate interests—not the good intentions of the allopathic doctors and practitioners within this system to truly help humanity—there is a distinct difference here. As with school teachers, most doctors are caught unknowingly within a system that never had any intention of allowing the knowledge of our energetic nature to be mainstream truth because healthy, awakened people are not profitable *or* controllable. However, at what point do we awaken and begin asking some important questions aimed at the pharmaceutical companies about their prescription drugs and vaccination agendas? There simply is no truth to the belief that vaccines save lives or even offer the prevention that they claim to—the non-octopus funded research shouts *very loudly* in the opposite direction. Ignorance and loud media spin keeps this non-truth going and is dividing the public. The octopus desires to take away your right of choice by claiming that non-vaccinated children harm vaccinated children. This makes no sense whatsoever since if the vaccines actually worked, then in no way would the vaccinated children be at any risk, regardless of their exposure! This is propaganda spin and the pro-vaccine clan is unknowingly and permanently harming their children's health and affecting their longevity and proclivity to vaccine-induced diseases. Allopathic doctors are ignorantly pushing the octopus' agendas, based upon the voice and so-called research from big pharma and their highly profitable vaccine industry.

If our vehicles deteriorate, it becomes much more difficult to be open to receiving the higher energies that facilitate our awakening. Our chakra systems begin to close down. Our once vibrant vehicle that was designed to interpret and integrate the higher vibrational energies can no longer perform.

Our pineal gland (our Third Eye that interprets incoming energies) becomes clogged with sediment from the toxic food and flourinated/chlorinated water supply. It is no accident that every tentacle within the old system is architected to shut down the human mind, body and spirit. If we awaken, we will stop participating in the programs. And yet, the deeper the rabbit hole goes, the more that people have simply obeyed and acquiesced. We stopped consulting our own *Inner Authority* and now we must take responsibility for allowing these systems to not only exist, but to flourish through our slumbering.

The Media Conglomerates

Many people are now realizing that most all of the mainstream television stations, newspapers and newscast are controlled and little is reported or discussed that is not preapproved. If you truly wish to unplug yourself from the fading 3D paradigm and raise your vibration, this would be an excellent place to start and stop feeding your consciousness with propaganda, fear and negativity.

TV news provides daily, highly censored *fear feedings* that lower mass consciousness vibratory levels. The octopus-controlled media conglomerates distort the truth. There are no benefits to watching the images of trauma and tragedy around the globe.

How many people ever question why 90% of all news consists of negative content? Do you really believe that there are not equal or greater events happening globally that are positive and of very high vibrational quality and would be uplifting and a joy to hear about? Do you question why these too are not being widely broadcast when we know unequivocally that what we focus upon grows energetically until it manifests?

There are excellent online independent sources for accurate news. The irony is that you are likely to find the reporting of the truth even more sensational because we have been sheltered from the truth for so long. Please filter everything you hear, see and read through your intuition. When you practice this art and master it, never again will anyone be able to push non-truths past you—your "truth meter" will instantly alert you to use your discernment. *We are our own best reporters of what is of truth.* You will not find truthful answers to any of your questions through these outlets as this "news" is packaged and delivered in a way that frames what the octopus wishes for you to perceive as truth. So many people believe everything that is reported on their mainstream news channels because they have lost the ability to decipher truth from fiction.

Be discerning about what you allow your consciousness to absorb through television, movies or other forms of news, media and entertainment. If it's full of low vibratory energies, you are being affected at a subconscious level. Some find horror movies "fun" but they are designed to further ingrain subconscious fear energy into your psyche. Like a sponge, you are allowing your vibration to be lowered via what you choose to permit into your life.

The octopus-owned and controlled media and television "news" cannot continue without your daily support of it. No viewers equals no money. An awakened population demands far more for the higher good of all. Much of television and a lot of the movie industry will be forced to transform into a higher expression of information and entertainment or cease to exist in our new 5D world.

Our Environment

The care and stewardship of Gaia is a divine responsibility for each of us, but it has instead become a political statement. It has been relegated to bills, laws and ordinances that govern what we can and cannot do with our planet, albeit ignored by the octopus. The 3D systems have harmed Gaia for well over a century with the many wars and the resulting energetic schisms left in these geographical areas. Oil and gas drilling, fracking, mining, industrial pollution,

Fukushima (which was octopus-driven), the global chemtrail (aerosol) spraying program, water and food contamination and pesticide programs add to her (and our) destruction. One of the latest programs is GMO food production *(easily, one of the most dangerous to date)*.

We have become so detached from our planet as the sacred and sovereign Being that Gaia is, that over the decades she has become essentially a dumping ground for our experiences. This abuse and neglect of our very platform for existence has left Gaia in a critical state where she cannot continue to support life. She is calling out for us to wake up, and is currently going through an enormous amount of clearing to heal herself. We are seeing an unprecedented amount of volcanic eruptions, tornados, hurricanes, freak storms and flooding across the world. This is far from coincidental—this is Gaia's way of relieving herself of the negative energy and low vibratory experiences that we have left her with.

There is no punishment involved here whatsoever. These geographical events are healing Gaia at her core level. She has graced us by acting as a playground for us to have our experiences upon, but this cycle is ending and it's time to return to the remembrance of our role as responsible Earth stewards.

Global warming is not an anomaly, but rather a by-product of the end of this cycle. Far more of the Earth is to be inhabitable and this requires the shifting of climates and land masses to allow for these changes. Our environment has obviously been greatly affected and harmed by industrialization and manufacturing. There is still some clearing that is to happen upon Earth but Gaia does not wish any harm to her beloved human family. However, she will continue to cleanse herself as safely as possible. The various relief mechanisms will continue until she fully rebalances herself, as we too are rebalancing ourselves to remain with her.

Parenting

The 3D model for raising our children is one that has served to develop only a small portion of a child's full capacity as a Being of

Light occupying a human vehicle. Because we as parents have forgotten how to access our own divine knowingness, gifts and talents, we have unknowingly taught our children the same. It has created generations of people who rely upon the octopus to direct their journey here, instead of being taught how to go within and remember the journey they themselves chose to have. Many parents are still very entrained within the 3D systems, so the current parenting model seems completely normal to them.

Most children are still taught that their birthright gifts such as their psychic ability, telepathy, playing with fairies and spirits are weird, frightening and unnatural. Many children are punished when they express their gifts, encouraging them to bury and forget about their divine nature. Eventually under this current 3D model, most children lose their natural abilities because of the strict conformity to be who they are not.

The children arriving upon this planet are far more spiritually advanced, energetically vulnerable and Light-filled than you may realize. They will not agree, even at a few months old, to follow the old paradigm. Expect much differentiation from them and strong opinions. They are not here to continue the status quo. They are here to influence and raise our collective vibration simply with their presence and their gifts.

These little ones are here to rapidly bust the old paradigm apart and assist others to do the same. They are born Light workers with great spiritual missions, arriving right in the thick of this grand shift. They will not be easily led off the cliff. Our jobs as parents is to allow them room to express who they really are, be creative, and protect them from the rigidity of the old paradigm. We need to help them maintain their strong, sacred connection and memory of their divine nature. They need our protection from the components out there designed to shut them down from their connected inner voices.

Create daily quiet times for meditations for your children and even make it a game of who hears, sees or feels what and then share it with each other. This helps them keep their psychic connections open and growing, as well as yours.

Pay special attention to your children's diets and help them avoid processed foods, GMO's, unhealthy school lunches, processed sugars and anything other than healthy organics, if possible. Drinking plenty of water is also critical for all of us and it should be pure, spring or filtered water, not tap water. Fluoride and chlorine both serve to calcify the pineal gland and harm their very delicate systems. These are documented neurotoxins and need to be removed from all water supplies.

When children are educated as to why healthy foods are in their best interest, they are innately more receptive to them because it is a truth that their inner Self knows and recognizes. Make healthy food fun and exciting for them to counter-act the corporate food programs they see in commercials and the temptations at school and at friends' houses.

Many kids love to cook (supervised of course) and help create and prepare their own foods, especially if they are encouraged to do so. Experiment with organic root veggies, raw creations, stir-fry, stews and soups, allowing your child to inject their own ideas for healthy foods into the daily routine. Make it fun. Buy some healthy cookbooks with lots of colorful pictures to read and encourage them to express themselves around creating their meals or helping in the kitchen in a fun and interactive way. Teach them that food has energy too and that the less the food is manipulated, the greater the energetic and nutrient content and the more it will raise their vibration, allowing their gifts to flourish. If you are able to grow a small vegetable garden and involve your kids in the planning, selection and care, they will have a greater appreciation and connection to the food they prepare and eat as they become more connected to Gaia. Teach them to consume their meals with intention and gratitude rather than mindlessly eating. Many children eat most of their meals in front of a television or video game and the parents wonder why their children are overweight, emotionally absent, chronically unhealthy and always hungry. There is no intention involved whatsoever and mindless eating (mindless anything) leads to a feeling of deep emptiness within us.

PART II

Who Are You Without the 3D Structures to Define You?

So who exactly are you if you do not define yourSelf by your success, your credit score, 3D status, job title, educational level, money, belongings or house? The current state of our global economy has been a powerful and effective catalyst to awaken people. Many feel led to answer these very personal questions about themselves.

We have deeply believed that we have to maintain what we have at great costs to our core Selves and our potential as powerful Light Beings. What we have failed to realize, or even contemplate for the most part, is that there are many options and choices outside of the prescribed agenda of the 3D system. Further, you become free to be the *intentional creator* that you are. With a fresh, clean canvas and paint brush, you are able to paint the life you really want; not the life that you were told you must live in order to be "successful" in this world.

There is nothing wrong with materialism, in and of itself, as long as it harms none, but that has not been the case. Many of us bought the concept that somehow more and more things could fill the void inside of us or make us feel more worthy, important or valuable in our society. Many people, especially in Western society, are hooked into the belief that accumulations, status, 3D power and wealth equals happiness, security, safety, respect and honor. Our educational attainment carries a large stigma around presumed intelligence and social status.

Maintaining the status quo is instilled within all of us. We feel great fear for our safety and many feel shame at a deep, subconscious level. Many people feel they have failed and done something wrong because they haven't achieved the false, glamorized ideal of success created by the octopus. They feel they are not good enough and did not "make it."

Belief systems around the meaning of wealth, certain professions and the social class hierarchy have led us to become our own "keepers." We are taught to categorize ourselves and others with labels and then place judgments upon which labels are prized and are to be rewarded and revered in our world—and which are not. We attach value and respect to those labels and we judge those people whose labels we feel are unacceptable.

As long as we obey the systems and buy into them, we are harmless to the octopus. We maintain our own separation from each other and remain immobile within our low frequencies. We have made it very convenient for them. And when they suspect that we might be waking up a bit, they simply pull out the trump card—fear, (terrorism attacks, fear of economic collapse or even their lab-created bird or swine flu in trying to create a global epidemic. Recently, it was the Ebola virus) playing it for distraction and control. Fear has always been used to control the people and it continues to work seamlessly with one exception—we *are* waking up en masse due to the higher frequencies pouring onto this planet and this frightens the octopus more than you can imagine.

Power, as we have known it, does not exist in the higher realms. All Beings are respected and honored within the oneness. As long as you are seeking power through the 3D systems, you cannot unfurl the innate and powerful Light that is within you.

Our collective path to freedom and enlightenment is clear—we must look at the systems of the octopus, acknowledge them and bless them as they crumble, so we may begin creating *new systems* that reflect our inner Light and sovereignty.

CHAPTER 8

Traps Within the 3D Matrix

As a master co-creator, you have full control and jurisdiction over yourself and no one can take that away from you unless you allow it. What is truly real is what you define as real, not what the systems tell you your reality must look like, feel like and be like.

How Fear Controls Us

Your vibrational state is greatly affected by fear. Your frequency, at any given time, is shaping what you see before you.

If you are stuck in negative thinking, beliefs and behaviors, everything that you see in the world is going to reflect those things back to you. If you are experiencing the world as incredibly awesome (and I hope that you are) it is because you are vibrating within a high frequency. It's much more than simply positive thinking, but positive thinking is a powerful paver on the path to positive experiences because positive thought raises your vibration. Our outer world is simply a reflection of our internal state.

If you fear this shift, you will magnetize plenty of reasons to give you fear, because that is how energy works to attract more of the same as your life experiences. Those that are convinced that we are headed for "Armageddon" are helping to manifest into reality just such a negative experience. You must heal your fears to raise your vibration. You will see and witness externally exactly what you believe that you will because you are creating it—either individually or as an integral part of the experience of mass consciousness. That's just how powerful you really are.

Fear Energy Is a Holographic Imprint Upon Mass Consciousness

Fear is generally related to something that could or might happen in your present or your future. Since you are a master co-creator and are in every nanosecond architecting your life through your emotions, thoughts and intentions, nothing happens in your "future" that you are not, in some part, responsible for creating. We create reality individually and as a collective consciousness. So when you align your energies with fear-based thoughts, you have then chosen to design and architect your future moments with energies that will indeed prove your fear-based thoughts as absolutely correct. The problem is that we have forgotten this tremendous truth. Also, this information (Universal Law) has been sequestered and hidden from us for a very long time. In the fifth dimension, this information is kindergarten material.

As you fear, so you create...

All of us have experienced great fear at various points in our lives. It is one of the most common emotions we experience and it is the easiest to be triggered. We are programmed by the systems to fear for our safety and survival in every way possible. Sometimes fear is instinctual, life-saving and vital (such as encountering a bear in the wild or a poisonous snake—it would not be a great idea to go pet the bear or play with the snake) but most often it is our largest barrier to creating our highest and best good. When fear runs its veins into mass consciousness, the results are extremely potent for those who give it their attention and energy. *It is the most powerful tool that the powers that were have used to further their desires.* That's why their operations have, historically, been so effective. The fear campaign keeps people inert within their systems.

Fear can be like a "shadow monster" that prevents us from boldly being who we came here to be. It can easily become an unhealthy filter between our Spirit and our consciousness and can affect our level of evolvement, not to mention our joy and happiness. It can (and does) hinder the ascension process for many people.

Fearlessness is inherent within a state of beingness and is completely natural beyond the 3D matrix. It resides at the Vista Point level of existence. The type of fearlessness that I speak of here is not the Hollywood version of violent characters toting automatic weapons on their shoulders. Those are the 3D versions of fearlessness in which one is supposedly not afraid of violence and bad guys. The type of fearlessness that I speak of far supersedes the ego's need to overpower others through violence. On the rooftop deck, there are no bad guys and no need for survival energies. This level of fearlessness comes through the heart and permeates our *knowingness*. It is the result of knowing who we really are and owning that divinity within ourSelves.

Spiritual awakening involves becoming fearless in a whole new way. When you remember your divine self empowerment, you know that predominantly, nothing outside of your chosen life experience (and karmic balancing) is going to happen to you. There is far more divine order and assistance happening in every single moment than we can fathom. When you remember how to let go and let the Universe guide you, fear becomes a distant reality.

The doomsday scenarios around massive destruction are a major trigger for us and designed to instill an internal sense of panic and terror. "The end of the world" scenarios trigger our subconscious, programmed minds. It is false information promoted by many who have aligned themselves with this large line of thought, rooted in fear energy. What it does accomplish is to assist in the creation of such scenarios because you are contributing your own manifestation abilities to this collective line of thought. The best paraphrase of this misinformation is, *"This is the end of a world ruled by the powers that were."* It is the end of duality among us and the transmutation of those energies across the globe. A peaceful and exciting transition to our new world is being offered to us if we choose to distance ourselves from the old frequencies of fear and resulting violence.

Fear Disrupts the Connection to Your Higher Self

When we fear change and are in resistance to the natural flow of evolution, we stop our growth and create stagnant energy in our lives. We feel stuck and wonder why we can't seem to move forward or achieve the things we so deeply desire. Fear is like a placard in our hearts and it marks us in ways we might not be aware of because it prevents a clear connection to the distinct wisdom offered by our Higher Selves. We have become so conditioned to living in fear within this matrix that most of us have no clue as to how it might feel to live our lives without it.

For those few who have overcome this element of duality and no longer live in fear, they are often seen by others as irresponsible, careless, even rogue citizens who refuse to follow the rules. There is a energy of calm and peace about them that is not understood by those who continue to be driven by fear and conformity. They have a distinct disconnection from the governing systems and a fearlessness that allows them to live in the moment and trust that everything is in divine order. In the absence of fear lies the foundation for peace and love.

Unplugging from the hologram of fear requires coming face to face with our own personal worries and traumas around feeling safe in the world. Fear wrecks havoc upon our bodies, emotions, mental stability and our Spirit because it drains us of our vital force. It can be a dark cloud over an otherwise stunning day. Fear greatly affects our connection to our intuition. It is also a tremendous depressive. Many people stay well-sedated with prescription drugs or alcohol and recreational drugs as a coping mechanism for all of their fear-based energies.

If we live in generalized fear for our safety, there is no castle or fortress on this planet that will protect us because our vibration will attract what we fear. Manifesting a sense of safety begins *within* us, not outside of us. Bolted doors and weapons will not keep you safe. Fear leads to apathy, depression and hopelessness, manifesting in our personal lives (as well as in mass consciousness) in ways that include:

- Alcoholism, drug abuse
- Paranoia
- Feelings of terror
- Obesity
- Grief
- Feelings of lack and loss
- Poverty
- Obsessive-compulsive behavior
- Hate, war, violence
- Taking jobs that drain our core vitality
- Avoidance of life because there are risks involved and we might be hurt
- Disease and illness
- Intolerance, homophobia, transphobia, racism, sexism and terrorism
- Greed and tyranny
- And the list goes on…

Fear might be so familiar to some of us that we have made it our very good friend. Fear causes us to miss out on amazing opportunities to grow and experience our lives to the fullest extent. For example, we might decide to turn down a challenging, but exciting, new career path that utilizes our divine gifts. We don't laugh too loud or aren't affectionate with our loved ones in public because of what others might think. We solve our fear-based issues with violence and blame. Fear often begins the day we are born into this 3D world and it is passed on to us in subtle ways through the systems and through our families and friends who themselves are stuck in fear-based patterns. Eventually, we are so well-programmed that it is our own internal voice that keeps us in line. Our self-talk then replicates and reinforces the messages and beliefs. Fear energies are also passed to us through our DNA—we literally inherit our ancestor's fears from their unhealed traumatic experiences.

Healing Our Fears

Acknowledging our fears is an incredibly powerful method for dissolving them. It is through our awareness of our fears that we can then name them, write them down, ponder them and then release them, knowing that they are just part of this 3D construct. As we release our fears from our mental, emotional, and physical bodies, we heal our Spirit and make far more vibrational "room" to hold a greater amount of Light within us.

There is nothing more important these days than raising our vibration and carefully selecting what we allow to permeate our energetic Selves. As we remember how to embrace our divine blueprint, we learn that setting up energetic boundaries with others (including the octopus) and with the world at large is critical to increasing our Light and keeping our vibration consistent. We learn to let go of those things (this can often include people and relationships) in our lives that lower our vibration and that hook us back into the 3D energies. We then graduate to the next step and learn how to be in the presence of any type of energy and truly not be affected by it or thrown off course. This level of mastery takes some practice and that is why I call it the next step. As ascended master, Lord Sananda (the aspect that was Jesus on Earth) taught, it is learning how to be in this world, but not of it.

When we are running fear energy, our internal GPS malfunctions because we are making decisions and going directions based upon a fear-induced emotional state, instead of making decisions from our highest perspectives and inner wisdom. We are *all* indoctrinated into the fear program of the octopus. The task at hand is for us to recognize and acknowledge our fears to heal and release them.

Explore your fears, write them down and ask yourself, "How does this make me feel?" Then use the powerful tools in this book to release them. No one is keeping you a prisoner of fear, but you. You may find that as you detach from the systems you will have to educate your loved ones as to what you are doing and why. You may find it helpful to explain the higher spiritual perspective to help them understand the importance of your actions. As you reclaim your own freedom, you are also helping to raise the frequency of mass consciousness, helping all others as well.

Betrayal/Guilt

As we detach from the 3D matrix, we often experience a period of feeling betrayed. The truth of this reality, once seen, can leave one feeling victimized, quite angry at the octopus (and all those carrying out its agendas) disillusioned, powerless and wondering how we could have possibly not seen all of this before. In fact, this is a very common part of the grieving process that happens when you wake up to the truth and realize that life is not what you thought it was. Your world can feel turned upside down for a little while as you go through the healing process and acquire new truths. You may well feel denial and loss before you reach acceptance and acknowledgement—the magical place to be. Just remember, there is no such thing as *normal* and everything you feel is always ok. It's what you do next that determines your evolution—a greater perspective is *always* a choice.

You might feel a sense of betrayal, not only by those you placed your trust in (such as your government, religious authority or any and all parts of the octopus' system that you personally connected with) but there may also be an *internal* sense of betrayal. In one way or another over many lifetimes, we have all bought into the manipulations of the powers that were. Whenever we realize that non-truths or even half-truths have gotten past our own internal gatekeeper, we can feel betrayed and often befuddled as to how we did not see what was right in front of us.

Many people have trouble identifying their feelings around this so that they are able to release them. Keep the roof-top vista in sharp focus and remember that you chose to come here to experience all that the 3D world has to offer. You cannot fully experience duality within this illusion unless you were slumbering to some extent. Give yourself a break and unconditional love instead. At a soul level, you have attained lifetimes of huge gifts and a wealth of knowledge from every experience you have ever had. No experience is ever wasted. Be gentle with yourself and others as you awaken from your slumber.

Judging Others

Being critical of others is another large trap within the 3D energies. The stance we take when we are judging others is most often from a place of ego and/or fear. We do not have a clue what someone else's soul path entails, nor their karmic balancing that they may be working on with other people (another soul might have agreed from non-physical to help balance the energetic scales). Any judgment of others only feeds our need to be right and feel substantiated. Compassion, forgiveness and empathy are all key to our ascension. It is time to heal, and to understand that what we perceive in 3D is extremely limited as compared to the Vista Point. If you wish to raise your vibration, this is a wonderful place to begin. Honor, respect, acceptance, appreciation and gratitude are all emotions that will take us far in healing our emotional and spiritual Selves.

Working Hard

Do you view your daily life as a struggle, or believe that you must *work hard* if you are to achieve anything of value in this world? The energy of "hard work" (created by the systems to serve the systems) is also connected to our sense of worthiness in the world. We are taught that if we work hard enough, we can then feel good about ourselves. We often feel that those who do not work hard enough by our standards are not to be respected or are lazy. In essence, it feeds our egos and ensures we feel good enough. The ability we each possess to manifest our reality from pure thought and vibration does not require hard, physical or mental work. In fact, it necessitates a vibrational frequency first and foremost, that is in alignment with our desire and then *followed by actions* that are also in alignment with our energetic intention. This may or may not require what we label, "hard work," but nonetheless the end results are the manifestation of our desires. It requires remembering how the cosmos actually works and using these cosmic tools to create from. It takes you out of the manifest world and into the unmanifest where all creation originates. Life was not meant to be hard. Anything that feels hard or difficult puts us into an instant state of resistance with what we truly want because it is not fun or enjoyable. If we shift our ingrained concept from "hard work" to *intentional work*, our creations flow with ease and grace. They do not feel hard at all; they instead feel easy, joyful and in full alignment with our purpose and reason for being here.

Worthiness

Your worth as a human being is inherent in your birthright as a divine aspect of All That Is. There is nothing that you need to *do* or *be* to be fully worthy of everything wonderful, sacred and beautiful in this world. You were born perfect and you will die in perfection, regardless of how you walk your journey while here. How can you be less than the Source that you are from and a part of? Beyond this costume you wear, you are a sacred Being in a Light Body consisting of pure, unconditional Love. Within this costume that you have perfectly chosen for your current experiences, still lies the pure unconditional Love and Light that you *are*. Someone once said that "what other people think of us is none of our business." This is a great truth, as we have no control over others' opinions of us and no one's opinion of us truly matters except our own. When we stop reacting to what others think and/or say about us, we take a solid step into the mastery of our emotional body. Our job is not to convince others of anything. Our job is to be *authentic* and allow others to have all of their chosen emotional and physical experiences, as long as we are not harmed in the process. The ultimate foundation and motto of 5D is "harm none." Your complete and absolute worthiness as a whole, beautiful, beloved and valued Being is as much a part of you as is your breath. Your complete worthiness of everything beautiful and wonderful in this Universe just **is**. The teachings and various doctrines within the 3D paradigm that might have taught you otherwise are illusionary and unreal, as they do not speak to the truth of who you really are.

The Need to Be Right

This is a very powerful energy and one can easily fall prey to its lure. It is seated in ego, feeling powerless and fear. When we feel that we must be right, it dishonors others who have an equal right to their opinions and thoughts and it prevents us from being open to learning from others perceptions. It also fosters an energy of competition instead of cooperation and collaboration. It truly speaks to how inferior and insecure the one that needs to be right feels inside. Very often, there is trauma involved where "being right" or being in control equals feeling safe in the world. In some families, being competent (which can include being "right") is critically important because competence equals worthiness and also feeling loved.

Many people feel they need to force their "rightness" on others who do not agree with them. It is an emotional field that creates duality within relationships, for if there has to be a right, there must also be a wrong. This yin-yang choice puts us in a tight box and limits our perspectives around life in general. It hinders our ability to learn and grow through cooperation with others and to entertain a wide range of viewpoints and different understandings. An expanded *Vista Point* approach is that there is no right or wrong version of reality, only many different perspectives and lens in which we filter what we label as real. Our own ideas around "right" might be very "wrong" for someone else's journey and it is not our place to judge where that may fall. Every human being has a basic divine right to be heard, respected as an important part of humanity and acknowledged and honored, *even if we strongly disagree with them.* Can you see how the 3D systems have taught us that it is ok to not only totally disregard and disrespect those who we do not agree with, but to also kill and eliminate them? The history books are full of examples.

Victim Consciousness/Powerlessness

At some point in our lives, we have all felt powerless and victimized. The octopus has taken this energy to the max, because a world that lives within the energy of powerlessness will never rise up against the systems that have been put into place. This is why a key message throughout this book is a remembering of humanity's active choice to participate in this 3D matrix. We are not victims of anything—we co-created a very potent stage for soul-level growth. Our memory of this truth then allows us to exit the stage any time we feel ready to do so. Accepting responsibility removes the illusionary chains that appear around us. Taking the reins dissolves feeling powerless. As we remember who we really are, this energy will be healed and released from the planet.

Martyr Energy

When you take on the energy of being a martyr, you attract people and situations that allow you to continue playing out your belief in this energy and your hook to it. This is true of all potential 3D traps. Martyr energy is very similar to victim energy, but with a slightly different flavor. It allows us to feel safe in the world and valued, through our chosen suffering. It is easy to feel angry at our plight and we place all responsibility for our circumstances outside of ourselves by blaming others. We might be subconsciously seeking pity, bravado and/or attention from others via a low vibratory pattern of behavior that serves to brings us more of the same.

Martyrdom energy can also be expressed as being selfless and sacrificing ourselves for others. Taking care of others can evolve into self-sacrifice rather easily and also allows us to skirt taking care of ourselves, or our path of healing and reason for being here. Many doctrines have taught us that self-sacrifice is a divine trait. It is not—it serves only to distract us from embracing our divine empowerment, creating major imbalances in our lives and relationships. We must put our oxygen masks on *first*, before we can truly assist others. We are here to be in service to each other, but not at the *expense* of our own Selves. Being in service to humanity, balanced with self-care, is optimal and does not require the lower frequency emotional patterns of self-sacrifice.

Addictions/Repression

A plethora of cultures around the globe teach people to hide and repress their true feelings and emotions. The results are tragic communication issues, wars, disease, rampant addictions of all kinds and desolate relationships. When we inhibit the healthy expression of ourselves, we wither inside and many then turn to substances that they think will fill the emptiness. Numbed out people are everywhere and it makes their awakening more challenging because they feel hostage to their unprocessed emotions, substances, people, or situations. They cut themselves off from their heartfelt feelings and expressions. Addictions serve to keep us stuck within the illusion. Some people are addicts because they are sensitive to energies in general and many are highly empathic as well. The addiction is a way of handling the bombardment of energies because no one has taught these individuals how to create energetic boundaries to keep the outside 3D world from permeating them to such an extent that it causes them intense pain. For many people, their natural psychic abilities have opened up and they do not understand what is happening, or how to direct them.

Highly empathic people feel the feelings and emotions of *all* whom they come in contact with. They also easily tune-in and actually feel the predominant energies of mass consciousness at a global level. This can easily fry their delicate nervous systems and adrenal glands, while they often have no idea why they feel so sick and unhappy. They can also pick up non-physical attachments quite easily because they are so energetically open and without the proper boundaries. This just serves to exacerbate the addictive cycle. In the case of an empathic person, many may turn to drugs or alcohol to try to escape the extreme sensory connection to the outer world.

Frequently, they are very gifted intuitive healers from birth. Most newly arriving children are coming in at this level of sensitivity too. They are *easily* overwhelmed by the 3D world because they are already entrained with the 5D world energetically and find it very challenging to make sense of the collapsing paradigm. Doctors and psychiatrists are far too eager to simply medicate and label these children with a "disorder" and the drugs effectively shut them down energetically, physically, spiritually and emotionally.

If you have an addiction in any form, there are many options out there that can help you let go. There are also many great healing modalities that will teach you how to create the necessary boundaries to stop the daily bombardment of the outer world upon your senses. Remember, the systems have taught us all to shut down. Highly sensitive, psychic and empathic people who choose *not* to numb out often find it very difficult to *exist* within the current systems unless they learn how to have strong energetic boundaries. Ever hear this topic discussed on your 6:00 p.m. news? Probably not.

Depression

If more "stuff" is the recipe for human happiness, then why do we have so much of it and yet millions of people globally take antidepressant drugs daily? The less we are able to be internal with ourselves, the more we rely upon the external to guide us and fill the void, and the more depressed we feel. We then pass our repressions, depression and addictions down through our lineages if we do not own and heal them. We are not taught that all physical and mental issues begin in our energetic fields. Instead, we are told that a chemical substance with a host of serious side effects will magically solve our problems.

Anger

Anger is most often a secondary emotion. It can mask fear, hurt, guilt and many other primary feelings. Anger can feel like a good spot to land in comparison to other more painful emotions, as it can feel empowering and like a step forward. Anger can also be an unexpressed boundary that can, through awareness, evolve into a more positive vibration. I have also known many people who use anger and hostility to feel emotionally safe because they push people away from them. They prevent being in a situation that would allow them to feel emotionally vulnerable. Anger definitely serves an important place, as do all human emotions within 3D, but problems arise for us when certain emotions become our main reaction to most of our life experiences. The neurotransmitter/chemicals that are released from the brain when one is experiencing anger can actually become very addicting at a cellular level. When this happens we will create situations and people in our lives with whom to play out this addiction. In fact, all emotions (including joy and happiness) can become addictive and literally be habit-forming at a brain chemical level. Anger can keep us in a cyclical state of volatility as well as in resistance to what we actually want in our lives.

Cynicism

Cynicism is defined by Webster's Dictionary as "one who is inclined to question goodness." When we do not *expect* goodness in our lives we, by default, manifest things we do not desire. The powers that were have promoted cynicism in our lives at every turn. We have been taught to question everything out of mistrust for each other and a great need to protect ourselves from hurt and pain. Cynicism in the extreme, has become a safety device for some people. For many, it has gotten out of hand and it overshadows their lives and dictates how they respond to *all* that life brings their way. When you respond to everything in your life cynically and suspiciously, you block those things you most desire. You are likely to miss out on opportunities that present themselves because you are too skeptical to look at them through a neutral or positive filter. Habitual cynics live their lives in the bottom, half-filled portion of the glass and things can and do become very negative and distorted.

Cynicism is a valuable part of one's intuition and discernment and is highly necessary when looking at the octopus, but for many, it has become out of balance and a filter for how they view life. All of us know one or two "Negative Nellies" who have a pessimistic attitude about almost everything. When presented with even the most positive of information, they immediately turn to skepticism and cynicism and they mistrust that the information could possibly be true or without some catch or trap. They also manifest from this energy and wonder why things never seem to pan out for them. They have forgotten how to use their intuition and guidance systems that infallibly registers truth from fiction.

As full consciousness returns to us, we will gently ease away from the above persona characteristics that have been so familiar to us in this dualic world. The beliefs, triggers and emotions that once kept us captive within states of disharmony will transform into the higher frequencies of love and acceptance. This transformation is occurring through the transmutation of the 3D hologram as it evolves into the 5D paradigm.

Non-Truths Seated Within Our Consciousness

Non-Truth: The world is a very frightening place to live. You survive through fear.
Truth: That which you fear you magnetize directly into your life experience through the Law of Attraction and Like Attracts Like. If you feel unsafe within you, you will automatically manifest more to feel unsafe about.

Non-Truth: No one is perfect. We are all sinners, punishable and unworthy. We must earn our divinity because we are unworthy sinners.
Truth: Sinful people do not exist. The concept of sin is defined as one who is creating through very low vibratory energies and frequencies. Those energies/thoughts/actions activate the Universal Law of Cause and Effect (Karmic Law.) You are an inherent and inseparable part of that which you call God. As such, it is impossible for you to be anything less than a divine and perfect Being of Light who chose

to manifest in a vehicle in order to experience life on planet Earth. You are a cosmic, galactic Being with ancestry from many star nations who has forgotten their divine nature and abilities. Your illusion of "less than" has been part of the 3D construct created by the powers that were. You are now being given the opportunity to wake up to the remembrance of all that you really are—if you choose to.

Non-Truth: Some people are more "Godly" and more worthy than others because they obey the rules of religious dogma.
Truth: Every single Being on this planet (or any other) is 100% equally loved by Source. Regardless of one's actions while experiencing here, every soul is as loved and honored as any other. There are no favorites and there are no "chosen people." This belief is manufactured ego and seated in self-righteous illusion. There are simply those that *choose* to live within the higher frequencies and those who *choose* to continue their experiencing within the low density of the third dimensional energies. Religion has nothing to do with Being Godly.

Non-Truth: We are separate from each other and must protect ourselves from each another.
Truth: We have never been separate from each other and the recall of our true oneness is coming to Light now as we climb the vibrational ladder of consciousness together. We are a unified, cohesive and coherent whole and when we reach a global tipping point of remembrance, the powers that were will fade because the energetic foundation will no longer support them.

Non-Truth: The world is full of evil and people are out to get you and your loved ones, so be very cautious, fearful and guarded. This greatly narrows and congests your heart chakra and puts your root chakra in a state of constant angst, anxiety and fragility.
Truth: The world is just as full of Love and Light—your experiences always reflect your fears, beliefs and thoughts, whatever they may be. If you believe that people are out to get you, you will experience lots of proof that this is 100% true for you. You are a Master

Creator and as such, you are determining in every moment what your life experiences will look like, be like and feel like.

Non-Truth: The world is full of lack, poverty and scarcity. You must work very hard to get ahead and survive. Good, decent people work hard to achieve what they want in life, otherwise they are lazy slackers.

Truth: Again, the world is full of whatever you believe it to be full of. What you project as your truth will simply be mirrored right back to you to prove you are right. Work can just as easily be fun, fulfilling, lucrative, short and quite easy, producing the exact same gains and results as the non-truth put forth by the 3D systems that you must work very hard to get ahead and be a valuable human.

Non-Truth: Success is defined through material wealth and gain; 3D status = respect and honor.

Truth: Success is truly defined as living your passions and expressing the divine gifts and Light that you came here to share with others.

Non-Truth: Nature (Gaia) is something to be overcome, used, conquered and dominated. The decimation of Earth's resources are unfortunately *required* for the survival of humanity. It's a by-product of our technological innovations.

Truth: Our inherent nature is to nurture and respect Gaia as our nurturer and sacred provider. The oil drilling, natural gas fracking and mining of Gaia's literal "blood" has not been needed for a very long time. Free-energy technology utilizing air and water to run vehicles and fuel homes has been known and perfected for well over 50 years now, but suppressed because of the massive profits to be made by the oil and gas companies. Our utilities could have also been provided for free through solar, water, wind energies and other even more advanced technologies that have long been known by the powers that were.

CHAPTER 9

The Global Band of Light Project

A 5D Model for Collective Consciousness

New societies and 5D systems are created first energetically, as a result of the expansion of our consciousness and the powerful portals of our hearts. They are manifested as the outcome of our conscious intention in action. This is the change that is occurring right now on the planet. Our actions are very important, both individually and collectively, but they are secondary to our increasing levels of consciousness as the impetus for massive global change. This metamorphosis is everything we think we know, flipped inside out.

When entirely new concepts and energies are introduced within a society, they can take quite a while to be understood and integrated on all levels. They trickle down into and through our consciousness to be embraced by those seeking them and those in resonance. They are often rejected by those who cannot step out of the box, or in the case of this cosmic shift—at a soul level desire not to at this time.

What Is *The Global Band of Light Project?*

Global Band of Light (GBL) is a 5D consciousness model and humanitarian organization created with the intention to help 3D mass consciousness evolve out of duality. We are a unifying interface between two distinctly different worlds. The door to the new world is through our hearts, for Heaven on Earth is a state of beingness that is within each of us, if we choose to tune in. Heaven is a vibrational quality that resides within us to be manifested on Earth and into form *through* us.

Sacred Architecture—A New Hologram for Humanity

Energetically, *The Global Band of Light Project* aligns with other similar organizations and projects to create 5D solutions and models for 3D issues. Through collaboration and cooperation, we can manifest high-frequency systemic changes within every new system being created and/or transmuted. *Global Band of Light* is contributing to the blueprint and hologram for the manifestation of our new reality. *GBL* functions as a bridge during this shift, creating stepping stones for others to walk across. This energetic anchoring is assisted as other like-minded companies, alliances, foundations, individuals and programs join together as new thought leaders. Together, we bring into being the new language of the 5D paradigm.

GBL assists in building new communities that will create higher vibrational results for the good of *all*. Solutions need not be earth-shattering to be very effective. In fact, we are returning to some very basic principles for living in alignment with Gaia and each other. Combined with the highly advanced new technologies that we're about to be privy to, the capacity to grow and flourish will skyrocket—sooner than you may think.

The *Light* that You Are

Have you ever turned on a lamp and then tried to separate the light in a room into little compartments and pieces? Of course not, that is silly, and you could not do it even if you tried. The light is coming from an energy stream we call electricity and most of us can't even explain how it really works. We just know that when we flip a switch on, we get light. An energy stream also inherently runs through every person on this planet. Some people may choose to bury and cover their Light, but it's still there, as Light cannot be divided or fractionalized and it is all from the same Light Source. We cannot be separated or divided from this Light Source.

Light can however, be *experienced* as divided. This is the essence of duality and the illusion of separation– an experience (and experiment) in consciousness where we believe that we are all separate and disconnected so that we may rediscover our oneness through our common Light. When we bring our Light together, we then create a colossal and powerful unified generator of Light—A Band of Light across the globe.

> *This is the essence and purpose of the **Global Band of Light** Project—a model for unified oneness across the globe that is intrinsic within all 5D systems.*

A Force-Field of Unconditional Love

I would like to clarify "oneness." You cannot understand oneness if you are trying to define it in 3D terms. I have encountered people who insist that oneness is bad and is the ingredient that socialism is made up of. This perception is a very linear, 3D, cognitive definition of oneness and it is not at all the intended meaning or energy of oneness in this book. Oneness is a *feeling, a knowing and a heart-centered truth, not an octopus-based political system*. Whether we understand or grasp it yet, we are all one in the sense that we all originate from the same Source. We are, as mentioned throughout this book, aspects of Source energy. We are like the leaves on a tree—each different and highly unique, yet each very much an integral part of that tree and the make-up of the tree. Oneness makes us a collective, comprised of the parts.

This entire chapter is devoted to capturing the essence of *Global Band of Light*, as it is multifold. In its greatest simplicity, it is a deep love for Self and for all others. This love has not yet been fully grasped in its totality or frequency on this planet. It has also been called Christ Consciousness, but in no way is this related to an organized religion. It is an *Unconditional Sacred Love* for *all*, with a full awareness that everyone and everything is an equally critical and highly valued part of the One.

GBL's foundational purpose is to help humanity return to the field of unconditional love that has been buried beneath centuries upon centuries of misunderstandings about our true nature. This foundational remembrance consists of truly loving others for everything that they are in the moment and everything that they are yet to become. It involves a deep respect for each soul's individual journey back to their highest nature, with an understanding that we are *far more* than the personalities we wear and the bodies we occupy. In this way, the *Global Band of Light Project* functions as a great gathering of Light and love that offers us a new way of being in the world, even though it is the return to our original make-up.

Reality Shifting: What about the 4th Dimension?

Fourth dimensional (4D) energies are a transitory phase and is where many people are right now. These midway, fence-straddling energies between 3D and 5D vibrations comprise the bridge itself. Just as an airplane lands in phases and degrees of altitude and doesn't just plummet 30,000 miles from the air to the ground, so too do we land at this new 5D destination in increments and varying levels of vibration. There are many already on the ground and out of the plane who have long been paving the way behind the scenes with new system models and spiritual emissaries who are to come forward soon. The powers that were are simply that—draconian energies that have played their part and are now released from that role by humanity at large. So hang on, this new land might be unimaginable to some of you right now and that's ok. Just find your knowingness inside of you, with the understanding that you are returning to who you really are and the energies from where you came. The instruction book that you feel you might be missing is inside of you—your own personalized manual for navigating 5D.

The walk across the bridge from 3D to 5D energies involves walking right through the 4D energies. The fourth dimension can be challenging because it is a heightened mix of frequencies and it takes intentional focus upon which vibration you want to reside within, or engage with. It's purely a choice we can make as we consciously alter our thoughts and feelings to match up with our new choices. Many people are having moments that feel like bliss one day, and then the next day, hour or minute feel as if their world is falling apart for no reason. This roller-coaster scenario is a normal part of dimensional shifting and inherent to going rapidly from a 3D world to a 5D world.

Remember that each one of us is evolving differently and at a different pace. Many people are unknowingly tapping into mass consciousness energies and picking up on huge levels of fear, grief and anxiety. They are feeling many emotions and do not understand what is happening. When this happens, it often means that we are participating in healing mass consciousness energies *through* us, along with our own internal traumas and issues that no longer serve us. It is common with these very fast moving energies to experience spontaneous and unexplained bouts of grief, loss and crying without understanding why, but then feeling so much lighter and better after the cleansing.

Episodes of great anxiety and stress are also common. These episodes are true blessings if you can recognize them as healing opportunities and just let them pass through and out of you with grace. As you do, you will likely find yourself feeling far lighter and feeling deep joy and happiness—just because. Welcome these healing opportunities, as it is evidence that your emotional body is cleaning and clearing and making space for the higher energies to integrate within you. Try not to judge or label your feelings, just acknowledge and welcome them. The more you are able to fully feel your emotions, the faster they will move through you, instead of getting stuck in your vehicle and psyche. Be kind and gentle with yourself (warm baths with sea salt can be very healing and relaxing when this happens) and know that it will leave as fast as it came when it clears out energetically.

Once you've been in 4D-5D energies, 3D frequencies no longer feel very good. You become more and more sensitive to the energies overall and dropping frequency feels very heavy and hard to navigate. When your vibration is going up and then down again rapidly, it can be confusing. Your physical body is learning how to integrate these new higher energies of pure Light at your cellular level and you might sometimes feel really exhausted and need more rest, food and water. Take good, solid care of your vehicle because it is critically important for your emotional, mental, spiritual and physical well-being. This also allows you to better handle the anchoring of more and more Light into your cells.

The fourth dimension (4D) is a fading of the intensity of 3D, while sampling the new buffet offered in the 5D reality. For every dimension, there are also many layers of vibration within it. You may find that your desires are rapidly changing and that people, relationships, homes and even foods that you once loved simply no longer appeal to you. Things may suddenly and abruptly change in your life—all unexpected. This is a very normal pattern for such tremendous internal and external change in such a short span of time. This is a Universal Recalibration for each one of us at the deepest level as we shed the old that no longer serves our highest good.

Many people are experiencing tremendous loss at this time, causing much grief. Please know that nothing is truly ever lost. All is being restructured into a higher expression that fits you better. Bless that which leaves you to make way for far more positive experiences than you can now imagine. Welcome the space that has been created for the new to manifest in your life.

If you have loved ones that have passed over, know that we never lose our connections with those we love. Even if they have passed over, they are still very near us in real and tangible ways. They are simply residing in a different dimension (and in their Light Body) that we cannot yet see, but we can certainly feel them if we try to connect. The veil has never been so thin and the higher you are able to vibrate your energy, the more that you will be able to communicate with them and can rest assured that they are doing just fine and will always be close to you. Death, as we have been led to believe, doesn't exist and there is no such thing as ceasing to exist—it is impossible, as we are infinite Beings. When we actually seat fully into 5D, we will find that we have a new ability to directly communicate and visit with our loved ones that have passed over as often as we desire. Much will be quite different on our planet and in our Universe, and all of these major changes that are happening are the result of the huge influx of Light we are receiving. This influx is rapidly causing humanity's shift into a higher frequency.

Understandably, the future painted here sounds very Utopian and very far away, if ever. 5D doesn't mean that all human problems just vanish, or that there are no longer any challenges for us as a global citizenry. What living in these new frequencies provides that is such a game changer is that humanity has their basic needs met. There is ample food, clean water and sufficient shelter for all (the resources have always been there, just not shared or implemented where needed). Instead of living to survive in a world that has long been "systemized" for lack, consciousness has shifted so that the global focus now is to remedy the needless poverty and sub-human living conditions created and nurtured by the powers that were.

The citizens across our planet are, for the vast majority, kind-hearted, generous, loving and welcoming to strangers—especially with the advent of global technologies and social media that connect us in ways that we have never enjoyed until now. It is the media (owned by the powers that were) that consistently paints such a frightening and inaccurate portrayal of who we really are. The focus has been on our differences (in a negative way) instead of how very much we are all alike and simply wish to live our lives in peace, joy and abundance for all.

Major Concepts of Our New 5D Earth & Its Evolved Systems

What will this New Earth look like when we are firmly seated within our new paradigm? How will the new systems be different from the current ones?

The new 5D paradigm already fully exists in holographic form. It is not a new reality that is coming sometime soon in our individual and collective futures—it is already here for each of us right now. As *we* shift, we allow more of the 5D paradigm into the material world that we are experiencing. It really is all about *allowing* it and acknowledging it through our willingness to heal ourselves.

Those who are embracing the higher levels of consciousness are already experiencing the incredible results of living in a 4D/5D world. The differences between the 3D and the 5D paradigms may seem vast and even surreal, but they are being anchored in right now and will become even more so with every passing day and week. Healing yourself in preparation for this new world is nothing more than awakening within the illusions that you live within and being willing to let go of misconceptions about who you and others are.

New Systems Thinking

New Systems Thinking is about building new systems designed to serve and help **all** of humanity. It is a model for oneness, as all systems within the 5D energies are interconnected and affect all other components of the whole.

Our new systems will be built upon divine integrity. If a particular system isn't in service to all people at a fundamental level, it simply will not be a part of the equation. This will require us to shed major levels of old, worn-out beliefs related to the concept that we are separate.

As we evolve in consciousness, a very genuine desire arises from the core of our Being: that everything good we wish for ourselves and our loved ones, we intend for all others as well. Further, we take the necessary action steps to ensure that this is so. In 5D, greed, hoarding and jealousy are long gone. Teamwork and unity supersedes competition, ego and the illusion that there are either winners or losers. We approach life from a win-win perspective.

Within the new 5D systems, both cooperation and collaboration are the new game. Everyone has a true voice that is heard and honored, whether it is within a family structure, a relationship, a business or educational structure or between nations. We work side-by-side in truth, integrity, honesty and heart-centered service to each other and to Gaia.

Basic 5D Concepts

Defining life within 5D energies is actually quite simple: It is in essence who we know ourselves to be outside of the linear, logical 3D world of polarity. So what does that really mean and how does it look in daily life? This higher state is not new to us, but it *feels* like it because with our descent into 3D we lost most of our memory and connectedness. It is a return to our core Self, while in a physical body and expressed in a far higher reality than what has been the norm on this planet for so very long. It is the next step on our infinite path of experiences as an aspect of All That Is.

Let's take a closer look at how these new energies might look and feel to us.

Heart-Centered Consciousness

Heart-centered consciousness can only be reached through our *feelings* and by embracing and accepting all as one. It is about shifting our perspective to the Vista Point so that we can see and *feel* the vista of higher consciousness. It involves a love for all lives beyond ours, honoring and respecting all people as they reflect our own "Selves" back to us. The only way to manifest a world seated in love, respect and peace is *through* love, respect and peace—at the heart level. We have been bred to shut our emotions down and protect ourselves from others. We are afraid of being hurt, both physically and emotionally, so we erect walls that we think shield us. Or, we believe in the falsity of gender roles and believe that showing feelings is a sign of weakness. Trauma becomes the filter by which we live and so often the filter is one that keeps the heart imprisoned and keeps us from experiencing life through our emotional body in a healthy way. It is time to heal our wounds and reopen our heart connection to each other and begin communicating with others from a loving, trusting foundation.

Unity and Oneness

We are returning to a profound respect and reverence for all forms of life, as we remember that we reflect one another to each other and in that reflection is our oneness with our Creator. We remember that we are here as individual aspects of Source and that every single life form is a unique and precious expression of this powerful divine energy. True service to others needs no self-aggrandizement. The reward is through the service itself and the soul-level contentment one feels. It is a collective relationship that is heart to heart. It requires knowing yourself as the divine Being that you are and trusting in the greater reality that we all exist within.

The Absence of Duality

As we walk the bridge from 3D to 5D, we are required to leave our old thoughts, beliefs and ideas that originated within the 3D world of duality behind. We have to release our traumas from all of our experiences in the old world. In essence, we must shed the 3D skins of feeling powerless and wounded. The "I" is shifting to "we" and our egos must come into alignment with our hearts, and our Inner Authorities. The old "Me, myself and I" mentality is changing into "How may I serve you?" because in 5D, we now feel fully complete and whole within ourSelves and find great joy in assisting all others through their wholeness and joy.

Through our countless 3D experiences and our karmic cycles, we are bringing many prized and invaluable gifts forward with us to our new 5D home. This next phase of our journey is a fresh new beginning and will lead us to astonishing vistas within endless vistas of experiences and discoveries about ourselves and others.

Divine Integrity

Divine Integrity can be loosely defined as living from a place of truth and honesty, with respect and reverence for yourself and all others. It involves decisions and actions that are fully in alignment with the greater part of you. It involves living from one's soul wisdom and understanding, not just the linear, logical mind and persona. It involves a strong integration with your Highest Self. Divine Integrity is a state of beingness that is very important in the awakening and ascension process. *Living in Divine Integrity is Light in action!*

If It Isn't Good For All, It's Not Good For One

In the new paradigm, all major actions and decisions are made from one basic tenant: If it isn't in the best interest of all people upon the planet, it is not suitable for one person either. Think Monsanto, GMO's, chemtrials, wars, greed, profit and environmental destruction—no longer will these destructive energies survive within the new frequencies that humanity has chosen as the new reality. This is at the heart of the shift into unity and oneness that I speak of. Indigenous tribes have always known and honored this as they understood (and still understand) the intricate connection and flow among all living creatures and the balance required between them, Gaia *and* the greater cosmos. From their perspectives, there is no separation from the Great Spirit and all tribal decisions give consideration to every member as part of the whole. The wheel (the Medicine Wheel is a great example of coherence) has been a predominant symbol for the understanding of unity and the circular connection of all life. We are now returning to this type of interaction and sacred connection between us. We, as a global and Universal village, are an energetic, aggregate whole.

Freedom and Sovereignty

This entails a return of complete individual freedom (this will begin with our financial freedom) and sovereignty and the pursuit and expression of one's gifts, birthrights and passions. In the 5D world, personal expression and creativity are highly prized as vitally important aspects of our society. We understand that our purpose in form is to express our divine Selves and contribute our gifts to the realm of the manifested world. Once the new 5D systems are built, in place and functioning, everyone is supported in that. There is ample free time in our lives to express our creativity and passions, because the new technology we are now privy to has automated much of our world, freeing our time for greater pursuits and interests. Remember that once in 5D, our consciousness and remembrance has increased so much that crime and violence is not a part of this new matrix—there is no desire or need for us to manifest these low frequencies any longer. Our needs are met through our manifestations and everyone is on a similar platform now. The energies of competition, debt slavery and tyranny are gone. We still work, have jobs and personal interests, but it is not driven by survival as before and our jobs are voluntary self-expressions of our real talents and gifts. We are *truly* free to simply "be" and enjoy our lives while we are in service to the greater good, because everyone's basic needs are met and maintained as part of the new systems' foundational purpose. As we delve into 5D energies even further, we will collectively remember that "money" is no longer required by us.

Living in the Now Moment

Linear time as we knew it in the 3D world has now shifted into living in the *now* of every moment. We have remembered that we are multidimensional Beings and that time—past, present and future exists all at once and does not exist on a linear continuum. We are at home within a cosmic reality that far exceeds our individual Selves, yet it includes every single soul as a prime factor and treasured jewel within creation.

The new systems that are arriving may sound like a fantasy or a science fiction movie. We are closer to this reality than you might think. The background work has been taking place for hundreds of years and the concrete results are coming forward very soon. We can either participate in and facilitate these amazing, sweeping energies arriving upon our planet or choose to live in resistance to them.

What kind of world do you visualize for yourself, your children and grandchildren? Your thoughts, beliefs and actions will make that so.

The Dimensionality of Our Ascension Path

What determines one's ability to ascend into the higher frequencies and higher vibratory energies is the ability to heal one's trauma at a multidimensional level. Traumas often include one's negative experiences and thought-forms as well as a tremendous amount of brainwashing by generations of the powers that were. As we heal ourselves and cleanse our DNA, we allow far more Light to enter our vehicles and consciousness. This allows our vehicles to ascend into the higher energies and dimensions. Our DNA is rapidly evolving towards a 4D/5D paradigm if we allow the higher frequencies to permeate us. Our ascension begins the minute we begin acknowledging our wounds and opening our hearts to oneness, forgiveness and love for all people, including ourselves.

5D World

Our/Gaia's Destination

Duality Does Not Exist Here

The Return to Galactic Citizenry and Full Consciousness

4D World

The energetic bridge to 5D, where many people already reside vibrationally

The healing phase required to shed our wounds, traumas and misunderstandings before moving to a higher frequency

3D World

Theatre of the Absurd

Playground for Duality

Historically controlled and shaped by the powers that were, who are losing their grip as humanity awakens

CHAPTER 10

5D Systems in Action

The old systems that are struggling to survive are being transformed into the higher energies. It is a process and will not happen overnight, but it has already started. The banking system is being forced to transform and the fiat dollar is soon to be replaced with an asset-backed currency, instead of being printed by the powers that were at their whim like Monopoly™ money. With Basil III's transparent banking system, fraud will soon no longer exist within our financial institutions without immediately exposing the perpetrator. Once we are fully into the 5D energies, fraud will not be a concern ever again because it will no longer be a part of our evolved consciousness to even contemplate such vibratory actions. Even the need for money is going to eventually shift and change as well.

So how do we, as citizens of this New World, participate in such a huge overhaul of everything we have known? How do we effectively change systems? For example, let's look at the educational system in the United States. How do we restructure it into a higher expression that reflects our new Universal consciousness? We cannot change it based upon its existing foundation that was designed by the octopus.

We begin with a fresh canvas and implement a *new system model* for an educational system that is built upon a foundation that addresses all children's needs, passions, gifts, talents and birthrights. No one needs to give you permission to begin creating the new systems right now—as citizens of this planet we will collectively feel empowered to move forward when we *own* our divine empowerment and begin living it in thought and action. We must stop asking permission of the octopus to reclaim our planet.

We begin creating our new systems and structures by asking brand new questions that are no longer based upon financial gain motives (as the sole impetus), power, hidden agendas and control over others.

Some of the critical questions for our new educational system might include, but are not limited to: Does this new system support our children's gifts that they so courageously brought into this life to share? Does it help them remember who they really are and nurture that expression? Does it teach them about their true cosmic connections and the energetic divine world that is the foundation of all creation? Does it teach oneness, how to be in service to humanity and how to honor and truly love themselves and others, as well as all of nature and Gaia? Does it teach them how to nurture the ego as a complement to their Highest Selves, not the ruler of It? Is heart and love energy, the highest frequency of all, at the center of all decisions and actions? Does it teach that all life is sacred and is to be revered and honored? Does it respect and honor these little ones as sovereign Beings? These questions and more will form the foundation for all other studies and teachings throughout academia. Academia in 3D was founded upon cognitive, linear logic that was shaped and tweaked by the powers that were to suite their desired outcomes. 5D academia is founded upon the integration of the heart, soul, mind and one's level of conscious awareness. Everything else that is based upon linear, logistic-type thought is equally as important, but it is seated within the context of a higher, more aware consciousness. This may sound like a small change, but it is a very critical distinction.

As an awakened and self-empowered society exercising our divine birthrights and gifts, we can and will jettison ourselves into an entire new vision for our global systems.

Predominant 5D Energies Underscoring All New Systems

Emissarial 5th Dimensional Leadership Across the Globe (Versus Political Parties and Governmental Control)

Within fifth dimensional energies there is no longer a hierarchy of ruling authorities that make decisions for humanity based upon power, force and greed. Decisions are made through the freewill of the people, operating from a far higher consciousness. It is our newly elevated consciousness that opens the door to our remembering that we are divine Beings. It is the expansion of our consciousness that raises our vibrational quality so that we seek out the foundational energies of the 5D systems.

An Emissarial Leader is a new breed of leader who is the voice representation for all people, appointed by and for the people and who embraces the great honor encumbered upon him/her. They are chosen for their spiritual mastery and divine integrity. They embody unity, oneness and "All for one and one for all" consciousness. Social class systems no longer exist and government in no way even resembles the old highly-controlled institutions. The use of force and weapons becomes non-existent. Humanity is long past believing that they are a threat to each other.

Citizens across the globe are self-ruling by their own divine nature which embraces the truth that we are all both leaders and followers in service to each other's highest and best good. The energy of being in service to humanity has replaced the old grid around 3D "leadership" where people handed their self-empowerment over to others and allowed them to make decisions without any oversight or accountability. (Albeit, we did so trusting those who were not trustworthy.) All leadership is now highly transparent and genuinely in alignment with the higher heart chakra where true integrity and compassion reside.

An Emissarial Leader understands the Laws of the Universe as well as divine truths, and is in service to mankind as a mentor and awakened diplomat. They lead by example. It is the difference between imposed, octopus-controlled tyranny, versus self-empowered governance by the people and for the people, encompassing *true* freedom and sovereignty. In our new societies, we know that freedom is our divine birthright and no one has the authority to alter that for any human Being. True freedom is collective sovereignty, not a monarchy. In 5D, we have a new society that has found the God within.

A Galactic Society

The veil that we agreed to experience here on Earth (as well as the powers that were/systems' suppression of the truth) has prevented us from remembering that we are very much part of an entire galaxy (among hundreds of thousands of galaxies). We have never been alone as we were led to believe. We have star families out there who love us as part of their ancestry and have followed our experiences here for as long as we have been here, lifetime after lifetime.

Our galactic family's presence is well-documented in many sacred texts and stories, as well as in a plethora of concealed archeology finds. As part of this large galactic society and because of this shift, we will soon be restoring our benevolent relationships and connections with our off-planet lineages. As our consciousness continues to open and expand, we will remember this truth. We will soon need no further reminders of our origins, as our greater capacity will show us this truth.

Abundance for *All*
(Versus a Debt Slavery-Based Financial System/Class System)

Once we are back in full consciousness, recalling and fully using our divine birthright gifts of manifestation, our abundance will be created through individual and collective consciousness. Eventually down the road, we will have no need for money to actually exist. I know this sounds far-fetched, but 5D is an entirely new paradigm in which our abilities to manifest through our intentions are beyond our current comprehension. We no longer live with financial portfolios or social tiers of status based upon one's material accumulations. Unlimited wealth belongs to everyone and it is called forth from one's ability to quickly manifest all that they need to live a comfortable life.

There is no lack in a 5D world. The irony is, we have these same abilities in 3D regardless of whether or not we remember them. However, the low density and limited consciousness prevents us from working with these gifts in their full capacity, confounded by a current mass consciousness that does not believe that this is possible. Our innate powers of manifestation have been forgotten by most.

The path to this new paradigm is not purely a reality where everything is just instantly made manifest from our intentions. We will still have housing, food production and other needs that will come from a societal effort and cooperative means. We still have a need for societal structures, but they will evolve in harmony and alignment with our new needs in our new world. And just as 3D has/had varying vibrational levels within the dimension, so does 4D and 5D as well. This means that someone with a 5D vibrational quality at the lowest frequency of 5D is going to have different manifestation abilities than a person at the top frequency level of vibration within the 5D dimensional "scale."

Planetary Stewardship (Environmental/Ecological Systems)
This paradigm shift greatly alters how we view our Earth. In 5D, we nurture our ecosystems because we know that we have the sacred honor of acting as the stewards of Gaia. As a living, sentient being, Gaia is now restored and pristine (thanks to her ability to rejuvenate herself and the advanced technology and help from our galactic families) as she too increased her vibration and now exists as a 5D planetary system. All of the land and sea upheavals while in 3D were to cleanse herself; releasing her wounds and traumas over the centuries. There is now a world-wide and galactic sacred respect and sense of responsibility for her and for all life forms that live upon her. Nothing is created by us that could harm her or us

in any way. We have transformed all of the old octopus-enforced energy systems into free energy sources that do not harm Gaia or use her natural resources in a depletive manner. Many other new avenues for living in harmony with our planet and each other have now come forward and continue to rapidly expand. This process is already well under way, even in this moment.

Spirituality

In 5D, all souls have remembered that we are all from the same Source energy and we live from that axiom. Spirituality is now within a cosmic and galactic framework that encompasses other higher frequency Beings in our own Universe and countless other Universes. We have become good galactic citizens. We are fully awakened and conscious of our role in the grand cosmic play and we live through our innate divinity and the awareness and honor of it in all others. We understand that in the expression of our divine Selves, we further the expression of All That Is and continue dancing in the cycles of creation and evolution through our manifestations. We remember and embrace all of the Universal Laws and Truths.

Health and the Absence of Disease

What does the concept of health and wellness look like in a 5D reality? In such a high vibrational state of beingness, physical disease, aging and breakdown of the body no longer occur. If there is an issue, it is easily resolved through the recalibration of our energetic systems by way of Light and sound. Sound, vibrational (Light) healing and frequency toning are used to restore balance in one's energy field and chakra system. Our physical bodies have returned to a very high state of vibration. In crossing the bridge from 3D to 5D, we shed our baggage and healed our bodies in the process, as this was a requirement to be able to handle the new heights of vibration. Our energetic systems are now far more pronounced as an inherent part of our new vehicles. The heavy density of 3D has been left behind and yet we are still in a physical body that is comprised of a crystalline structure.

Soul Expression and the Arts

Art is a container for the expression of the soul.

There are "portals" within us that provide direct access to who we really are and assist us in expressing our highest vision of ourselves. They are *windows* that open directly to the soul.

One such portal is our creativity. When we create anything with a feeling of passion and/or inspiration, we are directly accessing that greater core part of ourselves. If you are an artist, you know the state that I am referring to. It feels magical and it is. It gives us a very deep level of joy and satisfaction because we are expressing the divine within us. That alignment is transformative, not just for us as individuals, but to the world as a collective consciousness.

Art is a container for the expression of the soul. Our very essence is creative expression. No matter what form it actually takes, it is often the deepest expression of ourselves that we are able to share with others. It is said that our eyes are the windows to our soul, but I believe that our *creativity* is an even larger window to the Universal soul of mankind. It is our humanity brilliantly cast forth into the time-space continuum.

Universal Science

In 5D, our concept of time and space reality has opened to cosmic and Universal Laws. We embrace the quantum field and the understanding that Source energy permeates *everything* and *everyone*, regardless of form, location or density.

New modes of transportation are now common place, such as teleportation, propulsion Light craft that operate by means of conscious intention and much more that might currently sound surreal. Gone are the days of intrusive TSA airport security checks, limitations around our travel choices and limiting monetary factors. We are now able to travel anywhere on-planet or off-planet and amazing experiences are offered to us as we re-acquaint ourselves with our benevolent cosmic neighbors. There are definitely malevolent beings out there, but those who are assisting and protecting Earth are loving, benevolent, evolved Light Beings.

Media/Communications/Technology

Much of our interpersonal communication in 5D is through telepathic thought and it is as natural to us as breathing. We already communicate via telepathic thought, we are just not yet aware that we are broadcasting and receiving in the way that we soon will be. It's not a new gift, it's just far more accessible and usable in 5D because our higher frequencies allow clearer signals to be sent and received. Remember, 5D does not have duality as part of this reality. Everything is within truth and there is nothing to cover up, hide, covet or lie about. We now fluidly share all of the *wonderful* things that are happening across our planet and beyond.

Becoming an Instrument of Change

Forget everything you have learned and you will remember everything that you have forgotten.
~ Alan Cohen

Instead of standing idly by to see what will happen over the years to come, I invite you to become an instrument of change. Stop waiting for what you want to happen and start adding your personal ingredient to the soup that is making up our new 5D reality as we go.

We are all being asked to step up to the plate of life during this tremendous and sacred shift. Let's come together now and play a pivotal part in the evolvement of ourSelves and our planet. We have definite help in large ways during this shift, but it is our job and responsibility to help ourselves first and foremost.

I invite you to join us in bringing forth *The Global Band of Light* on this planet. Let's create a huge band of Light and love, completely enveloping this wonderful orb that we occupy. We are becoming a global, collective community in service to each other and conscious stewards of our Earth. Together, we can become generators of Light around the world instead of individual light bulbs. We are not organizing a revolution—we are **evolutionaries**, creating a New World *through* the truth of our unity, oneness and unconditional Love.

> *Every single event and interaction in your life is an opportunity and invitation to express your Light.*

3 Levels of Divine Responsibility

Personal Responsibility

You are the creator of all of your experiences. You are a spiritual Being having a human experience in a vehicle called your body. There is nothing for you to learn, only remember, because you hold the knowledge of the entire Universe within you, seated within your DNA. Everything in your life can be correctly viewed as just an experience within 3D for greater soul understanding, teachings, balancing from past choices and experiences and spiritual evolvement—everything. When you take full responsibility for your life and all of your experiences and expressions, you will be free. You must unconditionally love and honor yourself first, before you can go to the next two levels of divine responsibility.

Global Responsibility

We, individually and collectively, have a divine responsibility to create and enact global systems that are founded upon oneness, unity and transparency, and that honors every single Being upon this planet. If a system is not good for all, it is not good for one and vice-versa. We are sacred stewards of Gaia, the soul aspect of planet Earth and we are inherently responsible for her well-being.

Without Gaia, we cannot exist, and we are privileged that she allows us to have our experiences upon her, at her great expense and degradation.

Unified Responsibility

We each have a responsibility to honor all other Beings as aspects of All That Is. We have forgotten our oneness and innate cohesiveness. The "whole" cannot ever be divided or separated—that is an illusion within this matrix. We are here to be in service to one another. What affects any one of us, affects the whole. If you are in pain, I am also affected, as is the collective mass consciousness, as it is impossible to be otherwise. There is no separation. You cannot harm another Being and not also greatly harm yourself and all others. Alternately, when you extend love, compassion and kindness to another, you extend it to all, including yourself. Unified Responsibility extends beyond our planet, as the same principles apply to our effect upon the entire cosmos and the cosmos effect upon us.

CHAPTER 11

The Universal Laws

Many people say, "I'm not into metaphysics or that New Age spiritual stuff." That is like saying, "I'm not into that whole gravity thing." Whether you believe in gravity or not, it is still working 100 percent of the time and affecting your life on this planet. The same is true for the energetic Universal Laws and quantum physics. They are working in every moment whether you "believe in them" or not. However, if you choose to understand them, you deeply empower yourself to use them for your highest and best good, *by intention*. It is about understanding frequency and the interaction of frequencies between the unmanifest and the manifest.

The information in this chapter is my personal *interpretation* and understanding of the Laws of the Universe, albeit incomplete and written by many people throughout time. They are within my knowingness, and my own experiences validate them as true and as working in every moment, affecting my journey as part of the whole.

Through your understanding of the quantum and spiritual laws, you will know that life does not happen to you haphazardly and that you can stop the cycle of living powerlessly and by default.

The Universal Laws apply to everyone without any judgment, preferences or discrimination. They simply automatically react to whatever we cast forth. The systems created by the powers that were have buried the knowledge of the Universal Laws and how to work with them, but they should be elementary school teachings. The fact that we have forgotten the most basic tenants of how life is truly governed has left us playing baseball without a bat.

Because the octopus has ingrained that truth is only applicable if it's "lab-approved," (by their labs) the Laws of the Universe have been easily kept underground and away from mainstream knowledge. These laws are not scientifically "provable" by 3D standards, so you will never hear your 6:00 p.m. news anchor talking about the huge relevance of the Universal Laws and how they are seamlessly interacting with your life in every moment. Yet, all you need do is examine your life's experiences to find irrefutable evidence that it is you calling the shots, based upon your own vibrational interaction with these infinite and ancient laws.

The Universal Laws govern the entire cosmos and everything within it. Just like everything in nature, nothing exists in isolation and neither do the Universal Laws. All of the laws work together in a perfect, harmonious and fluid motion, interdependent upon one another like a well-oiled machine. They keep a perfect balance between all of creation. They beautifully intertwine with our freewill choices and offer us the ability to create unbridled joy, abundance, passion and oneness in our lives, if we choose to understand them.

The Primary Universal Laws

The Law of Vibration

When matter is deduced down to the tiniest, subatomic particles and atoms, it exists as a pure vibrational essence and a *signature of energy*. This applies to everything upon Earth (including us) and the macrocosm at large. Our thoughts, emotions, beliefs and words are vibrations moving at various speeds. The Law of Vibration works in constant unison with all of the other Universal Laws, especially

The Law of Attraction. You are creating and determining your own vibration with every thought you think and every word you speak in every nanosecond of your existence. It is your vibrational signature at any given time that is determining what is going to manifest next into your life. You have full freewill control over your own vibration. It is a *choice that occurs through awareness (or not)*. The more we heal ourselves from our current and past experiences and those of our ancestors, the higher our vibration goes.

The Law of Attraction[3]

This extremely powerful Law is quite simple: whatever vibrational frequency we are projecting energetically, will be matched and returned to us. If we are vibrating within a high frequency by running positive thoughts such as joy, love and peace, this is what our upcoming life experiences will reflect for us. Consequently, if we are steeped in negativity and low vibrational feelings, more of the same is reflected back into our lives. Because we have forgotten this basic Universal Law, the vast majority of humanity feel like victims of chance and fully believe that things just happen to them for no apparent reason, or out of punishment. This is how the entire concept of "bad luck" was created. There is no such thing as bad luck. The three possibilities for misfortune include: karmic balancing, one's on-going choice of vibration, or at a soul level we have chosen to have a particular experience regardless of whether we (as the soul aspect) label it "good" or "bad."

The Law of Cause and Effect (Karmic Law)

As we cast our energy forth into the world it is always *causing* an effect in some manner, often deeper than we realize. It is the forward motion from our actions and thought processes that create an effect. If we choose to harm another person, we then *cause* something in their life that will be returned to us at the same frequency, either in

---

[3] As coined in the book *The Law of Attraction: The Basics of the Teachings of Abraham*, by Ester and Jerry Hicks, Hay House, 2006.

this lifetime or another. You might think that the Law of Attraction and The Law of Cause and Effect are the same, but I have experienced that, although they are very similar, they have a different energetic signature. The Law of Cause and Effect acts as more of a *balancer* as it works *with* the Law of Attraction. As we cause our lives to happen and if we decide to infringe upon another's freewill, the Law then causes an equal effect and that deed is balanced to level the energetic scales. It is a rebalancing of energies that are out of balance and the balancing may, or may not, occur within the same lifetime. From non-physical, we often choose a contractual experience with another soul to balance a deed from a different lifetime with them. This could be experienced as positive or negative, depending upon the intent and vibration of the deed.

From an ever broader vista (our Vista Point), we experience firsthand what we have caused to happen to others, which balances the polarity of energies. Theoretical understandings about life are valuable, but there's nothing like walking in the shoes of another to extract experiential meaning at a very deep, personal and emotional level. All of us are *causing* something in every moment with every thought, action and reaction—we can't help but do this. The question is, what exactly are we causing and how does it affect oneself, the planet and others? Our futures are no great mystery. We need only take a closer look at our "now" moments to know exactly the *type* of experiences that the coming days are going to bring our way, both individually and globally.

The Law of Resonance

This law is actually the inner workings of the Law of Attraction. The Law of Resonance is the nuts and bolts of vibrational attraction and is kind of like the person at your bank who matches signatures. Whatever frequency or energetic resonance you are putting forth through your thoughts, beliefs and actions, this law automatically verifies a match to it. It identifies and matches your vibrational signature, thus allowing the Law of Attraction to return it back to you. Remember, like attracts like in the energetic world.

That is why I have said in previous chapters, that as this current world ceases to be dualic in frequency, what's left as this shift completes will be far higher vibrational signatures, which can then *only* attract more of the same to the New Earth. A non-dualic world means that no longer will incongruent (the polarity of positive and negative) energy signatures exist upon the same world at the same time. Only what is in full harmony with the higher dimensions will exist within the 5D paradigm and this is automatically achieved through *all* of the Universal Laws. Ancient religious texts refer to this huge shift as "Heaven on Earth" and indeed it will be because the lower vibrational frequencies will no longer exist here. This new incoming paradigm change is purely a dimensional/frequency shift.

The Law of Growth

With this powerful Law, we delve deeper into the understanding of how the Law of Attraction truly works. Basically, this Law states that whatever you seek to build is going to grow in the manner in which you constructed it. Your vibration carries a blueprint. Since you are the architect, your blueprint will be used to build and grow whatever you are intending to grow, whether you are consciously aware of it or not. If I build an empire on a foundation of greed and corruption, my harvest is going to be reflective of that energy. It will grow *through the energy of greed and corruption* from that trajectory point all the way to my retirement, if I make it that far. As one might predict, the end results might not be desirable and the interim ride is likely to be chaotic and tumultuous. If I create a blueprint however, based upon a high vibrational humanitarian intention, my construction and end result will equal that positive energy and original intention. You cannot put poison into a glass of water and then expect to drink a fine glass of wine—it will always be contaminated and toxic without some form of transmutation into a different frequency. The same is true of our intentions—whatever we cast forth to grow, will harvest at that same frequency.

The Law of Abundance

We are an integral part of an infinitely abundant Universe and it is our birthright to live in abundance and prosperity. It is through our descent into an energetically dense reality (and the brainwashing of the octopus' 3D systems) that has taught us to live in fear and lack. When we align ourselves with the Laws of the Universe, we can create anything we desire. When we look at nature, unhindered by man, we witness all life thriving and in perfect balance with new growth, death and rejuvenation. It is in complete harmony with itself and its original blueprint for evolution. Humanity on the other hand, is navigating within the land of emotions, fears, illusionary belief systems and societies built upon lack, corruption and deception. Because of these constructs, we have forgotten that we are privy to infinite and unlimited abundance, if we align ourselves with the same energetic signatures.

Lack is a manufactured reality that we believe to be true because the octopus has educated humanity to believe far more in lack and survival energies than in unlimited abundance for all people. There simply are no profits to be made (from the perception of the powers that were) from an awakened citizenry that has remembered how to manifest of it's own accord. Our fears around lack serve to create that very reality for us. The true key to unlocking our abundance is to remember how to master our emotions and thoughts, as well as heal our past experiences and energetic obligations. We can learn to have control over how we choose to react to life and to other people by learning how to be energetically neutral instead. Living within a high frequency on a daily basis (which then serves to manifest our wildest dreams) is a learned way of life. Lack has never been part of our divine makeup. We can choose endless emotional dramas over and over again (and manifest accordingly) or we can at any time step off the merry-go-round.

When we consciously decide to live in alignment with the Law of Abundance we will see our lives shift so magnanimously that it will appear to be a miracle. *We cause our miracles to occur by aligning ourselves with the higher frequencies.* It does take some time to shift what you are accustomed to, so be kind with yourself as you begin to catch yourself manifesting what you don't want and learn to shift it into conscious creation instead. Abundance is not about working hard in this world, it is about working in alignment with the Universal Laws and honoring your soul's purpose here. When these two aspects are implemented, work is fun and rewarding, as well as profitable.

The Law of Polarity
This Universal Law is what I liken to two different sides of the same coin. For example, one 3D matrix (the coin) involving two very different range of frequencies. Within the 3D construct, we have been blessed with an opportunity to experience both the Light and the dark energies—the Yin and Yang. We choose through our free-will which one's we intend to interact with. It is through the Law of Polarity that we are able to truly grasp how polar opposites can exist together within the same dimension from an energetic standpoint. This type of platform has provided our soul with an amazing array of choices, experiences and teachings that are not available in a 5D or higher frequency world. This stark contrast has provided us with priceless journeys within human consciousness.

As we begin to consciously create *with* the Universal Laws that govern everyone and everything, our manifestations will match our desires. Abundance, prosperity, joy and freedom are not pipe dreams—the Universe is as infinite as you are and in this new paradigm, these energies are basic foundational components for all people. Begin now to perceive yourself as you truly wish to be and all of the Universal Laws will work together seamlessly to amaze and delight you with your wonderful new creations.

CHAPTER 12

Unplugging from the Matrix

"When the Nazis came for the communists, I remained silent; I was not a communist.

When they locked up the social democrats, I remained silent; I was not a social democrat.

When they came for the trade unionists, I did not speak out; I was not a trade unionist.

When they came for the Jews, I remained silent; I wasn't a Jew.

When they came for me, there was no one left to speak out."[4]

How Are You Feeding the Octopus?

You cannot consciously stop playing a game (participating in the systems of the octopus) when you are not even aware that you are deeply involved in it. Once you understand the nature of this manufactured game, you will then know how to better navigate it.

---
[4] Published in the book, *They Thought They Were Free*, by Milton Mayer, 1955.

Unplugging from the octopus and the 3D energies is both an inner and outer journey. The first large step is in recognizing that the octopus has existed. Once we begin to feel the need and desire to detach from this reality, our true spiritual work really begins and involves an inner catharsis. This transformation allows us to uncover and heal all of our deep programming around survival and safety issues and the related traumas. It involves facing our own false beliefs about this 3D reality, ourselves, our capabilities and perceptions about others. In essence, we must face our deepest fears and discover that they aren't that scary after all. On the other side of this coin lies the discovery of our *Authentic Sacred Selves* that can see far beyond this matrix of experience and understands the panoramic view that the soul has painted for Itself.

How do we, individually and collectively, examine the 3D octopus so that we can see what it has really been up to? How do we acknowledge the manufactured reality it has created for us and then enact a spiritual solution instead of seeking revenge and a violent revolution or—getting stuck in anger or fear? I believe that it is all about our willingness to just *look* (from a heart-centered place) at what has been done over the centuries up until this moment in time, acknowledge what has been done (remember Karmic Law? Nothing and no one escapes this balancing) and then firmly unplug from the tentacles. These are the steps to healing and releasing our past, allowing us to move forward into what we want instead.

Once we remove our focus and energy from these dying systems, they will rapidly continue to fall. When we bless or release something, it does not mean that we agree to it or condone it—it just means that we shed our inner Light upon it to transmute it into a higher outcome and expression. As we do this, we free ourselves from that energy. It allows us to stop focusing upon what we no longer want to be a part of.

What systems are you feeding? Are you intentionally or unknowingly feeding the old 3D systems serving the powers that were, or the new 5D energies serving all of humanity? How *unconsciously committed* are you to supporting the agendas of the powers that were?

Every tentacle of the octopus' system needs your input, acquiescence, money, loyalty, and apathy to keep it alive and flourishing. The minute you awaken and see through the construct, you can disconnect with heart and intention. As more people awaken to the truths being revealed in this unfurling process, the systems will automatically fall because we will stop feeding them with our energies. There are 7 billion of us keeping these low vibrational systems running, either by working for them or feeding them with our money and blind loyalty. They cannot flourish, or continue to exist unless we continue to keep them alive and well. As the influx of higher energies seat within us, the octopus will not be able to continue. There are already many signs that confirm this changing of the guard is well underway.

Chasing the Dream

I have experienced all of the tentacles of the system just as you have. In the past, I have greatly flourished by 3D standards with a large income, more toys than I could ever use and a fat bank account. Yet, even with all the icing, I did not feel safe or secure. I was too stressed and consumed with the fear of losing what I had worked so hard to attain (just as my father was). The very things that I had thought would provide peace of mind and a deep sense of security had only brought a fear of lack in greater quantity. I was living out a very typical American dream scenario where we are taught to live to survive. The fear-based programming ran deep within me and prevented me from enjoying what I did have. I just could not relax and enjoy much of anything because I was too caught up in working even longer hours so that I did not lose what I had attained. I wanted to get far enough ahead so I couldn't fall behind. I was the greyhound chasing the elusive rabbit around the track. And guess what? I magnetized my deepest fears right to me. But, as painful as it was to go through it and like most platforms of deep experience, those years were great blessings and teachings in disguise.

I did indeed "lose it all" according to the American standard of success. My income plummeted due to the octopus created "recession" and I watched my client base dwindle to nothing. Every month I had to sell more and more of my "stuff" just to buy food and keep the utilities on. I fell behind on my mortgage payments, was forced to drop my medical coverage and trimmed down all of the extras until there was nothing left to trim. I had very intrusive creditors bullying me, threatening me and knocking at my door. I was terrified that I might get sick and need medical attention or that my beloved elderly pets might need medical care and I could no longer give it to them. I wasn't even sure that I could continue to feed them and for over fourteen years, they had been a huge source of love, support and companionship to me. I went through the barrage of emotional ups and downs and was forced to uncover all the boogie men in my own personal closet. I had to face my greatest horror of watching my castle crumble and the ensuing feelings of shame, failure, loss, grief, depression, disbelief, denial, anger, rage, fear and "now what?!" These are the feelings that the tentacles intend us to feel when we buck their system and no longer participate in their construct, whether by choice or not.

The concept that one can "lose it all" is very much an ingrained part of the illusion and the powers that were capitalize on it to keep us in line and plugged solidly into their systems. As long as we fear change in our lives and shedding the old construct that is in place to keep us entrenched, we remain firmly anchored into the 3D systems. We have bought into a false dream that never really existed. Money does not equal power. Houses do not equal security or success. Safety is inherent.

I was forced to take a deep inventory of my life and realized just how plugged into the 3D systems I actually was. I deliberately made decisions to detach and open myself up to new possibilities that were outside of the norm. The so-called recession had forced me to consider different choices, but it was a large gift to me from a higher perspective. My next decisions affected my home, what I ate (and where I purchased it) as well as a complete re-evaluation of my reality, what truly mattered and what no longer did.

Some of us are so terrified to color outside of the octopus dictated lines that we remain firmly in our hamster cages for life. My nose dive out of the 3D construct was life-saving and life-giving for me. I would not have done it willfully, but in hindsight it was like diving into an ice cold pool of water— somewhat painful in the adjustment phase, but very eye-opening, awakening and invigorating to say the least.

I eventually arrived at a point in my life where I realized that my own self-empowerment and *true*, not illusionary freedom, was outside of the rules and dictates of the highly controlled systems. For every fear that surfaces, there is a higher-frequency solution. From that Vista Point, our fears do not have the same power over us and we realize that the things that seemed so terrifying to us are just as illusionary as the entire 3D paradigm. If we can see that the current crumbling of our 3D reality is a tremendous gift to all of us in disguise, we can move quickly through the self-discovery process and forward into the amazing 5D energies where those imaginary shackles do not exist.

It was a challenging journey for me. Many days I felt totally hopeless as I dealt with each and every misconception that had been instilled within my consciousness for so long. I had to truly ponder the meaning of words like "security" and "safety" and what they meant to me personally. Just when I thought I had faced all of my 3D fears, more surfaced. Some days I wondered if it would ever end. But deep inside I knew that this was a necessary unraveling that I had to go through and that I could not go around it or side-step it. I could see the Light at the end of the tunnel and was determined to see just how bright it was. Was my security and safety truly within an IRA, the stock market numbers or even my home and hearth? No. My security was in my knowingness that when I detached from the matrix, the Universe was right there beside me to help re-create and co-create anything my heart desired.

I have never felt so supported, safe or secure. Where I happen to live and how many things I might accumulate is secondary to the contentment within and the connections that have deepened with my loved ones, friends and inner Self. The greatest remembrance was that I had to being willing to "lose it all" to truly gain all that ever really mattered in the first place.

The trance of 3D work (versus soul work that we came here to do) involving struggle, fear of not enough money, and fear of losing our homes or jobs is indeed at the heart of the rat race. The system was intentionally designed this way. And I learned that rat races are for rats, not for humans. The greatest gift that you can give yourself and the planet right now is to find the courage to unplug from the dying systems. Plug into your Higher Self instead, who sees right through the illusions created by the octopus. Once you do, you will find the freedom you seek from within. You will automatically gravitate towards work that is fulfilling to you personally, regardless of what that is. If you are wondering how to determine what your gifts are, look no further than *your greatest passions and talents*. Often, we must get past the societal voices that say "Oh, you cannot earn a living doing that!" If it's in your heart and soul and it Lights you up inside, it is within your capacity to be wildly successful at it and make a good living—*especially* in these new and unprecedented energies. Call in your Light Team and ask them to show you the path to reach your desires and open the necessary doors involved.

So—are you tired of dancing this dance? There is a new energy to be a part of. The masses are waking up, realizing that they can stop the madness and in the process, empower others to do the same. Funny thing about dancing—it usually takes two and when one person stops doing the dance and walks away, or decides to dance solo, the other is left holding an empty space energetically. When you stop dancing with the octopus you are no longer contributing to its systems and you leave an empty space. What happens to the octopus and its systems when we all stop listening to its highly mesmerizing music?

Our collective amnesia has prevented us from seeing and understanding that we are maintaining the systems that the octopus has created and these systems only operate because we participate within them and allow them to exist.

AWAKENING WITHIN THE SYSTEM

Breaking Some Eggs

When we ask 3D questions, we will receive 3D answers from our monkey minds. When we ask questions from our core Self, we always receive the truth—no exceptions. If you do not already set aside short periods of time to go within, (this can be a walk, being in nature, staring out the window, listening to soothing music, meditation, yoga or creating artwork) it's never been so important to do that. For every question you have, the answer is inside of you and it is custom designed for you alone. No one else can answer your questions. There is valuable inspirational help out there, but always go within and trust your own discernment.

Carol, a very wise friend of mine, said something to me years ago at a time in my life when I had some large life-altering decisions to make. I dreaded making some very big, but necessary changes because of the guaranteed major emotional upheaval involved. I was basically putting my future on hold because I did not want to rock the boat. As I described to her what I really wanted in my life, she looked at me and said: "Honey, it seems to me that if you want to make an omelet, you are going to have to break some eggs!" Those words of wisdom have stuck with me to this day and have helped me move forward on my journey with a firm knowing that sometimes you have to let go of relationships, belongings and situations to create a grander version of who you are and to get where you need to go. The magic is in how you decide to perceive it.

Beyond the Status Quo

Our lives are not going to return to the status quo of years passed. We are at the end of a very long cycle and the very nature of this shift is the ushering in of tremendous, *positive change.*

We are being asked to determine our priorities now—what is most important to us? How do we score our worth? Where is our security found at this point and what does it look like? Can we remember who we *really* are and just how powerful we are as Co-Creators with All That Is? Will we remember that lack is not real—it is only a program and belief that we purchased and installed? There is nothing inherently negative about having tons of money and belongings, as they are great tools to experience this reality with. It is when money and things become our *definition* of security, safety, self-worth, value, image, ego and status that they distract us from the truth of who we are and what we are here to be and do.

The fall and transformation of the current global financial structure is a perfect example of the transformation of one of many octopus tentacles. There are many more systems that will be changing soon, as we must release the old energies that are the underlying foundation of the 3D reality. All is unfolding beautifully, even if it currently appears crazy and chaotic. What some will find unfathomable, is that directly on the heels of the current failing financial system, a new one is already in place for the good of all people. Keep your eyes and ears open—it is coming from behind the scenes (it has been in the works for a very long time) and it is going to surprise you. The powers that were are soon to be bankrupt and out of business.

Resistance Versus Unplugging

It is wonderful that much attention is being placed upon some very low energies such as GMO's, the global banking system's illegal activities, chemtrails, environmental destruction, and many other global issues. People have simply had enough and the new energies are supporting this. These uprisings are a clear sign that people are indeed waking up and ready for large change. The list of crimes committed by the powers that were is in the millions. I could write an 8-inch thick book about all of their atrocities and that would barely scratch the surface, *but that is not where our attention and focus will enact change and that is why I intentionally left the details of these crimes against humanity for another writer. The more we place our focus upon what the octopus is doing now or has done in the past, the less we can move forward into the new systems that we desire.*

Your projection of compassion, love and Light is by far the most powerful way to enact change. So by all means, be a part of the groups for change, but ensure that your focus is in alignment with what you want for this planet, instead of energetically supporting what you do not want to continue. Fighting against anything puts you in an energetic state of resistance, versus ceasing your support of the system components that are harming humanity.

Self-Responsibility

My path to self-empowerment was to willfully take full responsibility for every single thing and experience in my life—from birth to the present moment, whether good, bad or neutral. I have spent much time reflecting upon the key people and events in my life, from childhood to the present, and pondered why I would have manifested those particular scenes with the various people involved. I extracted the greater meaning from each and I was left with a profound sense of gratitude for the teachings I received. *Outside of karmic balancing, it takes a deep love for another soul to agree to play a particular role for us, so that we can receive teachings and experiences that we ourselves desired as part of our own life plan.*

I took full responsibility for my entire life. If my creations are not what I want, I need look no further for a reason than my own vibration, beliefs, thoughts, karma and traumas (and those of my ancestors) from all of my vast experiences in 3D. There is nothing more freeing than *owning your own world and your own creations*—which encompasses every aspect of your life, good or bad. You cannot be both a victim *and* an intentional co-creator with your Source; one is illusionary and the other is your true nature.

My personal definition of self-empowerment is to *authorize yourself* through your own Inner Authority. No person, government or institution should possess the authority to authenticate your own truths for you. In fact, true wisdom is found when you question *all* social norms, morals, belief structures and systems, arriving at your own custom equation that fully resonates with your divine Self. Taking back our divine empowerment, individually and collectively, is critical to becoming 5D citizens and good stewards of this Earth.

> *It is as if we all agreed to attend a global smorgasbord of goodies, but once here, we were privy to partake in a few hundred delicacies out of billions. This evolved through our mass agreement to experience in a yin-yang world, encompassing a wide range of vibrational energies. Our abilities and abundance are unlimited, yet we have <u>allowed</u> the octopus to tell us how much we may have and how much we can be. We have allowed them to place a container around our consciousness and our birthrights. In essence, we have been co-opted by forces we didn't know existed.*

Questions as We Move into Higher Frequencies

- Who are you supporting? Where do you spend your money? How do you expend your energies? Are you supporting the old 3D octopus-created systems or are you ushering in our new 5D reality with your focus and money?
- What foods do you purchase and how are your choices supporting the powers that were and their corporate imitation food

programs? Do you purchase and consume GMO frankenfoods, pesticide laden produce, animals shot-up with antibiotics, steroids and hormones? Do your purchases support those cattle/animal farms that inhumanely raise, torture and painfully kill their animals? Do you realize that the life energy of those abused animals enters your body and affects your vibration? Or do you instead support local organic farming communities that genuinely strive to provide quality real food that is healthy to consume and who *consciously* treat their animals with love, compassion, respect and dignity?

- Do you provide your body with clean foods and pure water so that your vibration is higher and your body is able to absorb more Light though the higher frequencies?
- Do you allow your psyche and subconscious mind to absorb fear and negativity through low frequency television, news channels, websites, movies and books? Do your choices support a higher vibration or do they reinforce the 3D energies and lower your frequency when you watch, read or listen to these programs? Do your choices instill fear, anger or sadness within you or do they uplift, inspire and give joy?
- Do you allow other people to dictate, shape and influence what you believe, feel, say or do? Are you *consciously* architecting your life from your inner knowingness or do you live on auto-pilot and mindlessly follow the herd?
- Do you allow quiet, reflective time into your life so that you can connect to the divine greater aspect of who you truly are?
- Are you willing to ask your Higher Self to show you what's left that you need to heal and clear? Are you willing to simply look at what surfaces for healing and acknowledge it from a loving place?
- Are you able to look at all others on this planet from a place of love, respect, honor and oneness? Can you truly see them as a brother or sister, even if they are vastly different from you and you don't agree with their choices? Can you accept their personal journey as a plan they designed from their divine,

non-physical Self, understanding that you have absolutely no idea what they came here to master and learn at their soul level?
- Are you able to look at yourSelf with honor, love and respect, even if you are not yet (from your perspective) all that you wish to be? Can you get to the *Vista Point* so that you can see past the superficial and honor the beautiful, radiant divine aspect that you really are, beyond your vehicle and 3D persona that is helping you navigate this reality?
- Can you remember that you exist in many other dimensions and realities and that you are first and foremost a multidimensional Being who has come forth into this particular reality for the expansion of experience? Can you acknowledge that you are far greater than just this one expression of yourSelf?
- Are you willing to lovingly assist others to see all of the above and awaken within these dying systems so that we can get busy creating new systems that serve **all** people as we co-create a new and amazing global 5D society?

CHAPTER 13

Mastering Yourself

Some Thoughts About Mastering Your Life

How we might choose to unplug from the octopus is a very personal journey that brings new understandings about the deepest parts of ourselves. How I unplugged (and continue to do so) might not be the best way for you to go about it. The best course of action is to listen carefully to your inner authority and voice, as it will never guide you in the wrong direction. With practice, that sacred voice becomes louder and louder until there is no mistaking it. It is often a nudge from Spirit or messages from your Higher Self and/or your Guides and Angels that are working with you. They most often speak through our intuition, so developing our awareness is critical to hearing the incoming guidance.

As we are busy manifesting our new 5D reality, the most important thing that we can do (besides unplug from the old matrix) is to really focus upon *what we want instead*. This is the foundational energy that will form the next pavers upon our collective journey. This question, asked constantly, will greatly facilitate our arrival into the new and higher energies because it aligns us with our desires and instantly creates the focus required for manifestation. Can you feel the difference in focusing upon what you want instead, versus placing your focus and attention upon the people, things and systems that you dislike or disagree with? One feels good and one feels not so good, right? Manifestation always follows the path of focus.

We are talking about creating change in our world, but approaching it from 5D instead of 3D. We are reframing the old mentality that change is based upon attacking the issue from the energy of what we *do not want more of* and trying to get rid of it versus, first and foremost, defining what we want instead and then shifting everything about ourselves into that feeling, essence and outcome.

Many people are skeptical and will not allow themselves to truly believe that there is a global transformation underway. It's like they kind of want to believe it, but they have allowed themselves to put only one toe in the water, versus diving in with all of their might. I often hear "Well, I can't see it yet, so I'm just waiting and watching with caution until I'm absolutely sure that what others are saying is true." This mentality is the very opposite energy of manifesting *what we want instead*. This hands-off, skeptical, cynical approach stems from a deep subconscious fear of being disappointed. It is also a clear sign that one has shut down their soul's voice and direction. The fear is that what your inner Self knows to be real change (the global shift occurring) is actually not real and once again, the status quo will continue. It is a form of hopelessness from centuries of living under the influences and violence of the octopus. I believe that this violence has created a deep wound and scar upon our psyches. Can you feel this in your heart chakra?

There is a distinct difference between *intellectually understanding* a higher truth versus actualizing and living that truth. The path for most of us begins with a keen new awareness of (remembrance of) higher spiritual truths. It first seats in our minds, thoughts, linear perspectives and egos before it integrates into our hearts, psyche and intuition, becoming a higher level of consciousness for us. At this point, we begin *living* that truth and it permeates us as it raises our vibration. This is the essence of Mastery. *Truth becomes a part of our beingness and knowingness as we recognize, integrate and live it.*

There is a subconscious part of us that knows we are right on the cusp of massive and positive change (many can now feel it), but the ego monkey-mind can be a powerful cynic stuck in fear, denial and inertia. This hampers our embrace, participation and facilitation of exactly what we want so badly. Many have convinced themselves that life under the rule of the octopus is normal and they do not even realize that they are not truly free in the ways that they may think they are. They cannot remember what true freedom looks and feels like. Indeed, it has been a very long time since we were sovereign, free Beings and even far longer since we had full conscious remembrance of our divine, inherent abilities.

Neutrality—Intentionally Raising Your Vibration

Remembering how to live our lives in a high vibrational state is an aspect of our ascension. When we learn how to "massage" our emotions through the art of neutrality, we master our inner peace. *This does not at all mean that we shut down and cease to feel our emotions, nor deny them.* Quite the contrary, it means that we are far more in tune with our emotions than ever before.

The difference is, when you choose to live in the peaceful state of neutrality, you master the art of responding to life's dramas from the heart and a place of unconditional love. Otherwise, the "drama" will always suck your energy dry and lower your vibration. It may also cause trauma. As you become more aware, you learn how to catch yourself and then make a conscious decision about how you will respond to your experiences. With just a bit of practice, you will greatly want to make choices that will maintain your high vibration or increase it. Allowing your energy field to plummet with each and every little challenge in life becomes a painful, exhausting roller-coaster ride. You can live your life in peace and joy and if you choose to implement the tools in this book, it will become second nature to you.

Look carefully for themes and patterns in your life. Expect that even when you think you have mastered a situation, it may well revisit you. This allows you to practice implementing your new neutrality. Or, at a soul level, you may have agreed to help other people in your life move past their triggers around this same energy playing out. It does **not** necessarily mean that you have failed to heal and release it. It might not be about you, but either through karma or by an agreement made beyond your current awareness, you are still involved. Just stay neutral with the experience and in this way you continue to diffuse the energies around it as well as help others involved release their need to continue to play out that particular energy. Our Higher Self lovingly gives us repeated opportunities to display what we feel we have mastered. How else would you know that you have healed old beliefs and patterns if you were not offered chances to respond to them in brand new ways? You either got what you needed to get or you will recognize that you have a bit more tweaking to do.

Neutrality is about pausing your emotional-based reactive cycle long enough to make a choice about your response and then consciously choose a heart-centered response versus a linear, fear-based thought and emotion. How many times have you found yourself reacting in anger or indignation to something before having all of the facts or information, later realizing that you misinterpreted something or someone? Or quickly reacted and then once you "cooled off" you really regretted what you said or did? What if instead of making knee-jerk responses we practiced our neutrality and contemplated our choice of responses before we took action steps around it? If a grizzly bear is staring you in the face, you won't need to contemplate very long, but if the response is self-limiting, fear-based or octopus propaganda, wouldn't it be better to examine it thoroughly and run it through your inner guidance system before emotionally responding to it?

This *pause* creates the bridge for you to consciously shift from 3D responses (linear/logical left-brain reactions) to 5D heart-centered, intuitive gut-level responses instead. We are very programmed to quickly jump into low vibrational feelings. The chemicals released by the brain during our negative responses to life can be addictive and harmful to us. Running certain emotions constantly can cause us to automatically seek more of the same types of situations to feed this bio/neurological chemical addiction. The ground-breaking work of Dr. Candace Pert and her book, *Molecules of Emotion*, discusses this neurological release and the impact in great detail.[5]

Neutrality means that we consciously master how we decide to respond to life and to other people in each "now" moment.

The Cosmic Mirror

Others "out there" act as mirrors, *reflecting our internal landscape back to us and what we need to heal and release, or if enjoyable, expand upon.* Even the octopus is showing us what we individually and collectively need to heal and release within our own psyches, and this is a gift.

Other people can only appear to us as we allow them to be. The world is a large mirror for all that you are inside. You are the projector and it is the screen. If you are running low vibrational energies, that is what you will see in all others as well, and your experiences might reflect those same energies. Just the opposite is also true—if you are running high vibrational energies such as joy, happiness, love and peace, that is what you will predominately experience in the world. There is truly no one outside of you in which to blame for your pain, grief or unhappiness. You are the writer, producer, director, editor, stage help and starring actor. This is divine freewill in action.

We are led to believe that it is others who are creating our discomfort, treating us poorly and causing our pain and suffering. In a

---

5 Candace B. Pert, Ph.D., *Molecules of Emotion* (New York: Scribner, 1997)

literal sense this is perhaps true, but in an energetic, creational sense, it is incorrect. Everything within the systems of the 3D octopus reinforces this illusion. As we point our fingers and blame others for our miseries, truth is found by replacing every single "they," "you," and "it" with "I." When one finally grasps this deep teaching, everything in their world will shift and the result will be a powerful, divine Being who understands that there is no one outside of themselves that is creating these undesired experiences. When you get stuck within the illusion and blame others, you miss the opportunity to heal what it is within you that is *attracting* the situations and experiences that leave you feeling like a victim.

For instance, let's just pretend that I am a very fearful person in general. I worry frequently that I might be harassed or mugged while walking home at night. I may have even purchased a hand gun to protect myself. I diligently keep all of my doors locked and I approach all situations with great anxiety, caution and fear. If I am running the energy of fear of violence, that energy then acts as a giant magnet towards the energies that I fear. As discussed in a prior chapter, this is the Universal Law of Attraction and is entirely based upon what energy signature/frequency I choose to run in my energetic field. We run these frequencies without even realizing it and at a subconscious level, based upon our past traumas in this lifetime and many, many others as well. We also have the experiences of our ancestors embedded within our DNA and are tremendously affected by their traumas until we heal them. Healing ancestral trauma is a lot like a track and field relay race—it is the last person running around the track with the baton in hand that is fully capable of healing the issues and stopping the cycle of inherited trauma.

If you wish to play with the cosmic mirror, (and I encourage you to) practice using a person in your life that you do not get along with. It might be your boss, spouse, even your child. Begin by making a list of the main reasons that you think there is discord between you and begin each sentence on your list with the word "they." Go ahead, lay it all out. Then, starting at the top of your list and putting your ego aside, be willing to change each "they" to "I." Many of the things on your list are well-buried in your subconscious mind below your awareness. Nevertheless, these beliefs and traits that you are projecting out upon others *are either yours* too, or you are releasing a vibration that is magnetizing those things towards you. If you wish to gain divine empowerment, you must be willing to own and take responsibility for your energy signature. As you acknowledge these energies, they will release from you.

As another example, think of a person that sometimes irritates you. You might honestly determine that you do not share the action or trait that irritates you, but the question for you to ask is *why* do they irritate you so much—what else does it mean or represent to you? What actions do they take or what things do they say that trigger you? Why? Your answers are great clues that will help release the foundational issues that you might want to consider healing.

People also act out what we project upon them. If you wish to change another person and their behavior, change *yourself* first and they will automatically begin acting in new ways toward you. As you change yourself, that which is no longer in alignment with you will either go away or entrain with you and support your new level of consciousness. When people act as our mirrors, it is most often so that we can see what we need to heal within ourselves. Many of these acts are soul-level agreements and it takes a tremendous level of love for that soul to agree to act a certain way towards you. They are helping you gain something that you chose at your soul level to experience or simply understand at a deeper, core level. (Of course, if this reflects abuse or violence towards you, it's time to exit. I am in no way advocating a violation of anyone's personal boundaries or safety for the sake of gaining a new awareness.)

At a soul level, this person is extending a great opportunity and gift for you to reclaim your inherent power as the creator of your experiences. When you choose to get stuck in blame within the illusion of separation, you miss the healing opportunities.

Healing Our Lineages

The beautiful thing about choosing to release our trauma is that when we heal ourselves, we also release the patterning from our ancestors, current relatives, children and future generations. There is a powerful energetic reverberation that takes place across the dimensional lines and affects all involved. It is a perfect example of our oneness and capacity to heal each other through our oneness.

A few years ago, I became aware of a pattern in my lineage that I needed to address. It was playing out in my current life in many ways. Using some of the modalities discussed in this book under "Tools for Transformation," I traced the origin of this energy to my Cherokee lineage. It was hugely prominent for me and begging for my acknowledgement and release. I was experiencing frequent episodes of intense, deep grief and emotional pain and nothing in my current life warranted or explained these almost unbearable feelings. I also began to have frequent lucid dreams that repeatedly played out the scene in my mind's eye.

Through regression, I found myself observing the scene yet again, much like watching a movie. I was in a small village that was under attack by "white men" on horses and they had set fire to my Cherokee ancestor's grass huts. One tribal member ancestor was about 20 years old, married with a young son and daughter. He watched helplessly as his entire family was shot or stabbed to death and/or set on fire. It was a horrific scene and he could not save them. His name was Running Wind and he was a fast messenger between villages and tribes. After the attack, he was captured and forced to walk with others on a trail (The Trail of Tears) towards an encampment far away. It was cold and he was in total shock, deep grief and emotional pain. He walked for about two miles before he saw a large cliff and decided to end his pain by jumping off. He landed on his right shoulder and leg and he died a slow and painful death from his internal injuries. For years after the recall of this traumatic event, I had pain in both of these areas of my body for no reason. It would come and go and was completely energetic.

As I recalled that event and processed the resultant emotional pain and trauma, I was finally able to acknowledge it and the physical and emotional pain left without returning. Physical and emotional traumas surface for us when we are ready and able to heal them. I also healed the deep grief and sense of loss within me that was carried forward into my DNA from this significant lineage trauma. Running Wind had felt such deep guilt because he could not rescue his family. The rage was palpable as well. We all have the capacity to collapse these energetic holograms within us. I have no greater ability than you to do this work. It is readily available to all who wish to use the power of acknowledgment. So much trauma that we hold within us *is not even ours*; it is ancestral or from our other lifetimes. This is just one example in my own life that I have healed and released. Many of our most profound milestones in life cannot be seen or proven—they are simply experienced.

All healing translates into releasing the energy holding the trauma in place at many levels within us. It takes our willingness to simply look at it, feel it and then use the power of acknowledgement and love as the releasing agent. This is a large prerequisite for all of us as we awaken from our slumber and emotionally shut-down states. We must reconnect to our emotional bodies and our hearts with compassion to heal ourselves and evolve into our new trauma-free expressions within 5D. We have to relinquish the wounds from all of our 3D experiences and we are being given a tremendous opportunity to do just that in this lifetime.

I have revisited many past/concurrent lives and once recalled, all of them helped to explain things that were currently transpiring in this lifetime that otherwise made no real sense to me. We do not have a need to recall the vast majority of other lifetimes or ancestral experiences. *It is only those that were left unhealed that need our attention now, or the lifetimes that led us to the current themes that we are still living right now.* Remember, we are multidimensional Beings and what we are here experiencing now is but one facet of our total soul Self. Once fully seated in the 5D energies, we will return to full conscious awareness and remember all of our other aspects experiencing concurrently.

Soul Constructs and Rollovers

Each lifetime has themes that, at a soul level, we choose to participate in. There are countless themes we have each explored, such as poverty, power, greed, self-righteousness, warrior energy, subservience, being an attacker or a victim, selfishness, generosity, living in abundance, joy, peace, etc. Each one of these themes or constructs can easily carry forth (rollover energies) to the next lifetime and continue to play out, if 1) the lifetime ended and the traumas of it were not healed and released, or 2) the spiritual soul level teaching was not attained. The Higher Self will then construct future realities in which to try again until the aspect *(you)* truly gets it. All of these are energetic soul level modules and each one holds a specific "flavor" to it.

For example, there is a construct of poverty. One common reason (outside of karmic balancing) that someone may live in poverty is because they might have completely forgotten about their manifestation abilities. Remember, the octopus has been around a very long time and the brain-washing of humanity is centuries old and deeply ingrained into our DNA and lineages. It has deep roots within our psyches and belief systems. As such, many are quite literally born into poverty energy and carry that schism within them from the moment of their conception. Sprinkle the false teachings of the octopus on top of the existing lineage hologram and you can see how powerfully ingrained we are with false ideas appearing to be real. When we forget how to manifest, or that we even have that ability, life appears to be a frightening game of chance within the 3D illusion.

Through acknowledgment and release of the DNA imprints, one can then fully release the traumas from all lifetimes and the undesired lineage imprints from all of their bodies (physical, emotional, mental and spiritual). Acknowledging trauma allows one to garner the higher teachings that were chosen by them to attain. Once we extract the wisdom from our experiences, there is no need to repeat them, as we have "gotten" it.

I have assisted many others with healings that traced the energy patterning back to an incident that was in generations past or to a client's other life experience. When we do not heal and release our traumas after they occur, we die with those imprints still in place and then we bring them into the next incarnation, attached to our emotional bodies and DNA. That is why in this pivotal lifetime, we are all being asked to heal multitudes of outstanding past life traumas and to heal our lineages. This is why you might have noticed that so many people seem to be having a bombardment of issues going on. We have agreed to heal and release so much in this lifetime. We are in the PhD program and there isn't a moment to waste in getting started. You absolutely have the power and authority to heal yourself. No one can do it for you, but your Light Team is an invaluable resource to assist you in every moment. Your job is to *ask*.

Allowing Other People to Experience Their Freewill Journey

We humans like to fix things. That is fine and well, until we attempt to "fix" other people in our lives, or instruct them on how to live their lives. Many of us also give our power away to others who desire to fix us and this can leave us feeling hopeless, helpless and controlled. I call it the *Tumbleweed Effect* because these energies leave us feeling like tumbleweeds blowing around in the desert of our lives at the whim of other people's (and systems) opinions, influence and control.

When we think that we know more about how to run someone else's life than they do, we are disrespecting them at their soul level.

When we do not allow another person to gain mastery over their life choices and experiences, we are potentially interfering with their path and none of us have the right to do that. We cannot possibly know what another person has come here to experience through their freewill, or with whom they agreed to experience it with for their evolvement. It is ultimately a form of ego that leads us to believe that we "know better." It is a form of arrogance with a good intention. It is not trusting in the process and infinite intelligence of life. Respect all others, regardless of your judgments about them or their life. It is far better to simply hold them in your love, Light, acceptance and appreciation, all of which are very high vibrational energies.

Noninterference in other's lives does not in any way imply that we shouldn't be compassionate or helpful when asked. What it does mean is that we are not here to micromanage other people's lives and try to direct what is best for them—it's *their* journey, not ours. The distinction here is the difference between trying to direct and control others when they are not seeking your assistance or asking for your help, versus offering loving respect and compassion to all people, regardless of who they are. Energetically, the two intentions are worlds apart. We are responsible for our own healing; we are not *responsible* for another's healing, even though we may well choose to be of assistance and help in ways that others allow and desire.

Releasing yourself from the need to control others is not only freeing for you, but it frees them as well. Every single person is fully supported by the Universe and truly, all is in divine order without your approval, control or direction. We are not here to police other people. If you witness something or someone that is not in congruence with your own beliefs, your best bet is to stay neutral and away from judgment and ego. Go within your heart and send them your love and Light. Intend the highest and best outcome for them, as directed by *their Higher Self*. In doing so, you are sending yourself love and Light as well. This blesses their journey and frees you to pursue your own, while maintaining a high vibrational level.

You Can't Get It Wrong

Taking care of yourself and realizing how important your life is to the whole, is part of your awakening. As a master co-creator, you were brave enough to come here and experience all that you have created for yourself to experience. This braveness does not originate from the 3D ego. It flows from your divine Self who fully understands that you are infallible. Your soul knows that nothing is more prized than attaining higher levels of understanding in every way conceivable, whether it is gained on planet Earth or any number of other planets, dimensions and timelines.

Your Highest Self knows that there is no end to your experiencing. Death is only a transformation from one vehicle to another; it is a change of state. It is a method by which you can exit this experience when you have completed it and are ready to move on to your next journey. It transitions you from one experience to the next and it is you that makes the choice of when to depart. Most often, you make that choice before you even come into physicality. You are the travel agent and you decide when you will enter and how you will depart. You also decide where you are headed for your next grand adventure. Passing over (crossing from one dimensional state into another) leads you to a large *planning session* and reprieve for your next planned experience. It is a joyful reunion with loved ones, not just from this lifetime, but from all others too. We have been taught to greatly fear death, instead of remembering what it is really like. Most of us have incarnated so many times that we are professionals at this death thing. Death is much like visiting an airport where we depart one flight, rest and relax for awhile as we (with the assistance of our Light Team) map out our next destination and adventure of our choosing.

You are truly indestructible and the *you* that you are (beyond your 3D costume) will never cease to exist. You cannot get it wrong, but many spend countless hours and years worrying that they have, or that they might. *You are so very loved and cherished.* You matter more than you can possibly imagine to this puzzle called existence. You are needed and your life is a gift of immeasurable value.

You are the judge and jury of your life when you pass over. From this perspective, you remember what you had set out to do and to be in the lifetime you just left and whether or not you met your own goals or fulfilled your karmic plans with others, so as to balance the energies of prior experiences. If you strayed from your intended path you most often choose to incarnate again and continue on with your chosen path and soul experiences. Many have grossly missed their mark and upon their life review will see how they got sucked into the density of the 3D world and the low vibrations. The only judgment is by you, of you. If you strayed into very low vibratory energies while incarnated, you may well have incurred karma and will very likely choose to go back and balance out what you created.

This particular lifetime, however, is very different for all of us and is why it is called the shift of the ages. At a soul level, we have been eagerly waiting for this lifetime to arrive because it is so incredibly pivotal. We are all being given a huge opportunity right now to release all karma, wounds and trauma from our energetic bodies and harness the Light that we truly are. We have the opportunity before us to step off the karmic wheel, if we do the required internal work, and exit the dualic construct.

This is why the most important thing that you can do right now is to make a very strong connection and alliance with your Highest Aspect, your soul Self, and hand over the reins to lead the way. It is the difference between trying to navigate an expedition from inside a cave with little light versus being on a mountain top and able to see the entire landscape around you. Your Higher Self has the full perspective of where you want to go and knows the most appropriate path to get you there—if you are listening and living from awareness. It only requires a shift in perspective to greatly shift your consciousness.

If you did not have all that it takes to handle this shift, you would not be here right now. I encourage you to bestow the same incredible unconditional love upon yourself that your Creator has for you. Outside of this reality, you have full awareness of your place in the cosmos and how powerful and beloved you truly are.

Your Experience/God's Experience

Your experience is God's experience.

God sees nothing but pure perfection in each person as an aspect of Source energy. God gave each of us 100% freewill to go forth into many dimensions of time and space frequencies and co-create with our divine abilities and gifts. Your main directive is, and always has been, to expand at a soul level, *through* your many varied and diversified experiences.

You are having an experience with God through your physicality, whether you (from your limited 3D perspective) deem your life experiences as good or bad. God does not judge it, but simply observes it as an experience within duality. **All experience is valuable to our Source in the higher continuum.** Yes, your actions might well require some karmic energetic balancing if they have harmed other Beings, but that is part of the entire experience of living upon a 3D world. It is not necessarily a desired outcome by Source, but it is a potential reality within this dualic construct. You were well aware from your non-physical state that you would likely experience *all kinds of energies* here, and you have throughout many, many lifetimes.

God Does Not Get Angry

From the roof-top, full consciousness *Vista Point*, we are like small children playing on a large playground. Imagine for a moment that you've asked your parents to take you to the most amazing park and playground ever. You can't wait to go and experience all that it has to offer. Ah, the joy, fun and happiness you know you will experience in the adventure. But, it also offers the *potential* for you to experience physical and emotional harm. You might get into fights with the other kids, fall off the swing and injure yourself, be bullied and called names and incur traumas from all of these possibilities. And you probably will—it is part of your taking full advantage of the many rides and opportunities offered to you upon this playground.

Imagine that you do indeed fall off the merry-go-round and hurt yourself. You lie there in the dirt, all skinned up, bruised and even bleeding. You yell out to your parents, who are observing your experiences. You blame them for your accident. You get really mad at them for bringing you to this park and tell them that it's their fault that you fell and hurt yourself. You feel angry, abandoned and unloved. Or perhaps, you feel that your accident was somehow justifiable punishment because you feel unworthy and deserved to be hurt for partaking in such fun upon this playground. Perhaps you decide to beat up the kid on the swing next to you and expect your parents to punish you, but they don't. They simply continue to watch and be in joy for your ability to exercise the very freewill that they bestowed upon you. They do not *enjoy* watching you harm yourself or others, but they know that this is your current chosen experience through the use of your 100% freewill and that you are an indestructible aspect of Them and you will never cease to be. They also know that the very Universe that They created has a built-in, seamless system of energetic checks and balances through the Laws of the Universe that will always balance the scales of imbalanced actions for each and every soul upon the playground. They know that in the big picture, *all* truly is in divine order.

We are like the above scenario as we make determinations from our very limited knowingness about our God/Goddess, Father/Mother. We attribute human emotions and dualic characteristics to our Source. He/She has not, nor ever will, judge us for our experiences on this playground called Earth. Nor are we ever punished for participating in this dualic construct. Punishment and judgment are a manmade concept. And much of this non-truth has been perpetuated by the insertions of the octopus into religious doctrines. All of our pain—internally and externally, is caused by our lack of remembrance about how this reality truly works and our place within the greater cosmic matrix.

You are here as an eternal being of Light to experience *all* that this dualic 3D playground has to offer. And you have done so through all of the Universal Laws to maintain the energetic balance needed for your creations. And just as a parent watches their child at play with love, amazement and excitement, so has your Creator loved you through all of your experiences here. So many people ask how God could possibly allow so many atrocities to occur on Earth. The answer is, God didn't allow it or cause it; we created and played within them as a mass consciousness and it is we who must now balance and heal them, taking full responsibility for our creations.

Even if you play so hard within the energies of duality that you die a horrific death while playing, there is no sense of loss or grief from God, as God knows that you are as infinite as He/She is. You will simply transition and then design your next adventure with God fully supporting you in every moment of your infinite existence.

When we choose to limit our play upon the playground of life, we miss out on some amazing experiences and adventures that are awaiting us. Our fears and traumas can easily convince us to play it safe so we never risk being hurt, either physically or emotionally. When we live in limitation, we deny expression to the greatest parts of ourSelves. But, from the *Vista Point*, even that self-imposed limitation is still a valuable experience within the infinite experiences we will have. You simply cannot get it wrong.

CHAPTER 14

Awakening the Giant Within

The ability to manifest through your freewill is a very powerful force in the Universe. In essence, all healing and transformation takes place through your freewill intention to release old, stored energies. The bridge to the 5D paradigm requires that you heal all that no longer serves you or humanity at large.

What Is Ascension?

The new paradigm necessitates attaining an ascended state of consciousness and vibration to reside within the much higher energies of a new dimensional reality. The shift offers the opportunity and invitation to transcend from one dimension (level of consciousness, material density, and Light quota) to a higher vibrational one.

Ascension is the term used for this transformative process of evolvement. Very simply put, it is achieving a fifth dimensional frequency and vibration, moving each of us to higher levels of consciousness and much less physical density. Every single one of us has the ability to ascend if we, at a soul level, are ready and choose to do so. The path to ascension is all about healing the density we carry within us. What exactly is density? It is the low vibratory emotions, feelings, thoughts, beliefs, programming and trauma that are part of the old 3D world. Density is the level at which the lower energies saturate our frequency.

The more seated we are in the 3D world's negativity, the more dense our energy fields are. It is not something that you can see, (except for the manifestations) but you can certainly feel it. It is recognizable as the sinking feeling in your heart and solar plexus when you witness or participate in violence, persecution, hate, prejudice and emotional or physical abuse of any kind. It encompasses all of the ingredients that are not in congruence with our Higher Selves. These thick and heavy densities are the very opposite of peace, joy and unconditional love.

If we desire to ascend to a higher frequency reality, we must go deep within and ask of ourSelves, "What is within me that is not yet of unconditional love?" It is these things that we must heal and release. Humanity has never had this unique opportunity before, to raise our vibrations so drastically, while still occupying a vehicle. In a nutshell, our ascension is about a gradual, ongoing cosmic opportunity that will allow us to step off the merry-go-round of karma and duality.

Healing Is a Frequency Equation

As you release yourself from the 3D energies, your mind, DNA, psyche, energy field and chakra system, (literally, every cell in your body) makes room for more Light to occupy all of these spaces. As this takes place, your vibration and frequency goes up and the outcome is an ongoing expansion of consciousness. *Everything* is comprised of energy and you can transform energy for your highest and best good.

The equation is this: Heal our traumas = more Light absorbed. More Light absorbed = higher vibration + higher consciousness

+ higher frequency = an awakened state of beingness. Congratulations—you have made it out of the rabbit hole! As we release all of the false beliefs about our reality that take up space within us, we make room for Universal Truths to reside there instead.

Healing takes willingness and desire to let go in a new way. No healing modality will be effective for you if you are not ready to let go of your density, or haven't garnered the soul level teachings that you are seeking from your experiences.

If you feel that you need help with releasing and healing what no longer serves you, there are many wonderful and effective energetic tools and practitioners available to assist you. We are each healers with the innate ability to heal ourselves, while assisting others in remembering their own innate abilities. Also, because we are all one, we can actually assist others within that oneness, if their Higher Self is in agreement. We have no way of knowing whether or not a soul has chosen a particular experience, illness or tragedy as a part of their life plan. If this is the case, no level of healing will clear it, as it was chosen to be that way.

Healing ourselves results in a higher frequency signature. The higher your frequency, the greater the amount of Light you are generating out into the world. You can feel it and so can others, whether they are aware of it or not. Those unaware will be mysteriously drawn to you for no particular reason, while others that are more sensitive will actually *feel* your high vibration and recognize it. Practice loving *everything*—that which is easy to love and also that which makes your skin crawl. Whether you like a particular person or not, does not change the fact that they and everything in existence is still an aspect of All That Is. We can only transmute the lower vibrating energies into higher ones when we do not resist or push against them. We must love everything into a higher expression of itself, transforming ourselves and our world from the inside out.

We will continue to face the challenges of the lower dimensions until we each choose to master them at a heart-centered level.

The Power of Light Communities

I firmly believe and have repeatedly witnessed: Where two or more gather and expand their vibrational levels, the capacity for healing is amplified and exponentially increased. Prayer/intention groups can yield incredible results when we gather in the Light to heal ourselves and assist with holding the space for others to heal themselves. The next phase of this journey is one of building spiritual communities that come together with great intentions to heal our planet and each other.

You may be wondering after so much unplugging from the 3D world, what are we to plug back into? The new reality is not going to be laid out in front of us like the old one that we have, from birth, been indoctrinated into. This new reality is in the constant making as we move forward, step by step, into fourth density and then into fifth. We can be at ease and know that whatever the final picture looks like, it will be simply stunning and a collective portrait of a new humanity.

That being said, being at "ease" does *not* mean that we are not 100% participatory! We must recognize that apathy, manipulation and distraction landed us where we are and we must take responsibility for the creation of our new systems and way of life. We can no longer afford to be asleep at the wheel. We must unite and ensure that the antics of the powers that were stops and is healed. Look around you—our world is in serious trouble and we must take personal responsibility (every single person on this planet) to repair it. There is no question that we can indeed heal our world, but the first step is to *believe* that we can.

Fukishima is still a tremendous threat to humanity. So is the state of our oceans and sea life, the contamination of our food supply and drinking water as well as our highly diseased populations, caused by all of the above. The first step in taking the reins is to begin creating local think tanks and gather like-minded people together who are ready and willing to organize grass root changes. Once local community groups are organized, the next big step is to connect and align with other similar groups across the world to unite and share information with each other. This is where the true power for change begins.

We each have our talents and passions, so identify yours and take the lead by reaching out to others in your community who share your concerns and ideas for solutions, outside of the octopus' current system's so-called "solutions." There are so many choices that include: living off grid, organizing and leading healing groups, mentoring children with no direction, becoming a beekeeper (honey is very medicinal and GMO's as well as chemtrails are killing off our honey bees), rescuing animals, sharing "free energy" inventions and machines (and how to build these devices), helping the elderly, environmental clean-up projects, helping house and feed our homeless (and also involving them in all of these projects), group prayer and focused, topic-specific meditations, organic community gardens, purchasing parcels of agriculturally zoned land and using them as a co-op model for organic farming that will feed many people. Buy vacant buildings to use for larger-scale hydroponic vegetable gardens (as well as home-based or community-based hydroponic gardens).

Become a protector and steward of organic Heirloom seeds (which are rapidly becoming extinct because of GMO decimation across the globe). Run for a political office and BE the change you want to create. Grow herbal medicinal plants and teach others how to as well. There are so many lost arts from older days (that the powers that were have tried to terminate) that we can rekindle. Are you a natural healer? Volunteer one day a week (or month) and offer free clinics. Go beyond being a practitioner and teach others how to use their own energy for healing. Encourage them to pay it forward and also become a teacher. It's time to share our knowledge and reclaim our bodies, minds, soil, food and water supplies and remember how to live with Gaia and her lands and oceans. We must embrace the teacher within and share our innate knowledge with everyone who desires to know.

As consciousness continues to rise, people are seeking out the above information. Be a leader and take charge of teaching what you know—you will have a huge audience. This sharing is not about profits or making money (not that there is anything wrong with that, but we cannot continue to share our knowledge with only those who have disposable incomes). These are times when, because of the actions of the powers that were, masses of people are barely surviving and living paycheck to paycheck, or surviving with no income at all. More people than ever have zero disposable income. They cannot afford your services right now, but that should not exclude them from your help. Perhaps you can find ways to barter for your services or allow volunteers to help you as an exchange. Those that can afford your services will financially support your work. This is about the survival of humanity, as we rebuild and transform the damage left by the octopus, and we need every soul involved as quickly as possible. We can and are reclaiming our planet, but we must do it together from the Vista Point.

In essence, we are creating *Cities of Light*. These communities are already springing up around the globe and are founded upon peace, harmony, cooperation, collaboration, self-sustainment and green technology. They are 5D models that are paving the way for global transformation. These Cities of Light are serving as anchor points to ground the 5D energies within Gaia and within all of us.

Authenticating Yourself

We have been taught by the octopus and its associated systems that our inherent healing abilities are bogus and even "dangerous" and that we must rely upon outside octopus help. The knowledge of our inherent abilities has been very suppressed by the current systems, and many people deny that they even exist. Often, when those who are already awakened share their abilities to heal themselves and assist others, they are laughed at or shunned and discredited.

Many of us have been entrained with the false notion that all healing must happen "through God" and not us directly (remember, it is impossible to be separate), so we ask our Source for help and then sit back and pray for results. The blatant missing piece of the above is that we are all *part* of the same God/Source/All That Is, so this philosophy makes no sense.

As an aspect of Source energy, you have birthrights and gifts to heal yourself, while being the co-creator of everything you might need or desire in your life. As you utilize your freewill through Lighted intention, you are completely enmeshed *with* your Source—you are healing not only *through* God, but also as an integral aspect of *God*. Source graced us with these birthrights so that we could co-create our life's journey with Spirit. Give yourself permission and authenticity to take charge of your journey; the more that you do, the faster you step into the mastery of *you*, which is a very important component for ascension.

The Kaleidoscope of Healing

We are like giant kaleidoscopes. Every time that we heal even a *tiny* aspect of ourselves in any way, it shifts the entire picture in ways we can see and in even more ways that we cannot.

The expansion of our consciousness begins with the smallest seed of a new understanding. You can look through the kaleidoscope's viewfinder to see a snapshot of your life at any given moment. Many do take an honest peek, but once they observe it, they put the kaleidoscope down as if they are doomed to that particular image. Or they might think that it's an interesting picture, but they don't realize their ability to further the creation into a more complex work of art. If you do not like what you see, the slightest twist of the kaleidoscope's cylinder will create and manifest an entirely new picture. When you shift even a *minute* particle in your consciousness and DNA, you shift *everything*. It replicates and reverberates throughout your entire Being. You shift your consciousness the most when you allow in new beliefs, thoughts, concepts, ideas and perspectives that are in resonance with your Sacred Self.

Option Points

We often find ourselves in situations where we must make choices and decisions about our next steps in life. These *Option Points* are important markers as well as opportunities. We might recognize our *Option Points* only when we have big decisions to make or we reach a large fork in the road but the small, daily decisions are just as important. They are excellent practice for living our lives with direct, conscious intent.

> *If every person upon this planet became intentional with their Option Points in every situation and chose harmony over conflict and abundance over lack, we would have global peace and prosperity overnight.*

If you learn to intentionally look for *Option Points* within every situation, you get better at mastering your daily life and truly manifesting harmony within it. As you become more aware of what areas of your life need your attention, it is easier to make conscious choices about how you will react to any given situation or person that you encounter. You alone decide what energy you will project in every moment. Is the energy based upon peace, or is it based upon conflict? Is it about love, or fear? Your choice in that moment, your *Option Points*, will answer these questions.

Take note of the so-called "dramas" you attract to yourself, as they are golden bits of information that are telling you exactly what areas of your life need your loving attention. What are your "buttons" that prompt you to engage in trigger responses? What is the message underneath those buttons? When I am able to recognize a trigger and then through that awareness shift my response, I am able to heal and grow. Is this hard for me? Heck yeah! Of course it is, the path of healing is never perfect and the mountains before us are not always easy to climb. This is especially true as we clear more and more and begin to get down to the really large "chucks" that go very deep within us. That's where we really enter the PhD program of life. But it's also the golden eggs and what we are here to do, as hard as it is sometimes to walk through it. I feel very grateful for all of my *Option Points* because they provide me with opportunities to decide how I want to respond to life. And yes, sometimes my 5-year old self is the one responding—it's not always my grown-up version and sometimes it just "ain't pretty!"

If I were to instead approach these opportunities as a victim or blame someone else for my experiences, I would continue to create similar dramas over and over until I finally chose different *responses* and healed the issues in front of me, often flashing like a neon sign. It is because of the healing and releasing that the responses to our Option Points automatically change.

For every *Option Point*, you have the choice and opportunity to disengage from the lower vibrating energies and actively choose peace and love instead. You have the choice to stop dancing within the drama. It's a matter of participating or not participating with your energies and actions, and this happens because of greater awareness. Your *Option Points* are the energetic forks in the road that are the basis for your next experiences and manifestations.

Where Joy Resides

When you experience your own Light and what it feels like to live in states of joy and bliss, you will seek out those states.

With even a little bit of practice, you will find that more of your everyday life resides in these highly sought after states. As you take control of your vibration, the emotional roller-coaster turns into a flowing river. You create your own state of joy and it begins within. No one can create it for you or take it from you without your permission. *Joy is a conscious choice.* The octopus has taught us to seek happiness outside of ourselves. We often pour lots of money into people, places and things that we believe will give us joy, only to feel dismayed when the excitement soon fades and we wonder where the happiness went. Then, off we go to find the next greatest thing or person that might offer us some more joy.

Many people believe that if they can just shed all of life's burdens and responsibilities, suddenly joy is uncovered. But it's not life's challenges that stop us from feeling joy. Joy can be found *everywhere* if we focus upon that state of being. It's the fruit congealed within the Jello™. Joy can be extracted from the most dismal of situations if we realize that *all* emotions, deemed good or bad, are found within this matrix and it is our perceptions that frame our emotions. Mahatma Ghandi is my favorite example of the power of perception. Even though he was imprisoned for a very long time, he still found deep joy from within himself.

Often, the traumas seated in our emotional bodies place a large filter over our ability to feel joy. I spent many years feeling frustrated because my life experiences were amazing and should have felt fun, exciting and full of happiness. But no matter what I did, I felt numb and disconnected from all of it. In a nutshell, I was shutdown from the inside out. I had created this numbness long ago to cope and feel safe in the world and it clouded all of my wonderful experiences. The state became normal to me, as it is for millions of others too. As I intentionally began my own very personal healing journey, I had to allow all of my fears to surface, where I could then acknowledge them and let them go. It is an on-going process. As I did this, I consciously changed my focus to one of looking for joy *everywhere*, which greatly shifted my new experiences into states of joy. I aligned my inner world so that my outer world reflected this alignment back to me. The more I let go of, the more joy and happiness surfaced and stayed.

Paying It Forward

When we channel our energies into loving others, even strangers, we receive it back from the Universe in even greater amounts. This occurs because we are aligning our vibration with the highest vibration of all—unconditional love. You can make this a very fun and soul-fulfilling game each day and notice how your level of joy skyrockets. Give a bouquet of flowers to your neighbor, the homeless person on the street corner, a family member, a complete stranger or co-worker "just because." Or, if going through a drive-through, pay for the car behind you without them knowing. I was recently out for lunch with my family and after we had ordered and our food came, our waitress told us that an anonymous gentleman had already paid for our entire meal, including the tip, and that he had already left the restaurant. We were floored and all of us felt such joy and gratitude to this anonymous person who had so generously opened his heart to complete strangers. Our own vibrations soared because of this heart-opening act of kindness. This is what it's all about.

Paying it forward doesn't have to involve spending money. Giving a part of yourself can be even more meaningful to others. Open the door for someone, tutor or mentor a child, teach a free class, help the elderly or disabled run errands, clean their house, or cook for them. Spend time with someone who is lonely playing cards, games or watching a movie. Be that energy of love for all. Acts of kindness are about spreading the energy of oneness and reminding others that they too are very much an important part of the *All*.

Help others remember how much they truly matter, especially in the current global energies where isolation and hopelessness is all too common.

5D Boot Camp Training

5D boot camp is the re-training of one's mind, emotional body and physical body to allow for entrainment with the higher vibrations amongst us. Just as you might train for a marathon to create a solid foundation for your fitness level, so does it take awareness and training to restructure your mind, beliefs and thought patterns. It is your *intention* that opens the door. For example, I could have loads of laundry to clean, but if I make no intention or plan to get it done, it is not going to happen. I must put forth intention and effort on my part to accomplish my desire. This very simplistic example applies to all of life, doesn't it? However, when it comes to the energetic world, we often forget that the same simple path applies.

As you re-train yourself to keep your vibration high and Light-filled, you are making it far less possible for lower vibrations to affect you. You may say, "But there are lots of bad things in this world that happen every day to people right in front of my eyes and if I follow your advice, wouldn't I just be in denial of reality and even putting myself in danger?" What you label as negative in the outer world cannot touch you unless you align your energies with it, or you fear it. *Fear of it **is** the alignment.* It is Universal Law. Negative energies will not have access to you unless you allow them to affect you through your mental/emotional state of being. It is a conscious (or unconscious) choice that you are making in every moment of your day.

Society criticizes us for wearing "rose colored glasses," but I find this an amazing tool to use for manifesting what I want in my life. If I shift my perspective into *only* positive possibilities, I automatically maintain a high vibration. I can still make logical decisions about my reality, but I make them from higher vibrating energies. I love my rose colored glasses and have no intention of ever giving them up! Universal Laws always respond to your vibration by providing more of what you are broadcasting out, so start noticing what you are asking for.

CHAPTER 15

Foundations for Healing:
Bridging the 3D World to the 5D World

Diving into the Quantum Sea

We are being asked to go into the very far reaches of ourselves to see what's left that we need to transform, transmute, acknowledge and gently let go of. This cathartic process is critical to the healing of ourselves and our planet. We cannot easily continue into the 5D world unless we are willing to actively do this step. The "head in the sand" method that many people choose just isn't going to work this time around.

All of our experiences (including unhealed past life experiences) are stored and *recorded* within us until the time comes when we are able to deal with them. Most of us fear what is within us and it might seem easier to keep the doors tightly shut rather than fling them open and boldly look at them. We fear *feeling* our hurt, loss, grief, anger, abandonment and shame and these feelings keep us imprisoned within our own minds and hearts. Then it seems as if "all of a sudden" we have an illness or disease, when in truth it has been manifesting through our unhealed emotions for a long time before our symptoms became apparent. The so-called "weakest link" in your body is present because it is holding an emotional pattern or trauma within that particular area. Your body will absolutely tell you what you are repressing and what needs to be released with just a little bit of detective work. It is an amazing and beautiful system that is always supporting our highest good if we choose to tune in.

With the advanced healing modalities out there today (based upon cutting-edge *new* science) we do not need to relive our traumas to heal and release them. There are ways to get to the underlying energetic issues and release them without any need to retell our stories or relive what has happened to us that is painful. That is "old healing." From a place of Universal Law, retelling our "story" reactivates past trauma. This can often seat it more firmly in place, bringing more of the same experiences our way because we have placed ourselves back into that "like equals like" vibratory state of attraction.

When you relive something, your subconscious mind does not know if it is happening in the current moment or the past. This is a down side of traditional talk psychotherapy—we are accessing the linear logic side of the brain (left brain) when in fact, our stored traumas and beliefs are stored in the right side of the brain. When we then access the subconscious mind and heal the issue, it often seems like magic because the trauma was stored in a place that was beneath our conscious awareness.

The critical question in all healing is "*What do I want instead* of what I currently have, or how I currently feel?" The key to healing is in emotional, heart-felt acknowledgment of our journey and the resulting traumas. This release is not just a mental process: far from it, it is literally releasing the stored, repressed energies from your DNA, the cells of your body and your psyche *through* your emotional body. You are also deleting the monkey mind tapes that are on constant replay around the issue or trauma. This type of powerful healing is beyond what the octopus has taught us to believe is even possible. It is occurring at a quantum, DNA level.

Healing yourself is something that you can do in every moment of every day. Below, is one of my own examples, when many years ago I was having a major issue with someone I perceived to be a loud and inconsiderate co-worker. I became aware of my negative thoughts around this person and noticed with curiosity how the thought patterns would run through my mind and then *repeat* over and over. It was amazing as I allowed myself to become the observer of *me* and really notice this repetitive thought process that I was engaging with. It seemed to control me because the more I tried to stop it, the more frequent it became. I realized that to delete the programming, I would have to clear it from my consciousness. I was able to do this by actively catching myself in each repetitive thought-loop and then consciously shift it. How can a repetitive thought pattern be stopped? Below is my favorite method and is one that is a compilation of many tools, some centuries old and some relatively new.

The power of acknowledgement is not in any way a new concept and many great teachers have written about it over centuries of time. There are many excellent tools that are discussed towards the end of this book that can be used to release unwanted programming. As you use various energetic release tools, you will begin to customize them to fit your own needs and healing process.

The Conscious Acknowledgement Process

1. Awareness helps you to catch yourself when you are running a thought-form that is not of a high vibration. If, in response to the thought-form, you feel angry, jealous, revengeful, hatred, greedy, like a victim, hurt or any other low vibrational feeling, catch yourself in the moment and shift it. All of these feelings are simply part of being human in a 3D matrix and are not "bad" feelings. However, they can be harmful to your health when they are repressed and not felt and then released. As you practice doing this regularly, it becomes a way of life for you. Awareness is the key to everything and to all change. It is important in this exercise to use your linear mind only to help you *define the issue*, but once defined, the true portal that will unfurl the energy is done

through your heart chakra. You cannot "think" yourself through this process, as it must go through your heart and emotional body to be successful. Many of us are taught not to feel, or we do not feel safe when we are in our feeling state. Men, especially, fall into this trap due to gender socialization, so make sure you create an environment in which you feel safe to express yourself, *to your Self*.

2. Once you become aware that you are running some old, worn-out tapes, the next step is to stop what you are doing for just a few minutes and ask yourself: "How do I *feel* around these thoughts that I am running? Am I angry, frustrated, confused, hurt, frightened, vengeful or something else?" The key is to zero in on exactly how you feel about these thoughts. You might feel more than one emotion. Get a notepad or voice recorder in that moment and write or speak your feelings, as this will begin the releasing process. For those of you who are accustomed to repressing and stuffing your feelings and emotions, it is going to take some practice to even put a descriptor to *what* you are feeling and put real words (energy) to it. That's ok, keep working with this and you will very quickly become a pro.

3. The third step is to acknowledge these feelings internally. For example, with the co-worker situation, I identified that I felt furious at this person's perceived rudeness and felt assaulted by their daily noise level that was very distracting to my work. I was so irritated (and my body reflected that irritation as IBS and lots of skin eruptions). My next step was to dig more and ask, "How else do I feel underneath those feelings?" My answer was that I felt powerless to change the situation and it just fed my anger. I said to myself, "Ok, I acknowledge that I feel powerless to change this and I also feel assaulted by the noise and that makes me feel very angry at her and even abused." Your acknowledgment is your allowance/expression (the opposite of repression) of your feelings.

4. The next step is to (silently or out loud) say, "How I feel is OK. I do not judge how I feel and it is OK for me to feel this way and

I honor my feelings and mySelf." This process creates a state of acceptance, surrender, ownership and neutrality within you that *opens the energy* to shift into something else that better serves you.

5. Now it's time to release it. To do this, say to yourself: "I allow these feelings to completely release from all four of my bodies; mental, physical, emotional and spiritual and I am grateful for this opportunity to let go of the feelings that used to serve me, but no longer do." Make sure that you take four to five deep breaths and focus upon (visualize) these energies exiting your body with every exhale.
6. The final step is very important: ask yourself "What do I want instead of 'this'?"

For the problem with my co-worker, I truly desired to have a kind, harmonious work relationship with this person that was based upon mutual respect and consideration. I also wanted a quiet work environment where I could focus and not be distracted. I wanted peace between the two of us and friendly, stress-free interactions. Since we have no power over changing other people's behavior directly, when we change our own internal landscape we automatically change those around us. *This final step is what 5D is all about. It is the step that allows us to become the change we wish to see outside of us, by first becoming that within us.*

After defining what it was that I wanted between myself and my co-worker, I stopped the repetitive cycle of negative thoughts that I was running daily. The noise at work ceased. The environment became miraculously quieter and peace was restored *because* I restored it within myself first. It was never about the co-worker to begin with.

The 3D version of this scenario might have been: file a report against my co-worker with our supervisor, gossip about her behavior to other co-workers, blame her for her perceived rudeness, treat her unkindly or make snide comments under my breath hoping she would hear them, along with many other 3D responses that would have been the surfboard gliding on top of the anger, victimhood and revenge. This was my own personal *Option Point*. The 3D method might also have produced "quiet" for me in the end by way of company policy, but meanwhile, I would have lived my life running very low vibratory emotions and thought-forms and still felt stressed out when I was around her. I would have manifested more of the same kinds of things into my life and in the world because I would not have addressed my underlying emotions that needed to be acknowledged and released so that I could move on. And, I would have never achieved my stated goal and desire of goodwill and true harmony with my co-worker. During this process, I had to give up some key negative emotions within myself such as feeling self-righteous, needing to be right and feeling like a victim. I had to firmly push my ego out of the way and command that it align with my Highest Self.

This entire 6-step process takes all of about 5–10 minutes once you get used to it. Remember, it is a process that you are doing within yourself and the heart is the portal for alchemy to occur. The more you catch yourself running unwanted scripts and then do these steps, the faster they will simply not exist within you anymore because you are unwinding these stuck energies.

There were days that I thought the mental scripts would never end, but I persevered and realized that many of them had been sent to the delete file. They were just no longer running in my monkey mind or my vibrational field. My life began to really reflect these changes as I enjoyed my newest manifestations that were in harmony and alignment with my heart and what I really wanted.

In retrospect, my co-worker played a very important role at a soul level in helping me to heal some emotional triggers that I was not even aware that I had. Some of my strong responses were rooted in childhood memories that surfaced during my deep sea diving. After all, no one else at work seemed bothered by this person. It was a blessing and gift to discover the issues and heal them. Anyone that desires can do this process themselves. All that it takes is a willingness to step into a neutral self-detective role and self-healer. Observation, in and of itself, creates large change. The willingness to observe ourselves with humor, compassion and unconditional love is what moving across the bridge to 5D is all about.

Allowing drama in our lives only serves to keep us anchored into the low vibrations and is harmful to our vehicle. You will find that when you have truly released the foundational energy beneath an undesired pattern or trauma, you will automatically have a feeling of neutrality and inner peace around the issue. The charge or "button" is simply gone. Often, you may not be able to recall what it was that you were so upset about! This is actually quite common and it is a neurological event at a physiological level within your brain. At a physical level, you have closed the neurological pathways that transmitted the thought and associated chemically-induced feelings. Your brain has stopped firing the chemicals that activated those particular neurotransmitters and the familiar chemical reaction ceases. You have also allowed the cells in your body to release stuck energy in a particular area where the trauma or emotional impact was seated. Once this healing takes place, neutrality about the incident is almost instantaneous, if the root trauma was fully uncovered and acknowledged. You might be able to recall the issue, but there are no negative feelings or "hot buttons" around it now because you have released that trauma within you. You may also notice that with each release, many physical problems improve, if not altogether disappear.

Meditation

Like a lot of the population, I did not grow up practicing and learning the art of meditation—far from it. However, I did grow up believing that people who meditated had some special skill, or gift and they somehow knew how to achieve a unique guru state of mind that was different from the rest of us. What I learned over the years is that anyone can meditate and it is very simple to do. In fact, the secret to meditating is not "doing" anything, but rather shifting into our natural state of beingness.

I also believed that I had to follow a particular protocol before I could participate. I thought I had to be able to shut down my thought processes while sitting quietly with my eyes closed. It not only sounded incredibly boring to me, but darn near impossible. I am such a "thinker" and highly visual, so blanking out my mind and imagination seemed very unlikely. I later discovered that staring at a wall can be meditative. Day-dreaming is meditative and can be taken to a much higher degree quite easily. For many people, exercising, gardening, walking, listening to certain types of music, or even taking a shower is meditative if one allows the mind to defocus and relax. I have had amazing realizations in my shower as well as on my treadmill. These activities do obviously require your attention for safety, but the focus is far more non-directed as compared to say, doing accounting, driving or buying groceries.

Ideally, you create a quiet space for yourself where you can relax and close your eyes. There are no absolute rules to follow or a particular protocol for meditation because each of us achieves things in our own unique way. *All* of it is valuable and valid. There is no right or wrong way. In my opinion, the ultimate goal of successful mediation is in learning to place yourself into the expanded state of consciousness referred to as *beingness*.

Beingness

It wasn't until I embarked upon my own healing journey in earnest that I began to really understand how to quickly go into a meditative state. I realized that I didn't need to make a big deal out of it, nor did I need to make time for meditation (which I then found cumbersome and never seemed to have the time for). A relaxed, meditative state automatically took me out of my beta brain wave state (which is a linear, action-filled place of very fast brain wave frequencies) where most people reside, day in and day out. It is where our monkey minds take place.

Meditation is a tool that can lower our brain-wave frequency and allows us to consciously enter into a far greater state of awareness and capacity. It took a little practice to get myself into a lower brain-wave frequency, but it is not difficult and is highly relaxing and healing.

At first, I became familiar with what it felt like to shift from beta into an alpha state of beingness (consciousness). Then, as I played with other tools and modalities, I began to easily take myself into theta states of beingness (an even slower brain-wave frequency). The more I practiced these states of consciousness, the more I found myself *living them* automatically in my daily life. In fact, I found out very quickly that I *craved* residing there, because the fast-paced, stressful, overly logical world of my beta mind was becoming less and less enticing.

Now, I often use the term "beingness" in place of the word "meditation" as it more aptly describes where we are when we enlarge our consciousness and lower our brain wave state. Our beingness is that unlimited, greatly expanded part of our core Self that knows no boundaries. It is a state that crosses the veil of our amnesia and unites us with our higher non-physical Self.

I found that when I was in deep alpha or theta states of consciousness, I had very significant light bulbs going on and that physical, emotional and spiritual healings began taking place with simply my intent. I found that my creativity soared and my spiritual awareness was heightened. I found myself in a place that felt so familiar to me deep inside, yet within this 3D world was labeled "woo-woo." I had rediscovered my inner Self by getting out of my programmed, brainwashed state of consciousness. I utilized my intention to achieve this state of beingness, where far greater recall is possible. Not only is it possible, it is relaxing and blissful.

Through practice, these heightened states of awareness increased my intuition and my sensory receptors became sharper. My perception and connection to All That Is became so strong that I could literally feel and experience my own Light and oneness. I lost sense of where I ended and the Universe began. To my surprise, the line simply vanished. During one amazing meditation, I became a diffused particle of Light while in this expanded state of consciousness; an infinite, inseparable drop in the ocean of Prime Creator. I *became* beingness, which is best described from my own personal perspective as a feeling of existence as pure Light and consciousness, completely transcending the physical 3D world. In essence, I was in a place of non-actuality, yet 100% presence.

The deeper I delved into beingness, the more I became pure consciousness and it was incredible and indescribable with our limited language. And yet, I was sitting in my favorite living room chair. Once, after a particularly peaceful experience in beingness, I walked out to my backyard and noticed a huge dragonfly pass by. I have always loved dragonflies and I decided to talk to it and call it over. I found that it responded to my thoughts and intentions and it flew closer and closer to me until it finally landed about five inches from where I was standing on my patio. It stayed there a very long time, and it felt magical. I continued to talk to this new friend and could literally feel the connection between us. I have learned that I can talk to dragonflies and call them to me and they will come. Try it—it is an amazing reminder of our connectedness to *all* things, large and small. When we are in beingness, magic occurs.

Meditation, however we choose to go about it, is an intimate, personal and experiential journey of rediscovering who we really are. Sacred energies are very subtle in how they communicate with us. We must quiet the very loud 3D world from our senses. When we deliberately take ourselves into a deeper state of awareness and expanded consciousness, we can then hear, see and feel many subtle energies communicating with us. These subtle energies remind us of our true state beyond this physical journey and within the matrix of duality.

We can easily forget who we really are in the fast-paced hustle and bustle of our society. We are encouraged to stay very busy and distracted with the pursuit of material acquisitions and the illusion of 3D success and survival in this world. The secret is this: what we so intensely search for in 3D to fill the void within, is found within these expanded states of consciousness. These higher states are not just some place that you go visit for 15 minutes each day—with a little bit of practice, they will actually *become* your daily states of awareness when you integrate them frequently into your life. The state of beingness can indeed *take you home.*

Using Tools to Bust the Illusion

Meditation is one of the most effective tools to help break free of the illusion that the 3D world is fixed and non-malleable. It is also one of the most powerful tools to instill deep inner peace and calm. Many of the healing tools that are mentioned in this book utilize various methods to guide you into a meditative, beingness state. With a little practice, one can close their eyes, expand their energy and be in a theta brain-wave state within seconds or minutes.

There are many cutting edge tools in this book that are aligned with our newly expanded capabilities in these times. We already have the advanced abilities to heal ourselves and manifest realities in the blink of an eye. Trust is all that it takes to move forward. The tools are simply platforms that allow us to utilize what is inside of us until we no longer feel that we need the structure. They are like training wheels.

We must be very clear and concise with our energy, as manifestation means that we not only manifest those things we desire, but equally those things that are undesired, by default. This is why healing our wounds and traumas is even more critical now—the cleaner that we think, feel and act, the more beautiful our manifestations will be. In these times of tremendously amplified energies, our abilities are greatly enhanced and will continue to escalate as we move along this ascension continuum. Practicing with powerful tools helps us refine and heal our thought processes, becoming masters of what we choose to think and feel. It's about learning to be *selectively reactive* to life, for it truly doesn't matter what life presents—of far greater importance is our *reaction* to life and how we process and release the experiences we have that create trauma.

Our Native Elders completely understood the journey to the inner world, but unfortunately their Shamanistic rituals of seeking out their Highest Self (and their other aspects) were all but lost with the enforcement of the white man's ways and the octopus' agendas. Our Native ancestors understood the great importance of regular spiritual quests and the expansion of our consciousness. With the proliferation of dogmatic religions that condemn and discourage these sacred inner journeys of self-discovery, our sense of oneness with our Source became very muddied and distorted.

How Meditation is Healing on Many Levels

Much scientific evidence shows that meditation (slower brain-wave frequencies) provides a long list of health benefits. We already know that 90% of our reality is unseen and energetic and not validated through the limiting parameters of 3D science and medicine (although the use of Biofeedback by some medical professionals is really a great step in helping patients better understand their abilities to direct their bodies into ease). It involves self-experiential proof and knowledge, not solely Petri dishes in a lab, test tubes, animal testing or octopus-funded test trials.

Through meditation, we are able to reach the *Vista Point* that I have spoken of. Enlightenment is not unfurled through the linear, fact/fear-based mind. There is much that we *know* without a shadow of a doubt that we cannot prove through the cognitive mind. I *know* with 100% accuracy that I am (and you are) an infinite, limitless, Being of Light who came to experience this time, place and dimension by choice and with intention. I know that this illusionary matrix is my playground for acquiring those experiences that I want to acquire and heal anything that needs to be healed or balanced with others energetically. I know that we are all invaluable components of a magnanimous Source Energy. Our greatness, as such, is not measurable, for measurement has a beginning and an end. As infinite Beings, we do not.

Through meditation and expanded states of consciousness, we also greatly influence our DNA. In fact, we can direct our meditations to cleanse and clear unwanted thought forms and belief patterns that are *attached to our DNA strands*, as what I call "historic cellular baggage." There are so many things about each of us that are fragments from our ancestors' experiences and traumas, as well things we brought in with us from our other lifetimes. We each have the ability to transmute and release these cellular attachments that greatly affect our current lives and our state of health and happiness.

The Chakra Connection

We each have seven major vortexes within our energetic bodies that are known as chakras. The word "chakra" means *wheel* in Sanscrit. These unseen, but vitally important, energy centers look like wheels or cones and they both receive and transmit energetic information. The chakra system is a critical component to our enlightenment. Our chakras are a major *link* between the physical world and the antimatter Universe.

When our chakra systems are open, healthy and functioning at a high level, we have access to the deep wisdom and knowledge that resides within us. It is our "Life 101 Handbook" that connects us in far deeper ways than most of us realize or take advantage of.

The chakra system is also critical to allowing dimensional transformation to occur within us. The system functions as energetic portals, connecting our physicality to the essence that is our soul. They serve to maintain our feeling of connection with Source Energy as well as to cosmic Universal intelligence. This is especially true for our higher chakras, such as the third eye, heart and crown. When our chakras are congested, we feel disconnected from ourselves, our Source and from the truth of who we really are. For this reason, a very basic overview of the chakra system is included. We each possess more than seven chakras (if you wish to delve further) but for the purposes of this book we will briefly touch upon the basic seven:

The Root Chakra (Red) is located in the hip area at the base of our spine. It is related to our sense of stability, survival, structure, safety and security.
The Sacral Chakra (Orange) is located about two inches below the belly-button. It governs our sexuality, abundance, sensuality and pleasure in life.
The Solar Plexus Chakra (Yellow) is located at the stomach level. This chakra is related to our self-worth, self-empowerment, and is the center of our creativity and sense of freedom.
The Heart Chakra (Green) is located in the middle of the chest and is related to love, peace, oneness, unity and cohesion.
The Throat Chakra (Turquoise) is located at the throat level and is connected to speaking one's truth, communication, expression and integrity.
The Third Eye (the Pineal Gland) Chakra (Indigo Blue) is located in the middle of the forehead, right above the nose and between the brows. It is the gateway to your intuition, psychic abilities, inner wisdom and higher knowledge.
The Crown Chakra (Violet/Purple) is located at, and slightly above, the top of the head. It is the connection to the greater divine essence that permeates all of life and all realities. This chakra is most utilized when in meditation.

The entire Chakra system is a beautiful representation and model of the ascension process. We began our collective human experience on Earth solidly seated in the root chakra energies of survival and safety. We will exit this dimensional reality by ascending upwards, fully activating the crown chakra—the gateway to our Higher Selves. Over linear time, we have had collective, historical experiences within the energies of each chakra. From our earliest times upon this planet, we have, decade by decade and century by century, evolved through each chakra's energies, It is through the 5D energies that we will soon fully experience the higher heart chakra, third-eye and crown chakras as our prime connection points to the greater Universe.

When our chakras are healthy, fully open and functioning properly, they are magnificent interfaces between the greater realities we are experiencing and our physical vehicles. It is through our chakras that our intuition can be heard and honored. It is the healing and coherence of all of our chakras that will assist us in our ascension process and into the higher dimensions.

Our chakras operate at *very* subtle levels. When we live our lives in fifth gear, or simply live to survive within the 3D systems, we are not aware if one or more of our chakras are partially shut down. Remember, the intent of the 3D octopus has been to hide the nature of who we really are through every 3D system that exists and this very much includes the basic knowledge about our subtle energy systems. When we understand how to operate our energies and bodies cohesively, we will enjoy brilliant health. We will then feel empowered and knowledgeable of how to do our own internal analysis of our energy flow and nip energetic congestions in the bud before they ever manifest into a physical disease.

Balanced Energy

When our chakras are congested, we are easily thrown into emotional states where we become highly reactive to others. Through this imbalance, we may give our power over to other people or try to take power from others. We may also believe that violence or bullying can solve all of our problems. We tend to make poor decisions that can greatly impact our lives (and others) in ways that are damaging and self-sabotaging.

All four of our energy bodies (physical, emotional, mental and spiritual) ideally work harmoniously together to create an optimal state of balance for each person. When any one of them is out of balance with the whole, it becomes difficult to hear or feel our inner wisdom and guidance.

Living in a state of energetic balance is *key* to hearing and following our Inner Authority at all times. We achieve balance by taking responsibility for our growth, body and conscious advancement. It requires a dedication to our own highest good and the proper care of our energetic Selves. You are a sacred Being and you are critically important to the whole. Everything about you is unique and precious—exactly as you are in this moment.

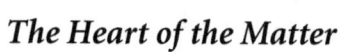

The Heart of the Matter

If the key to living life in the 5th dimension is through the heart chakra, then how do we access it? The vast majority of people have heart chakras that are partially closed down, or at the least, greatly affected by experiences and resulting traumas in the lower energies. We have lived in an octopus-created and controlled society that teaches us from birth to hide and repress our feelings and emotions. Deep, core level expression has not been encouraged or socially condoned, especially if you are of male identity. We often learn early in life to squash our feelings and emotions that run through the heart chakra and as a result we create blocked energy there. This imbalance in the heart chakra leaves us feeling numb and disconnected from life and others. An open, healthy, loving heart chakra is so *incredibly powerful* that it deeply scares many people! They are so accustomed to being emotionally numbed out, that even intense feelings of love or compassion can be overwhelming and frightening.

We literally create *trapped feelings* within this powerful and vital energetic portal when we are not able to express life's pain, hurt, loss, grief, disappointment, anger and fear. Equally important, we often don't even know how to express our love for each other. As a result, we have exorbitant rates of heart disease in our country (as well as divorce) and people who have no idea how to connect to others through feelings of love, compassion and oneness. Sadly, it is all too common that people project suspicion, skepticism, mistrust, judgment, fear and hatred through the heart chakra, until and unless they are willing to heal.

Opening the Heart Chakra

By taking a close look at your everyday life, you can see exactly how much your heart chakra is open. When your chakra system is clear, clean and functioning optimally you feel great love, respect and compassion for yourself and all of humanity. You also feel safe, nurtured, self-empowered (divine empowerment) and your ego is the *servant* of your heart. You are able to properly speak your truth. Your natural birthright abilities are available to you, such as your psychic and healing abilities. You see, feel and hear Universal information because it freely flows into you as *truth*. You have a strong connection to your Highest Self and feel a deep level of joy and happiness. Your life experiences are filtered through the energy of love, gratitude, appreciation, acceptance and oneness, first and foremost. But to get to this state of beingness, most of us have to clear some debris. How do we clear the debris? We express and acknowledge the underlying emotions and we allow them to release. We learn how to embrace the so-called "debris" as some of our most valuable life experiences.

The Interpreter

Our chakra systems interpret and process the outer experiences that we have, based upon our responses to them. Each chakra frequency corresponds to certain colors, sounds, tones, organs, foods and emotions. Each also has its own special purpose and function and is in constant communication with all the other chakra portals. If any chakra continues to have congested energy, it then begins to manifest *inwards* towards the physical body as an illness or disease. The vast majority of all diseases are caused by the unreleased, suppressed emotions and traumas that have not been healed. We were not energetically designed to hang onto lower vibrational feelings, and we have not been taught how to let them go after a traumatic experience occurs. There is nothing stoic about denying your feelings - it doesn't make you "tough" or resilient, it just eventually makes you quite ill and very unhappy.

All illness is synergistic with the particular chakra or chakras involved. For example, low back pain and hemorrhoids (and other issues in this vicinity) are very often the result of money worries and/or feeling unsupported and unsafe in the world as well as not being able to let go of the past. Breast cancer is highly connected to "mother love," or lack thereof. It is often about the relationship one has with their mother and themselves. Throat issues (including thyroid problems, tumors of the throat, neck pain, etc) are often related to the inability to speak your truth, or find your voice and your expression. Once you get quiet with yourself and ask your Higher Self to show you the message that the disease or discomfort has brought to you, you are then able to heal and release it. I assure you that there is always a message if you are willing to stop and listen. The soul uses the vehicle as a tool to bring in higher knowledge about ourselves and what we need to heal. But we must ask and listen carefully.

The Power of Acknowledgement

How do we clear our chakra blockages? As I mentioned earlier in this chapter, it can be as simple as *acknowledgement*. For now, keep on the back-burner of your mind that simple, conscious acknowledgement is extremely powerful in releasing stagnant unwanted energies that no longer serve you. Trauma leaves a cellular imprint or hologram upon the DNA (and other parts of the body as well) that can be transmuted and healed via your conscious intention and conscious acknowledgement. Remember that I said you have no idea just how powerful you really are?

We cannot stop life or our experiences from happening, so the cycle of repression becomes larger and more cumulative if we have forgotten how our energy works. *We also cannot shield ourselves from experiencing trauma in our lives, but we can **learn** how to heal and release it right away so that we do not store it within us.*

The more we close ourselves off from feeling our feelings and do not release our experiences in the moment, the greater the suppression is in our mental, emotional, spiritual and physical bodies. After decades of this vicious cycle, we end up like zombies going through the motions in our daily lives, unable to truly feel much of anything (except pain) and wondering why we are so unhealthy and unhappy.

The energetic body serves a critical function and our chakras are key to understanding ourselves and our relationship to the outer world.

Working With Your Guides and Angels

We all have higher dimensional, nonphysical spiritual guides and angels that are present with us. They have spanned many lifetimes with us, often knowing us better than we know ourselves while we are slumbering and experiencing within 3D consciousness. Our guides are Beings that we know well from our non-physical state. But once we incarnate, the veil often prevents our memory of this and the awareness of our chosen agreements. Our guides and angels are our mentors and muses. They often act as our protectors and cheerleaders, greatly assisting us from behind the veil. They are there for us in every moment, but they will never interfere with our freewill. We must ask to receive their help. Sometimes we ask and do not receive the help we think we need. It might be that we chose a particular experience in order to reap the benefits in ways we cannot yet understand from this position.

There is so much happening beyond our conscious awareness that is conspiring for our evolution and enlightenment. As master co-creators, we each have a plan that our lifetime is following; a charted course and direction that might sometimes be seen by us as undesirable, but in reality is exactly what we came forth to experience. There is growth and new understandings in every single moment of our lives, but our perception can be the opposite of this. Our experiences are not punishments. Often, we cannot see or understand the gift offered within a situation that we deem undesirable until long after the dust has settled. And many never seek out a deeper meaning underscoring any of their experiences.

Many various guides and angels will work with a person throughout their lifetime. We all have one or more birth guides that are with us throughout each incarnation, but many others will also be a part of your journey. We often "call in" certain masters, guides and/or angels at critical junctions in our lives because we are ready for the next step. It is our highest Self calling them to work with us, so we may not be consciously aware of the new assistance. It is easy to learn more about your guides and angels and connect with them directly—all that you need do is (with respect and gratitude) ask them for a stronger connection and how they work with you and why.

When I first began to really connect with my guides and angels, I asked them for concise ways to let me know that they were with me. From that intention forward, it has been a magical journey and my gratitude, love and appreciation for them is beyond words. They have my back in every moment and I know that I am never alone on this journey. They make themselves known to me in a myriad of ways. They let me know when I need to be paying close attention to something in my life and also when it is time to make a shift. They place external clues at every turn that I cannot ignore. The messages are very clear, both internally and externally, *if I am listening and asking for information*. The secret to a close and cohesive relationship with your guides and angels is in the asking.

A Note about Healing Tools

In the next chapter, we will take a look at some wonderful and effective tools such as Reiki, Rapid Personal Transformation (RPT), Acupuncture, Crystal Healing, Homeopathy, Herbal Medicine, Sound and Color Healing, Aromatherapy and many others. I encourage you to do some research and see what appeals to you. The more you utilize these modalities, the more you will raise your vibration and open your consciousness. However, there is no single tool that supersedes another. For some people, a particular tool might shift their entire life and for another it could seem ineffective with no apparent results. As much as we are connected, we each have our own highly unique energy signature that resonates with various energies in different ways. If we identify ourselves with only one particular modality or healing tool, we limit ourselves from being activated by other amazing tools that may also help us. Often, we are drawn to a certain tool to use in healing ourselves and then decide to become a practitioner of the tool. This can be great, but use caution that you do not hand your power over to the modality instead of *incorporating it into your own gifts and then expressing it through your individual perspective.*

Each and every tool is a stepping stone on our path to full remembrance. Each is there to put into our respective tool bags, amalgamate and then reconstruct into *our own expression of it*. Use caution with any tool, person or modality that has rigid lines around it and prohibits or discourages you from following your own instincts around how to utilize it. I have had a few experiences of being introduced to a fantastic healing tool, but the "bringer" of the info got very caught up in their own ego and recognition, sharing their tool and knowledge in a competitive way. We are here to help each other grow and evolve, not limit our understanding.

Effective healing tools help us walk the bridge between the old 3D reality and the new 5D paradigm. They are wonderful agents to help open our bodies, minds and spirits to new levels of consciousness. They serve to remind us of what we have forgotten about ourselves and what we are capable of, as they help reconstruct the picture of our true Selves.

Soon, the time will come when we will no longer need tools because we will become these tools ourselves, bringing them forward from the inside out. In reality, we already are the tool and any tool that we employ is simply an extension of our birthright abilities.

Every tool carries a frequency and vibration that we employ for healing ourselves, but that same frequency also exists within us and we can bring it forward through the power of our imagination or "pretending." I have had healings from just *thinking* about taking a certain homeopathic remedy. I connected my energy to the frequency of the remedy (I just held the vial in my hand) and got the same effect as taking it. This is how very powerful we truly are. Many might call this the placebo effect, but the reality of a placebo effect is that we are the one's innately healing ourselves *through* our belief and intention that a particular substance is going to work, regardless of what it is. It is your *intention* to entrain with another energy that makes it so. Your intention is a command. When you command your body, cells, mind, consciousness or thoughts to do or be something, they all say "Ok, we're on it," as does the Universe. You are indeed in complete control of your body, mind and health. What intentions you broadcast out (through your thoughts, beliefs and feelings) creates that truth.

The Cycle of Trauma

Trauma (and 3D programming) are seated within our minds, bodies and DNA via our inherited trauma and past-life imprints that remain unhealed and unacknowledged.

Leads us to negative thoughts and lowers our vibration, keeping us stuck in the 3D illusion.

Leads to emotions that are on a lower vibrational scale such as fear, anger, hostility, shame, blame, judgment, hopelessness, depression and worthlessness.

Leads to negative beliefs about ourselves, the nature of our world and reality in general.

Leads to negative decisions and actions based upon the illusion created by our trauma and misperceptions about ourselves, others and our world.

Law of Attraction draws more of the same to us to validate our perceived reality.

The low frequency we are running energetically moves into our physicality and seats into the vehicle as an illness or disease, providing us with a larger healing opportunity to clear the trauma(s).

When we do not heal our traumas, we pass them on to our children and future generations, including the propensity toward the same diseases, emotional issues and undesired life experiences.
The Cycle of Trauma continues until it is healed.

How the 3D Systems Suppress the Chakra System

CROWN CHAKRA (Purple)

Most religious dogma teaches separation from our Source and completely omits the reality of our cosmic family. Denial and suppression of divine gifts and birthrights such as telepathy, innate psychic abilities and our capability to ascend. The taught notion of "original sin" as a means to control the masses. Guilt and fear congests the crown chakra and blocks the receiving of vital, divine information trying to reach us.

THIRD EYE (Pineal Gland–Indigo Blue)

Suppression of information about our divine abilities to "see" higher truths and ascertain truths through our psychic senses. Greatly affected by the rampant use of processed foods, prescription drugs, vaccinations, fluoride, chlorine, chemtrails and other toxic chemicals, known to calcify and shut down the pineal gland. Our 3rd Eye is one of our major "truth" barometers and a direct connector to Universal energies as well as our Higher Selves.

THROAT CHAKRA (Turquoise)

Suppression of our individual and collective voice. Repressed through every tentacle in the current system, created by the powers that were.

HEART CHAKRA (Green)

We are taught to close the heart chakra down through fear, the illusion of separation, competition, aggression, war, lack and violence. All of the octopus' tentacles have greatly promoted heart, spiritual, mental and emotional suppression.

SOLAR PLEXUS CHAKRA (Yellow)

Our "Power Center" and also connected to the throat and root chakras. Energetic blocks are created through the 3D matrix where power is championed through tyranny and control versus divine empowerment. Without self-confidence and a sense of worthiness, we feel powerless and fearful, which is greatly promoted by all of the tentacles.

SACRAL CHAKRA (Orange)

Defines our sense of "worth" in the world and the knowingness that we are enough and that we have enough. The sacral chakra is about creating abundance, our sexuality and feeling pleasure and joy in life. Through the various tentacles, we are taught that there isn't "enough" (i.e., lack) and that we are not enough. As a result, many people continue their never-ending search for satiety—emotionally, spiritually, physically, mentally, sexually and financially.

ROOT CHAKRA (Red)

All of the current 3D systems work to suppress our sense of safety and security in the world. Our connection to Gaia is greatly suppressed through industrialization, pollution and concrete cities. There is a gross lack of understanding that Gaia is a living, breathing Being too, with consciousness, and not simply dirt, oil, air, trees and water to be exploited for profit.

CHAPTER 16

Tools for Transformation

The following tools are ones that I have personally found to be highly effective and powerful in my life. They are but a small sampling of tools and modalities out there. Sometimes you must try a tool many times to get the hang of it and find your own way to make it work for you personally. Be playful in your use of these and all tools. When we approach healing modalities[6] without expectations or requirements, they are more effective. The energy of "need" creates resistance, so be wide-open to what your Higher Self, the Universe and Source will deliver through you, as it may be far more than what you expect! Openness, awareness, allowance, acknowledgement and intention are the key ingredients to all healing. So is the energy of gratitude and appreciation, which I have listed as an actual healing tool.

---

[6] FDA Disclaimer: Statements, products and services mentioned in this book have not been evaluated by the US Food and Drug Administration. None of the statements/products/services are intended to diagnose, treat, cure or prevent any disease, nor to dispense medical advice or make claims regarding the cure of diseases. Those seeking treatment for a specific disease or illness should consult a qualified licensed health care professional for a complete evaluation.

(Note: The following tools are in alphabetical order)

BodyTalk™

BodyTalk™ was founded by Dr. John Veltheim. "The BodyTalk™ System seeks to address the whole person. This means that no aspect of the human psyche can be overlooked, be it emotional, physical or environmental. In BodyTalk™, we have developed a whole-healthcare system that supports and promotes the wellbeing of any person, animal, or plant. As WholeHealthcare™, BodyTalk™ understands the profound influence the psychology of the body has on our health. Instead of focusing on the symptom, BodyTalk™ finds the underlying causes of illness by addressing the whole-person and their whole-story. The BodyTalk™ techniques provide insights to the areas of your body that need attention. What might seem like an obvious problem to you is not necessarily the one your body wants to address first. This is the beauty of BodyTalk™. It respects the body's own needs and determines your body's priorities for healing. Then with the use of a variety of non-invasive techniques, BodyTalkers refocus your body's natural healing response to establish better communication within the body." (Courtesy of www.bodytalksystem.com)

Diamond Alignment™

Per Jacqueline Joy, Spiritual Leader: "Diamond Alignment™ is a sacred technology offering high-speed connection and alignment with the Divine Power within, through a revolutionary online phenomenon: the Diamond Alignment™ Activation. Divine Energy is an inherent part of all of us, yet our fast-paced demanding lives often prevent us from finding the time—or even learning how—to consciously Connect and Align with our Inner Power and Wisdom. Diamond Alignment™ offers an unprecedented service that answers this great need. It is convenient and profound, taking technology to the next level. Diamond Alignment™ **is** a Divine Energy Transmission that focuses our energy, so that we are aligned with our Highest Potential while enjoying the undisturbed, infinite peace that comes from the Divine Energy within us. Diamond Alignment™ is **not** a religion, spiritual practice, dogma, or self-help course. This Energy-based technology is designed to help us thrive in our everyday world…spiritually, mentally, emotionally, physically and materially." The 6-minute Diamond Alignment™ Activation is accessible 24 hours a day, 7 days a week, by subscription. (Courtesy of www.diamondalignment.com)

EFT™ (Emotional Freedom Techniques)

Per Gary Craig, the Founder of The Emotional Freedom Techniques™: "EFT is an emotional version of acupuncture, except no needles are used." It employs finger-tapping on certain body meridians to release stuck energy that can result in physical healing by allowing the energy or chi to resume its natural flow of movement. EFT™ often produces amazing results and is suitable for adults, children and animals. It is a simple and highly recommended tool to release emotional issues and traumas. I commend Gary for offering a free tutorial on his website, so that everyone, regardless of income, has access to this tool—way to practice 5D consciousness, Gary. Please visit www.garythink.com or www.emofree.com for more information. This healing tool is very simple to learn, yet powerful in results.

Ho'oponopono

We are each capable of taking conscious and intentional responsibility for *everything* we see, feel, hear and experience, whether or not it belongs directly to us or a stranger on the street. This is how we heal ourselves and each other through the power and truth of oneness. When we take responsibility for something, whether we perceive it as being "ours" or not, it gives us the ability and divine power to change it. This truth is at the heart of the ancient Hawaiian, Shamanic healing tool called Ho'oponopono, brought into mainstream awareness by Dr. Hew Lin. It stops denial and energetic resistance so that stuck energy and trauma can shift. Because we are all one, you can individually own something for someone else and heal it on their divine behalf. If the issue is in their soul contract to experience, or if it is karmic, it simply will not release. There are built-in checks and balances. Dr. Ihalekala Hew Lin accomplished an unimaginable feat and quite literally emptied a Hawaiian state hospital for the criminally insane, solely by employing Ho'oponopono. He was hired as a therapist for the hospital from 1983-1987, but he never saw one single patient in person. Instead, he went directly to work on *himself* to, as he says, "clean up his own subconscious mind." This affectively healed the patient that he was focusing upon by himself, behind the closed doors of his office. For additional information please look up, "Dr. Hew Lin." His story is absolutely fascinating and a prime example of oneness and compassion in action.

The One Command™

The One Command™ is a fun and effective healing tool that can dissolve and release limiting beliefs and thought-forms from your DNA as well as your mind, body and spirit. I have had great success with it. It is also a highly effective tool for manifestation. The technique teaches you how to enter into a theta brain-wave state and employs a simple six-step method. Old science would say that the theta brain-wave state cannot be accessed unless one is sleeping, but that is simply not true and anyone can access it with very little practice. This tool and program was brought forth by Asara Lovejoy. For more information please visit their website at www.successbyyourcommand.com.

Radical Forgiveness Program™

Radical Forgiveness™ is a wonderful body of work by Colin Tipping that is very empowering. It touches deeply on the self-empowerment attained by taking full conscious responsibility for all of our creations and our dance with others who help us see the issues we need to heal within ourselves. His work beautifully portrays all of us as the master co-creators that we are, and as such, how to leave victimhood behind. The healing shift that is offered through Radical Forgiveness™ is one of a large shift in perspective and a new realization that no "wrong" has actually been committed from a higher spiritual understanding. I highly recommend Colin's work. He also offers many free tools on his website and many powerful programs that target both individuals as well as the corporate world. Radical Forgiveness™ offers a large step into 5D consciousness. Please visit www.radicalforgiveness.com for more information.

Rapid Personal Transformation™

Rapid Personal Transformation™ (RPT), previously known as "Reference Point Therapy," is a very powerful and beautiful healing modality. The premise is that trauma (both from this lifetime as well as ancestrally) can be released through the Triune Brain Model™. It is a cutting-edge tool that was brought forth by Simon & Evette Rose and anyone can learn to utilize it. Unlike many healing modalities, RPT™ gets to the base foundational component that is holding a particular pattern of trauma in place, whether the trauma has manifested emotionally, physically, spiritually or all of the above. Many tools simply band-aid our "stuff" and it may get better for awhile, only to resurface down the road because the root energy was not found or released. RPT™ assists you in getting to the foundational issue and releasing it. Its beauty is that you do not need (nor is it helpful) to re-visit the trauma for it to work. RPT™ helps us remember ourselves as sacred Beings of the whole. Once you have taken the basic level one and level two classes, you will have ample knowledge of how to use this tool on yourself and others. The level three class is an extensive journey into the deepest parts of one's self—I highly recommend it. For videos and more information, please visit their website at www.rapidpersonaltransformation.com.

The Sedona Method™

The Sedona Method™ is a technique that teaches you to unwind suppressed emotions by identifying the emotion, feeling it and then letting go of it. Most of the emotional release techniques mentioned in this book have a similar foundational structure for releasing and healing, but they all have a different flavor about them in numerous ways. Some people may find a particular technique to be enormously successful, while another one may not seem to work at all for them. It's best to keep working with various modalities until you find the one that you personally resonate with. The Sedona Method™ was developed by Hale Dwoskin. You can find more information about the Sedona Method™ at www.sedona.com.

Quantum Jumping™

This is one of my favorite tools. Created by Burt Goldman, Quantum Jumping™ is fun and effective. The program teaches us how to navigate within our multidimensionality and also how to explore our other aspects that I have mentioned throughout this book. You learn (remember) how to access your other soul aspect's talents and gifts and how to bring them forward into this current experience. Burt Goldman's guided, advanced visualization programs will take you on the great adventure of discovering *yourself*. Please visit www.quantumjumping.com for additional information.

Other Helpful Tools

Acupuncture

Acupuncture is an ancient Chinese healing method originating over 5,000 years ago. It employs tiny needles inserted at various energy meridians on the body to stimulate and balance the Qi (pronounced "chee"—life force energy). There are over 1,000 acupuncture points on the human body. I have used acupuncture for years for various reasons and have experienced very positive results overall. I have found that not all acupuncturists treat patients from a holistic perspective and some do not support other energetic practices. Determine your needs and then speak to a number of qualified professionals to find the best fit for you personally. Acupuncturists must be state licensed in the USA with ongoing continuing educational requirements. Acupuncture is an amazing and effective alternative healing modality. Many people are turned off by the idea of needles, but they are so incredibly small that I have never experienced a session as painful or uncomfortable. For more information visit www.aaaomonline.org.

The Amazing Power of Gratitude and Appreciation

We are in every moment maintaining a vibration that correlates directly to where we are giving our attention and how that makes us feel. The Universe is constantly matching our vibration, automatically. So if we consciously choose to create states of gratitude within ourselves, we maintain a higher vibration *deliberately* and with intention. The more we feel gratitude and appreciation, the more we manifest things and people to be grateful for. It is about "frequency matching." Frequency matching is another, more specific term for The Law of Attraction. It is of course not a "law" in a 3D sense, but rather a naturally occurring resonation between us and a larger frequency that is innately part of the greater cosmos.

You might be living in a state of poverty or illness at this particular time, but there is still so much to be grateful for. Find beauty in nature, the love of others, the dew on the morning grass, or just look into the mirror and appreciate your own radiant beauty, because you are indeed staring at a reflection of All That Is—manifest. Your life, no matter how hard it might appear to be in this moment, is a huge gift and you are invaluable to the oneness of life. We are all lucky to have you upon this planet. Thank you for choosing to be here. It doesn't matter if you collect garbage for a living, or if you own a multi-billion dollar company; your worth and value as a human Being as well as your contribution to the whole is *equal*, regardless of what you may have been taught by the 3D systems.

Appreciate your life and know that you yourself chose it exactly as it is for a specific reason. If it doesn't feel right to you, you have the power to change it through your vibration and your very next thought. Learning to live in gratitude for all that you *do* have and for all that you *are* is one of the most powerful healing tools we can utilize.

Aromatherapy

Aromatherapy* uses essential oils and aromatic plant compounds that are able to influence one's health and mood through the olfactory system and sense of smell. It is a holistic art and science that I was a bit skeptical about myself until I tried it. I was amazed at the positive effects upon my mood and in treating migraines, sinus issues, insomnia and fatigue. Aromatherapy is now a regular part in my overall health plan. For additional information visit www.naha.org

Astrology

Understanding your solar birth chart and how it is like a blueprint (that you yourself chose from your non-physical state) for your life path is very helpful. It will show you what you came into this incarnation to accomplish, to heal and to be. Remember when I spoke of the great planning that you did from your non-physical state of beingness? Your birth chart helps you understand those decisions and life plans. It is a wonderful navigational chart to help you *remember* your life path choices, karmic energies, talents, goals and personal evolution. When you understand your own greater intentions, things in your life make far more sense. Your birth chart offers guideposts for your life and insights into your journey here. I recommend finding an astrologer who can take the technical aspects of reading your chart and break them down into what that actually means to you in simplistic, everyday terms and language. Astrology is not woo-woo. It is a very science-based tool for growth and awareness. The irony is that the powers that were extensively use astrology *daily* to plan their agendas. They understand the power that lies in astrological alignments, as well as numerology, for timing of events. Isn't it time that we educate ourselves as well around this ancient and accurate science?

---

* Author's Note: Homeopathy and aromatherapy often do not complement each other very well, as aromatherapy can cancel out or neutralize the homeopathic remedies. Speak with a homeopath if you plan to use both.

Body Work/Massage

Manual body work is important to our overall healing because it helps us release toxins, relax our muscles and reduce stress levels. As we begin to unwind the emotional patterns that have been stored in our bodies, a good massage practitioner can facilitate the release of these energies from our cells. This clearing allows our bodies to hold an even higher vibration. I recommend a practitioner that is skilled in not only massage, but also as an energy practitioner and/or medical intuitive. The combination of the two is priceless.

Clean Your Basement

Make a written list of all of the negative thoughts and habits that you feel you are practicing. Go into a meditative (beingness) state while holding the list in your hand. Intentionally acknowledge each and every item on your list. Then, imagine piling all of these things into a huge garbage bag to bless, thank and take out to the curb. Repeat: "I am a powerful creator and All That Is delights in my remembrance of my divine nature and gifts that are my birthright. I now release what no longer serves me, allowing the Universe to pick it up at the curb and carry it away for me. I am far more than my thoughts, beliefs, habits and actions. I embrace my new, higher vibration."

Color Therapy

Color Therapy, also known as Chromotherapy, is a form of vibrational healing through electromagnetic energy. This modality has historically been highly underrated in its power and effects upon the body, mind and spirit. I have found that when I use color therapy that corresponds to a particular chakra or chakras that I sense are congested, the clearing and release is far faster and more complete. We can use color as a modality in numerous ways, whether we simply visualize it in our meditations, wear it on our bodies, decorate with it in our homes, or use colored lights in a healing session. I know of one practitioner that streams colored lights through large, clear quartz crystals in her sessions and the color healing is amplified because of the energy projected by the crystal. We are highly affected by the frequencies held by various colors on the spectrum. As we intentionally interact with various colors in the light spectrum, our energetic field responds and entrains. We are naturally drawn to use certain colors, often without even realizing it. Have you ever felt depressed and felt an internal nudge to wear yellow? Or how about being drawn to green when you needed to feel calm or soothed? Many people find that it's hard to sleep well if they decorate with red in their bedroom, as it encourages action and movement. What paint colors would you pick for your home? They are likely ones that would benefit you at this time. Many people wear a lot of browns and blacks because it helps to ground them. Start experimenting with colors and use them intentionally during meditation or otherwise. There are many gifted professional color therapy practitioners available to assist you in a more in-depth manner. If you cannot find a practitioner in your local community, try searching in a larger city because most will be able to Skype™ with you or offer phone consultations. For more information visit www.iac-colour.co.uk

Cranio-Sacral Therapy

Cranio-Sacral Therapy (CST) is a gentle, hands-on approach that releases tension deep in the body to relieve pain and dysfunction, improving whole-body health and performance. It was pioneered and developed by Osteopathic Physician, John E. Upledger, after years of clinical testing and research at Michigan State University where he served as professor of biomechanics. Using a soft touch, which is generally no greater than 5 grams, or about the weight of a nickel, practitioners release restrictions in the soft tissues that surround the central nervous system. CST is increasingly used as a preventive health measure for its ability to bolster resistance to disease and it is effective for a wide range of medical problems associated with pain and dysfunction. Please visit www.upledger.com to locate a practitioner in your area.

Crystal Healing

I have been the steward of a large collection of crystals since I was about seven years old. I was instantly mesmerized when I saw my first large crystal. Now, over forty years later, I am still captive of their power, beauty and ability to assist in healing the body, mind and spirit. Crystal therapy[7] is used frequently in conjunction with Reiki, meditation, massage and other energetic tools, because they greatly *amplify* and stabilize the work being performed. There is a crystal, or a number of crystals and stones that identify and resonate with every human illness known to us. Their energies can be highly effective in working to release the issue. Crystals, just like us, are composed of pure vibrational energy, frequency and Light. What appears solid is most assuredly—not. Crystals can ground you, help you meditate or travel out of body, dispel negative energies, protect your energetic field, calm you, elevate your mood, help you sleep, jettison your spiritual development and so much more. These amazing tools are Gaia's gift to humanity. They help us remain in resonance and harmony with her, while also attuning us to the rest of the cosmos.

Most often a crystal practitioner will lay a particular crystal "grid" on the person, or around them to interface with their auric field. I use various crystals in my meditations and now easily attune with their energies as soon as I am in their presence. During this ascension process, our physical bodies are changing from a carbon-based template back to the crystalline template that better supports our Light Bodies. Working with crystal energies helps us cross this bridge with greater ease because when in the presence of crystals, we are aligning our energetic body with the desired frequency. We then entrain with the stones, as they act as a catalyst to help raise our vibration. This may sound far out to many people, but our vehicles evolve just as we do spiritually. Duality has necessitated a very dense and heavy physical form for this experience, but the end of

---

[7] Please visit the "Resources" section for a list of excellent books about crystal healing and the properties of each stone.

this cycle requires a vastly new and improved body that is able to hold the higher frequencies of Light. Our old carbon-based bodies could never hold these energies and survive them. The very nature of healing and emotionally releasing our old 3D experiences enables us to attain our new Light Bodies. Find a local rock shop or check out Ebay™ (with a little bit of practice, you can actually feel the energies of a stone via a photograph online) and see what crystal or stone you feel drawn to. Consider purchasing a number of them to use in your meditations, walks, massages, or even at your work desk and on your nightstand. We are usually drawn to the stones and colors that we need to work with at any given time. Once that need is filled, we might feel prompted to gift it to someone and then see what stone calls us next.

Flower Essences

Developed in the 1920s and 1930s in the U.K. by Dr. Edward Bach, (a well-known bacteriologist, physician and pathologist) flower essences are made through the infusion of the energy of a flower or plant into a base of water via sunlight or a special boiling method. The process captures the energetic signature and blueprint of the flower, becoming a part of the water. The tincture is then diluted with brandy which creates a mother tincture. These remedies are homeopathic in nature and pack a powerful (yet harmless) boost that gently assists with a wide variety of issues—emotionally, physically and spiritually. I have had wonderful and powerful results in my usage over the years. For additional information, please visit www.bachcentre.com or Google: *Bach Flower Essences*.

Herbal Medicine

Herbal remedies have been used very successfully for centuries all over the world and are made from plant or plant extracts. They treat a very wide range of conditions and are often prescribed along with other alternative healing treatments. Herbal treatments are used to either boost energy (qi) or disperse it. They are very commonly used in Ayurvedic, Chinese and Naturopathic medicine.

Many acupuncturists prescribe herbal medicine to support their treatments. Herbs are used to treat disease and maintain good health. Most pharmaceutical drugs are manufactured with an extracted main ingredient from a plant and then synthesized into a chemically-based product instead of an herbal-based product. Much fear has been generated by the octopus around herbal supplementation. It is always advised that one consult a professional (I highly recommend a quality Naturopathic doctor, as allopathic medicine is not knowledgeable about herbal, plant-based medicine) when consuming herbals and especially when mixing pharmaceutical drugs with herbal treatments. Just as many prescription drugs should not be prescribed for certain illnesses, the same is true of certain herbs. Please use your own internal compass and a professional herbalist when determining what is in your best interest on your healing journey. Make decisions from your *Inner Authority*, not out of generated fear by the powers that were.

Homeopathy

Homeopathic Medicine* is a very old, proven and extremely powerful alternative solution to treat all illness and disease. Homeopathy can also bring about the energetic release of trauma and emotional patterns that are stored within the tissues and cells. When the correct remedy is administered, the effect is quick, thorough and healing takes place at the root cause of the issue. Homeopathy has been around for hundreds of years and is still widely used in Europe. With the advent of Western allopathic medicine, insurance companies and octopus-influenced pharmaceutical companies,

---

* Author's Note: The author recommends consulting with a professional for the use of homeopathy (as well as herbal remedies, flower essences and aromatherapy for the best results). Although these treatments are overall safe to self-administer, a professional will be able to customize your treatment based upon a total picture (historically and current) of your mind, body and spirit. The homeopath will then prescribe the appropriate remedies for your individualized needs. As with all energy-based alternative healing modalities, the treatment focuses upon the entire person as a whole and does not simply mask, or band-aid a symptom, which serves to further suppress the foundational root causative factor(s). These treatments support the body's own ability to return to its original, healthy blueprint. Alternative medicine is akin to gently and safely unblocking a dam to relieve stuck energy, allowing the body's natural and innate brilliance to take over, creating a fully balanced and harmonious state of health.

homeopathy became far less popular and even questioned as "valid medicine." Many people confuse homeopathy with herbal medicine, but they are very different. Homeopathy is also not a "placebo" as many people are led to believe.

Homeopathy is a form of medicine, first proposed by German physician Samuel Hahnemann in 1796, in which practitioners use highly diluted preparations that support the body's natural propensity to heal. It works under the *Law of Similars*, or "like cures like" through the use of highly diluted micro-dosages and potencies. The idea is that symptoms are signs that the body is healing itself and homeopaths work to support, not suppress, these symptoms. There are no side effects, the cost is minimal and homeopathy is used to treat every ailment or disease known to mankind. My entire family has used homeopathy for decades with tremendous success. For more information visit www.nationalcenterforhomeopathy.org, or contact a homeopath in your area. Most homeopathic physicians can effectively treat patients either in person or by phone or Skype™.

Love Yourself to Health

What you don't love about yourself, you automatically reject energetically. What you reject is known as resistance. Resistance stops the healing and manifestation process. Our self-judgments are largely based upon the teachings of the octopus and self-condemnation prevents us from actualizing the love that we truly are. When we dislike, judge or hate ourselves (or anyone else) we cannot also be in unison with All That Is. We block that beautiful flow of divine energy if we judge ourselves to be unworthy, unlovable and not good enough. It is time to honor this experiential journey for what it really is and deeply love ourselves for who we are, outside of this illusionary matrix. Whatever you may believe about yourself, I assure you that you are far greater and this truth has nothing whatsoever to do with the ego. As our consciousness levels continue to rise, we will return to the knowingness that there is nothing to *"not love."* We judge ourselves, often harshly, by our chosen experiences and decisions, but we are not comprised of those things. This is a basement perspective, not a rooftop vista. You are *amazing beyond belief* and as you realize this, your vibration will soar. Unconditional self-love is a critical key to your ascension.

Myofascial Release Work

Myofacial Release is the light manipulation of the connective tissues to release tightness that is causing pain and pulling the body out of alignment. Myofascial therapy gently stretches and loosens the fascia to return range of motion, induce muscle relaxation and restore the body's alignment. I have found this treatment provides very positive results and is one of my favorites. Much trauma is stored in our fascia and healing occurs when it is released. John F. Barnes is the international leader, trainer and authority for Myofascial Release. For additional information visit www.myofascialrelease.com

Past Life/Concurrent Life Regression Work

Past life issues often resurface in this lifetime to be healed. The problem is that most people are not aware when their current life issues are connected to another lifetime or are an inherited energetic pattern. As discussed in prior chapters, the emotional traumas that we carry with us when we transition manifest in future lifetimes. Linear time (as we now understand it) does not exist outside of this 3D Earth construct. Therefore, the term "past lives" is not as accurate as the term "concurrent lifetimes." Because we have forgotten our multidimensionality, we have also forgotten that our many soul aspects exist in many dimensions and places *all at once*. These aspects are experiencing in many various time and space constructs. From our current standpoint, we have a very difficult time wrapping our brains around this. Our current lives affect all of our other aspects, and their life experiences are affecting ours, in every moment. As we revisit and heal stuck energies from other lifetime experiences, we heal all of our aspects at the same time. I have had much past life recall in this lifetime—scenes (and emotions) that played out in my inner (third eye) vision with clarity. These memories always seem to have patterns of emotional trauma that I can easily find within this lifetime as well. They are coming forth, asking me to acknowledge and release them. These memories act as pieces of evidence that can point us to the underlying traumas if we willfully take on the role of detective. It is a fascinating journey into the totality of one's self. Remember, repressed energies are simply waiting to be acknowledged before they can release—both for the wisdom and understanding that they are gifting you as well as the literal energetic release within your cells, DNA and psyche. A past life regression practitioner will have the ability to act as a guide so that you reap the deeper understandings of the recall. They will also have the skills to help you release what you are ready to let go of.

Reflexology

Reflexology is a method of exerting fingertip pressure to the feet, hands and ears at certain reflex points to affect specific organs, bones and body systems for healing. It also stimulates the nervous system, allowing the body to repair itself intrinsically. Reflexology is an ancient healing practice with evidence pointing it all the way back to ancient Egyptian times. It is successfully used to treat illnesses and ailments as well as maintain good health and harmony. For additional information visit www.reflexology-usa.org

Reiki

Reiki (pronounced ray-key) is a Japanese word meaning Universal Life Energy. It is a very old spiritual practice that utilizes the Universal energy that is all around us to facilitate relaxation and healing though the "laying on of hands." Usui is the most widely known and practiced form of Reiki, developed by Dr. Mikao Usui in the early 1900s. The beauty of Reiki is that anyone can give or receive it. The person giving Reiki becomes the channeler of the energy, sending it to the person receiving it, including oneself. There are various levels of Reiki attunements that are prerequisite to practicing Reiki and classes are available in most all cities these days, taught by Reiki Masters. Reiki energy works to balance and heal the entire body, mind and spirit. Reiki promotes self-healing and balancing within the body. For more information visit www.iarp.org

Sound Healing

The next great shift to higher vibrational healing for every human condition is going to be sound healing. We consist of vibratory frequency and Light. Sound is a frequency of light and vibration and has a tremendous ability to heal and create complete balance within every particle of our existence. The type of sound that I refer to here is produced by certain frequencies and is created in a variety of ways, from crystal or Tibetan bowls, to tuning forks or studio-produced sound waves. I like the apt term, "Sacred Sound" the best. High vibrational sound healing has been successfully used in pain management, restoring a diseased body to full health, consciousness elevation, inducing deep theta brain-wave states, relieving stress, increasing joy and achieving a deep sense of inner calm and peace. Sound healing goes back to ancient tribal cultures and has been used extensively as a healing modality and to assist in Shamanic traveling. Since our bodies are made up of 70% water, sound waves reverberate deeply into our cells, creating a resonance between the vibration of the cell and the note, or notes being produced. The components of the cell actually entrain with the frequency of the sound waves. Sound can easily alter our vibration, changing our state of consciousness up or down, depending upon the type of music or sound. The cosmos actually produces a "sound" that is an extremely high frequency and some of the best sound healers out there are channeling in these Universal harmonics that can assist with the healing journey. For more information visit www.worldsoundhealing.org, www.tomkenyon.com and www.marceyhamm.com

Uncovering Your Passions

Here's a good test for you: If money ceased to exist tomorrow, would you still do what you are doing for a living? Would you quit your current job or keep working at this profession? Why? Why not? If not, *what would you choose to do instead?* If you would choose to stay, what is the draw? What are your greatest passions? What makes your heart Light up, sending excitement racing through your veins? Whatever it is that jump-starts you out of bed in the morning and is something that you would do regardless of compensation, is your *true calling* from your soul level. Your core Self knows your path and if you are listening, the path will be unmistakable and your heart will show you how to get there. If you are feeling an undefined urge from the center of your being to do *something*, but you don't know what, it is your soul calling you into action. Perhaps it is time to shift into the work that you came here to do. Listen carefully for guidance and it will unfold. Sometimes, what we deeply desire is manifesting for us, just perhaps not at the speed in which we want it. Watch for the signs and know that if you are truly seeking the highest and best expression of yourself, you will indeed find it at the exact right time and in the perfect unfolding of *you*.

Yoga

Yoga is far more than a stretching or exercise modality. Yoga is a complex (as in the results are so far reaching, it is hard to put a box around it) platform by which one can create an energetic alignment within themselves on every level. Yoga can open and clear chakras, free the mind, heal the body and connect the spirit. Through the asanas (yoga postures) and proper breath work, the body becomes the portal to the higher realms. There are many different styles of yoga, so do your research and try all that sound interesting to you. Each has its own flavor, level of difficulty and particular intention or focus. My practice of Hatha Yoga has provided so many positive changes in my life that I can't even put words to many of the sensations and benefits. I also really enjoy Kundalini Yoga. For more information visit www.yogajournal.com. This website offers a state by state search engine to locate yoga classes near you, as well as a list of yoga associations to explore.

CHAPTER 17

The Return to Cosmic Consciousness

You have a Universal capacity as a divine human Being having a physical experience, but you have only been aware of a tiny percentage of your innate powers and abilities. The vast majority of you have zero memory of your greater cosmic lineage and your place within this family during your many lives upon Earth. The octopus has ensured that your recall stayed dormant and that any mention of your off-planet relatives and ancestors resulted in fear, laughter and/or denial.

What is Cosmic Consciousness?

The global movement underway reaches far beyond the powers that were systems comprised of non-truths and illusions. We have been severely bruised by the hyperbole of their promises, designed to keep us quiet and in order. We have heard endless campaigns of promises from those who serve themselves.

This newly arriving energy is restoring our memory of who we really are as sovereign divine Beings and Universal citizens. Our core Selves will be our guides and the lighthouse for answers. As we learn how to tap into this cosmic consciousness, we will realize and recognize the oneness of our Light. In essence, cosmic consciousness is being able to lovingly and respectfully interact with all Beings from the Vista Point. It is the knowingness and remembrance that we are an integral part of a greater Universal family that has been hidden from our awareness.

As we awaken, we start to remember that one of the greatest fallacies from the octopus has been that we are alone in this Universe. We have forgotten that we, as the family of Earth, are part of a far greater landscape. We have forgotten that we *agreed* to participate in this 3D lower dimensional reality for our soul's evolution and also to assist Gaia during this cycle's end. We agreed to come here to collectively help release Gaia and humanity from the octopus and its current systems. We left behind our higher-dimensional star families to do so, many eons ago. However, throughout our so-called linear time, our star families have always been very present behind the scenes, guiding and assisting us to the completion of this very long journey.

Spiritual Maturity

As we move into higher states of consciousness, we also move into far greater levels of accountability and *spiritual maturity*. As our manifesting abilities return to us in increasing intensity, we must become acutely aware of our thoughts, beliefs and intentions. What we manifest affects all others. *With these returned gifts and responsibilities, divine integrity must become the foundation for all manifestations.* We are the hologram and blueprint for the new paradigm and our entire concept of power has to now shift into divine empowerment. We have a common destiny with Mother Earth. We talk so much about our rights as human Beings, but we talk so little about our responsibilities and accountability as stewards of this planet and of each other.

We will truly honor, respect and love each other unconditionally when we remember that we are all Sacred Cosmic Beings. We are far greater than just our current expression upon this one world, among countless worlds. If we are willing to do the inner healing work, we will be given the opportunity to return to cosmic citizenry and the remembrance that most of us have native homes within many various star systems.

There is much in this chapter that might be a great leap for many of you reading it. You might seriously question my sanity and legitimacy. But I highly encourage you to read on and open your mind beyond the 3D construct. Explore your own truths about who you really are at a cosmic level.

Truth Meter

Our internal knowing could be aptly termed our *truth meter*, as it will most assuredly show us what is valid and real and what is not. Carefully filter what you hear and use great caution around what sources of information you allow into your awareness. Some are very obviously of the octopus and with a little practice you will begin to know what constitutes propaganda and what does not.

Our internal truth meters are imperative during this shift and we need to greatly develop and depend upon them. Stop letting others define "what is real" for you. This applies to the entire "alien" drama that has been sold to us through Hollywood movies. Just the word *alien* triggers fear in many and laughter in others, as it was intended to do. This tremendous lie is busting open at the seams and full, truthful disclosure is near.

It is important to note here that the powers that were have many very advanced technologies (given to them to use for all of humanity, but they did not honor their agreement) that we do not yet know about or understand how they work. Be very careful not to *automatically* believe anything put forth by the mainstream, octopus owned and controlled media.

The truth is that we are surrounded by a huge family from many star systems and planets. This is common knowledge within the ranks of the octopus, with much to lose if the truth is recognized by the masses. Many insiders within NASA (including many astronauts) and the military are coming forward to speak their truth around their knowledge of the above. I applaud their courage. The frightening fairy tale that the powers that were have created to hide the reality of our benevolent, spiritually evolved star families is soon to come to an end.

Our Future Selves

Have you ever considered that the powers that were have historically done everything in their power to ensure that any belief in life beyond this planet is perceived as ridiculous and is ridiculed? Why would that be? Could it be that if we knew the truth we might instantly understand our own capacity? This is exactly what has transpired and to this day a Universe teeming with countless other occupied planets is denied any relevance beyond science fiction or hypothesis. Earth is one of many, many playgrounds. We are and always have been greatly assisted by our star families to the dismay of the powers that were. As this colossal revelation continues to unfold, the octopus is well aware that its days are very numbered.

These Beings *are who we are becoming*. We individually have a choice now whether or not to remember our galactic citizenry. There is an entire cosmic community that is waiting to greet us if we embrace them. However, the only way that we will be allowed to reconnect to our greater cosmic family is if we shed the lower vibrations and walk the path to higher consciousness. Those that seek and ask are being shown the way.

Many people cannot fathom these truths because they have been brainwashed to believe that we are all alone within this massive

Universe that is within countless Universes. Ships (many comprised of pure light) are regularly crossing our skies and at least some governments are now actively reporting the public sightings of them, worldwide. These sightings are increasing as our star families try to gently unfold the truth and remembrance of their existence. They are indeed experts at shifting realities and dimensions, as they have already ascended and live in a fifth dimensional reality or higher. There is nothing but pure love for us and positive intentions. They have no agenda except to help us return to who we really are and regain our ability to be galactic citizens. To do so, we must attain spiritual mastery over duality and achieve the energetic vibration required to rejoin the higher realms without being a threat to others.

Most dimensionally advanced off-planet societies no longer have a monetary system, as it is no longer needed. They have evolved beyond that construct. Eventually, we will too.

Our cosmic relatives have no desire to interfere with our freewill, control or save us (they know that we have to "save" ourselves). However, without their help, our ability to shift into 5D systems could be futile, as the roots of the old 3D systems are very deep and well-anchored. The help that we are getting from our star families and Light teams is critical to our journey out of this dimension. If you tune in to their presence, you will feel an amazing level of unconditional love for us. It has always been so, but well-hidden behind the fear created by the powers that were to keep us isolated from the knowledge of our cosmic heritage.

We are fast approaching a time in human history where we will not need anyone to confirm the existence of ET's beyond our planet. We will have no need for so-called "experts" to provide evidence or footage because as you awaken and remember where you truly came from, proving the obvious will seem silly and absurd. And yet, because we have been slumbering for so long, it might still seem very far out. With the incoming energies and large shifts occurring, this will soon change.

Navigating the Galactic and Solar Influences

Earth is experiencing a tremendous increase in solar flares and coronal mass ejections and the frequency and intensity is escalating. This is barely discussed on the mainstream news of course, but the information is out there for those that care to look. What has facilitated this change?

Our planet and entire Universe is moving deeper into the galactic center in space, where the charged particles are very different from anything we have ever experienced. These solar influences act as *catalyst* for tremendous changes in consciousness to occur on Earth and to our entire solar system. Simply being within these highly charged particles is what is facilitating the final purging of the old paradigm. No one will be unaffected by these intense energies, regardless of their awareness of them. If we welcome these new energies they will be magical because they help us build a new foundation for higher consciousness.

At a purely 3D scientific level, increased solar activity can take out entire power grids and satellites and cause much havoc upon technology. But of *far more significance* is how they are affecting our mind, body and consciousness levels. For those of us who are highly sensitive to energies, we are like barometers and can literally feel when they occur. The increased solar activity is affecting many people, days before and after the event.

It is important to drink lots of pure, healthy water during this time as we can become easily dehydrated and our bodies utilize the water to protect our nervous systems from the solar intensity. We are operating at a higher "combustion level," so to speak, than ever before.

Organic foods are also highly recommended. Avoid processed foods, sugar, GMO's, soda pop and alcohol during these times, as all of these lower the body's vibration at an energetic level. Many people are reporting increased headaches, internal heat surges, high fatigue levels, sleeplessness or increased sleepiness, irritability, anxiety and even increased muscle and joint pains.

Please take extra good care of your vehicle during these times of change and transformation. What you choose to put in your body (and on it, as what you put on your skin and hair goes directly into your blood stream and cells) is of critical importance now and directly affects your frequency and vibration. Food is energy and is either vibrating high or low (or somewhere in between) based upon its purity or toxicity. Organic produce and humanely raised grass-fed meats and non-GMO's are important to protect the body from added toxicity.

You may wish to investigate the plethora of highly effective natural solutions. Many physical and emotional symptoms are literally being caused by the ascension process. These symptoms do not necessarily mean that you are ill or have a disease, as most simply come and go with the changing frequencies. Many symptoms will come on very suddenly and leave just as quickly. Your entire chakra system and all associated organs are being recalibrated to a higher octave of physicality.

These highly charged electromagnetic energies are *greatly* affecting humans and animals alike in every way. They also significantly influence our weather patterns globally and can trigger major storms, earthquakes, tornados and hurricanes. Combine the solar influences and the arrangement of the planets (and their influence upon us) and we have a sum of causative factors that are exerting tremendous force upon our metamorphosis.

There is absolutely nothing to fear, but so much to be incredibly excited about. These new particles are literally encoded with our next phase of evolution. I like to think of them as highly intelligent "Divine Sparks," that assist in raising our vibration and consciousness higher and higher. They are affecting our DNA and helping us to evolve. If you tune in, you can feel them.

These "sparks" are the substance that is causing the transformation of our carbon-based vehicles to morph into our new crystalline template. We are of the exact same particle substance as our intelligent Universe was created from, so it's no surprise that it is in this manner that we are evolving. In fact, how amazing it is to witness all of this transpire at an experiential level!

Remembering What You Already Know

As we awaken, we realize that we have never been alone on this planet. We remember that we are surrounded by other planets teeming with highly spiritual and technologically advanced life, many who look just as we do or very similar. There are over 20,000 known galaxies *just within our Universe alone* and these are only the ones currently known to 3D science.

The octopus-controlled scientific community has not embraced that life is highly multidimensional by nature, so how could they understand that life upon other planets is a dimensional state of existence—dimensions that we do not have access to with our 3D sight. The lack of understanding our own Universe has left 3D science unable to validate life upon other planets by nature of the different vibratory rates. The powers that were are fully aware of the dimensional differences, but will not allow their financially-controlled scientists to reveal this truth.

Traditional (old) science remains draconian to protect the many agendas of the 3D systems. What has come forward out of science is only what the octopus has permitted to come forth. The technologies and discoveries that would in any way expose the agendas and/or hamper the plans of the powers that were are confiscated and never reach the public, regardless of whether they would help humanity or not. You can be assured that anything that would truly advance the evolution or freedom of humanity is not going to be in the best interest of the octopus. As long as we continue to give validity to the 3D science models to provide proof of our true history and capabilities, we will miss the truths right under our noses.

The world's ancient indigenous tribes are, by far, our most advanced cultures in spirituality and direct understanding of connectedness and enmeshment with Source energy. The octopus would like for you to believe that they are still quite "primitive" instead of the Keepers of the Truth and the ones who refuse to be Followers of the Lies. Most all of the indigenous Native tribes across the globe speak of an off-planet origin and of our benevolent, higher spiritual nature. Their artwork often depicts crafts and Beings from off-planet and their own links to them. They remember their cosmic connections that most people have all but forgotten.

It is a fading triumph that the octopus was able to hide the reality of our greater-evolved star families from us for so long. Hollywood has also promoted fear of off-planet Beings with ridiculous sci-fi, fear-based depictions of "alien" monsters intending to take over the planet. Hollywood is infiltrated with those there to further many agendas by shaping public opinion. Many of these movies depict keeping the ET's away from Earth to protect us, but has it ever occurred to you that perhaps the spiritual hierarchy has quarantined *Earth* from interacting with the higher civilizations comprising our Universe? We are the ones who can't seem to let go of violence and separation, which would allow us to evolve into benevolent spiritual Beings and reunite with our galactic families. Be that as it may, we are currently being offered a tremendous gift to do just that, if we choose to heal ourselves and embrace our Light. From *The Galactic Federation of Light's* perspective, unless we make a soul-level choice to evolve, giving us the greater body of cosmic knowledge would be like putting rocket science (and rockets) into the hands of children.

Cosmic Oneness

Each of us is self-defining within the Universal and galactic oneness as aspects of Source energy manifested on this planet. Self *is* Source. Our oneness is defined by our substance as the pure consciousness of All That Is. We share something very sacred, and that sacredness is at the heart of that which we call God (or Source, Prime Creator, Christ, Buddha, Allah, Great Spirit, All That Is or whatever sacred name you prefer for this same divine energy). We are like grand adventurers and explorers within this particular time-space consortium and our collective oneness far surpasses our brief experiences upon Earth.

> *When one relies on sight to perceive the world, it is like trying to stare at the galaxy through a crack in the door.*
> *~ Kreia to Jedi Exile*

What Are Our Divine, Universal Birthrights?

Basic Tenants Regarding Our Divine Birthrights:
- They are non-negotiable.
- They are not defined by any border, country, political institution or government.
- They are not subjective, nor for morphing into subjugation by the powers that were.
- They are not philosophical, political or affiliated with a religion.
- They are currently disregarded in the manufactured reality of the 3D octopus-controlled matrix.

They Include:
- Healthy non-GMO food, shelter and clean, non-fluoridated and chlorinated water, readily available to every man, woman, child and animal upon the Earth.
- Free utilities (such as heat) based upon free energy.
- Freedom from a highly controlled global financial network that ensures debt-slavery for all citizens.
- A quality 5D *education*.
- True freedom and sovereignty.
- Respect and honor as sacred aspects of All That Is.
- Freedom to live out one's chosen life path and journey without the powers that were's influence and obstacles.
- Abundance for ALL people, not just the .001% upon the planet, i.e., the octopus and its worker bees.
- Human equality. All women and men are created equal and are to be treated with equal regard and respect.
- Freedom from tyranny, control, war, subservience, racism, sexism, fascism, religious and cultural supremacist ideologies, suppression, cruelty, torture, inhumane treatment and sub-standard living conditions.

- Freedom from thought influence (i.e., mind control, which is used extensively in television and other media), freedom of speech, diversity, creativity and expression.
- Freedom of gender choice. One's physical vehicle *does not* determine what their true gender is. There are gross misunderstandings around this and the current draconian attitudes that are prevalent in most societies must be healed.
- Freedom to love whom one chooses. Freedom from societal bias and persecution because of whom one chooses as their mate. No one has the right to interfere (judging others is interference at an energetic level) with another person's choice in this deeply personal facet of themSelves.
- The inalienable right to justice (not bought-out judges that are currently running the vast majority of the 3D judicial systems and enforcing the laws of the powers that were, which is US corporate law here in the states), equality, liberty, peace and *true* freedom.
- Equal opportunity to employ our freewill choices. In 5D, this basic tenant automatically assumes the vow to *harm none*. Since harming none is an integral part of who we know ourselves to truly be outside of the 3D matrix, there is no need to even enforce this tenant—it simply **is** because we have awakened to our true nature.

AFTERWORD

The opportunity to awaken is an individual, soul-level choice. Some will make a conscious decision to awaken and go through the ascension process, while others will choose to remain in their slumber so as to continue experiencing in a 3D reality. Either choice is equally valid. There is no right or wrong decision, only decisions around advancement or a dimensional graduation, if you will.

Awakening requires that we consciously heal and release all of our past traumas and wounds across many lifetimes and dimensions. We are being given that very opportunity and blessing in this lifetime. It is your birthright to awaken from the illusion, when you are ready to do so. It is your desire to awaken and willingness to heal that creates the opportunity for you. The steps that you are led to take to awaken yourself, helps awaken others as well. There is absolutely no judgment involved in this soul-level choice.

What's Next?

The first dominos are finally beginning to fall in a way that is noticeable to anyone paying attention. There will be much more breaking news in the coming times that will bring strong evidence that this shift is *well* underway. The key component is to know that all is right on target and that the new paradigm is on the heels of the old one. In fact, the new systems are already being put into place, some running in the background until all is ready to announce to the public at large. There are already a few systems that have been remodeled and there are many, many more to come.

What keeps us from embracing these wonderful new energies is obvious—fear and gross misunderstandings about the reality in which we live. If you but peek at the world's history of violence you will instantly grasp why every one of us has DNA that is affected by the fear factor. It is deeply ingrained and we tend to go there immediately when we are faced with great change. It is normal, but it does not have to be. We are very capable of healing and releasing fear at the cellular level. It takes conscious intention and a commitment to our spiritual growth and mastery over the third dimension.

When we are in touch with our Higher Selves, we know that we are completely prepared for whatever may come. Listening to our inner guidance is imperative now, as it's true that Angels whisper. So please slow down, stop talking so much and *listen* far more. You have a very important reason for being here right now and for many, it is to simply awaken and hold the Light on this planet during this Universal event.

It's a time to come together and remember that there are no true walls of separation between us. We must learn to recognize the dramas that are created to further the agendas of the powers that were. Transparency in all systems is the new game and so is our active participation in our new governments and all new systems that we each will have a hand in collectively creating.

If you still believe that one country is superior to another; one race, gender or religion is better than another, you are promoting the separation of mankind. Divine Integrity is about honoring every other soul upon this planet and their chosen journey—just as you desire that they honor and respect yours. Bless them and know that what others are doing or Being, from the Vista Point, is perfect for them and what they came here to learn, experience, contribute or balance through karmic agreements with others. This applies to the powers that were as well, but honoring another's journey doesn't provide the right to harm and imprison others. This choice has repercussions—and no one is immune from karmic balancing.

The Landing Phase

We are currently in the *Landing Phase* of this journey. We can see the runway for our new destination and we have much help in the tower navigating us safely to the ground. Yes, there seems to be a little turbulence, but it won't last long. Meanwhile, we should buckle our seat belts and stay seated in our Higher Selves. Just as a plane lands in phases and degrees of altitude and doesn't just plummet from 30,000 feet, we too land at our new destination and dimensional change in stages. It has been a very long plane ride my dear friends and we are all exhausted, but let's land with care and intention. There are many people already on the ground and out of the plane who have long been paving the way behind the scenes with new systems and leadership that is to come forward soon. We can anticipate some very interesting and amazing adventures ahead that will be welcomed by everyone.

Within these *new 5D systems* there is abundance for all people and you can hang your hat on that. In fact, as we proceed along this ascension path, you will be creating your own abundance in a literal sense. That is why it is so imperative that you become a clean and clear co-creator.

So hang on—this new land might be unimaginable to you right now and that's ok, just know that we are returning to who we really are and the energies from where we came, long ago. The instruction book that you feel you might be missing is inside of you, just waiting to be uncovered.

Taking This One Step Further

We can greatly contribute to this shift by taking the healing and acknowledgement process one step further. As we witness the collapse and fall of the 3D systems and all of its low vibratory tentacles, we can apply the same six-step *Conscious Acknowledgement Process* discussed in prior chapters. For example, if you were to hear that the octopus is attempting to cut out a program that assists the elderly or children, you can help heal this attempt to create more fear and feelings of helplessness by going through the six-step acknowledgment process. How do you personally feel about this action? Go beyond fear or anger—dig deep. Bring it up and then acknowledge it.

Releasing this personally helps release it from mass consciousness and disempowers the powers that were. When you hear other people talking about one of the octopus' antics or witnessing part of the 3D collapse, teach them the process of acknowledgment too. Explain to them that they too can choose to feed the octopus through anger, fear and acquiescence, or they can assist to quicken the fall and hasten the arrival of a new age of oneness and peace. The final step is to ask: *"What do I want instead of this action?"* Then allow your imagination to run rampant without limitation and become immersed within that picture as though it is happening right *now*. As we each do this and help others to remember who they really are, the slumber stops and we walk across the 3D to 5D bridge together.

It is Within You

The truth is, after this recalibration period, *all heaven* is about to break loose across Earth. It will be an awe-inspiring sight to behold as a unified force of awakened consciousness. You have been preparing for this transformation across many lifetimes.

Allow yourself to actively imagine what Earth and your daily life feels like with the octopus completely gone. Create the sights, feelings and sensations. Really visualize what you want it to be like. This way, you are feeding what we all want instead and shortening the manifestation time. Surround yourself with others who can also see the greater vision. The more that we allow only the higher energies into our lives, the faster we create. Bless everything else and hold the space for the transmutation of it.

When you no longer look outside of yourself to co-create with All That Is, you will be able to manifest so fast it will astonish you. There is the most inexplicable joy in the awakening and ascension process if we can view the massive and seemingly chaotic changes for what they are. Large change requires just that—things changing. It is the *movement* of the old that paves the foundation for the new to arrive. Embrace the salamander at your door.

As we unfurl and create more Light communities, we will begin to assemble and organize ourselves so that we can get to work healing our beautiful planet. We have much to do. Earth *will* once again flourish with our full attention, love and reverence. It is time to embrace the stewards that we are, not the conquistadors that we played out upon the stage.

*In every second you are either contributing
to humanity's oneness—or separation.*

Building a Lighthouse

We each have the capability and power to change the world simply through our beingness. What does that mean and what does that look like? Simply put, it means that when we learn how to harness and maintain our own vibration in the face of adversity, we become a beacon of Light for others who might still be struggling within the systems.

When we cross paths with someone still entrenched within the lower energies and feel unaffected ourselves, we are able to project our Light to them, becoming huge catalysts for change. This means that wherever we go and whomever we come into contact with, we have a very positive impact. We need not do anything, or even say anything to those we encounter—we need only be in our own high vibrational state to effectively share our Love and Light with other souls.

In our everyday life, we can each Be a lighthouse for others. This is not the same as proselytizing or "preaching" to others—it is not our place to convince others of *anything* for it is not our journey, it is *theirs*. It is not our place to assume that our chosen path is in any way superior or better than anyone else's chosen journey to rediscover who they really are. Self-righteousness is ego based; simply being a beacon of Light for others is an entirely different energy, seated in oneness, love and *all-encompassing* acceptance.

Tick Tock

The octopus is desperately fighting to keep you sound asleep, powerless and unaware of the matrix in which you live. It is time to wake up.

We have all been deeply asleep, but the alarm clock is ringing. If we so choose, it is now time to awaken from the dream. The drama that seems so big and scary collapses when we remember that we have been sound asleep within a matrix designed as a spiritual playground. In our awakened awareness, we can find deep gratitude for this journey in consciousness that we are now completing—even our journey dancing with the octopus.

Soon, we will look around us with deep respect and see that we, and *all* of our fellow travelers have been sleeping giants. As the curtain closes upon this particular dimensional experience, new opportunities will be presented to us for growth, healing, unlimited abundance and tremendous joy. It's all part of the transformation and transmutation of the collective "us."

May we embrace all of our experiences with deep gratitude, knowing that we came here by choice and to evolve *through* the experiences offered by life and the plan that we architected. It has been our willingness and eagerness to participate that has allowed our souls to shine. The time has arrived for us to shine brightly—*together*.

Nathan Z Townley
(Website: www.NathanZTownley.com)

FAITH

*When you have come to the edge
of all the Light you know,
and are about to step off
into the darkness of the unknown,
Faith is knowing that one of two things will happen:*

*There will be something solid to stand on,
or you will be taught how to fly.*

~ Anonymous

RESOURCES

Recommended Books
- *Ask and it is Given*, Ester and Jerry Hicks, 2004
- *Beating Cancer with Nutrition*, Patrick Quillin/Noreen Quillin, PhD, RD, CNS, 1994
- *Before There Were Words: The Energetic Meanings of Runes*, Kriss Erickson, 2012
- *Effortless Healing*, Dr. Joseph Mercola, 2015
- *The Biology of Belief*, Bruce Lipton, PhD, 2005
- *The Body Knows*, Caroline M. Sutherland, 2001
- *The Book of Chakras*, Ambika Wauters, 2002
- *The Celestine Prophecy: An Adventure*, James Redfield, 1995
- *The Complete Book of Essential Oils & Aromatherapy*, Valerie Ann Worwood, 1991
- *Confessions of an RX Drug Pusher*, Gwen Olsen, 2009
- *Contacting Your Spirit Guide*, Sylvia Browne, 2005
- *Conversations with God: An Uncommon Dialogue, Book 1*, Neale Donald Walsch, 1996
- *Crystal Enlightenment*, Katrina Raphaell, 1985
- *Crystalline Communion*, Collen Marquist/Jack Frasl, 2000
- *Energy Medicine*, Donna Eden, 1998
- *Essential Reiki*, Diane Stein, 1995
- *Genetic Roulett: The Documented Health Risks of Genetically Engineered Foods*, Jeffery M. Smith, 2007
- *Healer Wisdom*, Valeria Moore, 2008 (online Wiki subscription available)
- *Healing Ancient Wounds; The Renegade's Wisdom*, John F. Barnes, PT, 2000
- *Healing Back Pain*, John E. Sarno, MD, 1991

- *The Healing Power of Water*, Dr. Masaru Emoto, 2004
- *The Healing Tones of Chakra Bowls*, Renee Brodie, 1996
- *The Hidden Messages in Water*, Masaru Emoto, 2005
- *The Holographic Universe*, Michael Talbot, 1992
- *Homeopathic Cell Salt Remedies*, Nigey Lennon/Lionel Rolfe, 2004
- *Homeopathic Color and Sound Remedies*, Ambika Wauters, 2007
- *Homeopathic Medicine Chest*, Ambika Wauters, 2000
- *Homeopathy for the Soul*, Cassandra Lorius, 2001
- *Love is in the Earth*, Melody, 1995
- *Metaphysical Anatomy*, Evette Rose, 2012
- *Matthew, Tell Me About Heaven*, Suzanne Ward, 2001
- *The Mindbody Prescription*, John E. Sarno, 1998
- *Molecules of Emotion*, Candace B. Pert, PhD, 1997
- *Myofascial Release: The Search for Excellence*, John F. Barnes, PT, 1990
- *The One Command*, Asara Lovejoy, 2008 (Revised 2012)
- *Radical Forgiveness*, Colin C. Tipping, 2002
- *Seeds of Deception*, Jeffrey M. Smith, 2003
- *A Shot in the Dark*, Harris L. Coulter/Barbara Loe Fisher, 1991
- *The Source Field Investigations*, David Wilcock, 2011
- *Stones of the New Consciousness*, Robert Simmons, 2009
- *Stories Along the Way*, Margaret McElroy, 2008
- *Vibrational Medicine*, Richard Gerber, MD, 2001
- *You Can Heal Your Life*, Louise L. Hay, 1984

Articles

- "Scientists Prove DNA Can Be Reprogrammed by Words and Frequencies," *Galactic News, Health and Nutrition*, August 12, 2014. http://wakeup-world.com/2011/07/12/scientist-prove-dna-can-be-reprogrammed-by-words-frequencies (All information in the article is taken from the book *Vernetzte Intelligenz* by von Grazyna Fosar and Franz Bludorf, ISBN 3930243237, summarized and commented by Baerbel. The book is only available in German at this time. www.fosar-bludorf.com)

- http://humansarefree.com/2015/03/the-united-nations-exposes-chemtrails.html

Healing Music and Sound
- Marcey Hamm—www.musicbymarcey.com
- Tom Kenyon—www.tomkenyon.com

Individuals and Organizations
- www.AVEEZ.org
- www.gwenolsen.com
- Humanus Corporation (www.humanus.ca)
- THRIVE—The Movement (www.thrivemovement.com)
- www.trivedifoundation.org

Movies/Films/DVD's
- www.thrivemovement.com
- www.zeitgeistmovie.com
- Chemtrails: *The Movie—What in the World Are they Spraying?* (www.vimeo.com/16219493)
- Black Whole, Nassim Haramein, 2011 (www.Gaiam.com)

Websites and Links
- David Wilcock—www.divinecosmos.com
- Dr. Joseph Mercola—www.mercola.com
- Dr. Rima E. Laibow, M.D, Medical Director of the Natural Solutions Foundation
- One People' World Trust—www.peoplestrust1776.org
- Citizen Hearings on Disclosure—www.citizenhearing.org
- www.HAARP.net
- www.bariumblues.com/haarp1.htm
- Google: "HAARP Jesse Ventura"
- www.forbiddenknowledgetv.com
- www.carnicom.com (Clifford Carnicom—chemtrail information)

- www.willthomasonline.net (**William Thomas**—chemtrail information)
- www.aircrap.org
- www.stansberryresearch.com/gerald (**chemtrail information**)
- www.NVIC.org (**information on vaccinations**)—Barbara Loe Fisher
- www.foodpolicyfund.org (**GMO information**)
- www.nongmoshoppingguide.com (**GMO Guide**)
- www.morgellonsexposed.com/MorgellonsGwenScott.htm (**detox information**)
- www.in5d.com
- www.damanhur.org
- www.drrimatruthreports.com
- www.earthjustice.org/fracking
- www.agriculturalmissions.org/Netline_2011_002.htm
- http://articles.mercola.com/sites/articles/archive/2010/06/03/another-despicable-monsanto-move-seeks-to-devastate-haiti-further.aspx
- www.seattleglobaljustice.org/2010/08/for-immediate-release-gates-foundation-invests-in-monsanto
- www.globalresearch.ca/gmo-scandal-the-long-term-effects-of-genetically-modified-food-on-humans/14570
- www.responsibletechnology.org/gmo-dangers/gm-hormones-in-dairy
- www.chemtrails911.com/lab_tests_and_effects.htm
- http://articles.mercola.com/sites/articles/archive/2011/04/29/the-emergence-of-vaccine-induced-diseases.aspx
- http://rense.com/Datapages/morgdat1.htm
- http://rense.com/general74/chemma.htm
- www.activistpost.com/2011/10/flu-shots-contain-more-than-250-times.html

GLOSSARY

3D (Third Dimension): The dimension that we have been living in for a very long time. 3D is comprised of very heavy, dense energies in which duality (positive/negative; yin/yang) is highlighted and heavily experienced. Consciousness is limited in 3D; the veils are thick. Earth and most of her residents have or are moving out of the third dimension and into the fourth. Some are already living within the frequency of the fifth dimension.

4D (Fourth Dimension): This dimension bridges where we have resided for so long and our next destination. Many people are already carrying the frequency of the fourth dimension. It denotes a higher level of consciousness, a deeper spiritual awareness and awakening. Seeing through the charades of the octopus is as well as envisioning what a 5D world will be like. Their vista is now much higher. This "bridge" is a period of so-called "time" where humanity will go through a tremendous cleansing, both internally and externally, as all that is not of these much higher energies will simply fade away. In 4D, the global focus is one of not just rebuilding and healing our planet and ourselves in every way, but also upon transforming all systems upon this planet into the new 5D energies and frequencies. We are not that far away, regardless of how it may appear to look. There is so *much* going on behind the scenes that will soon be apparent.

5D (Fifth Dimension): This is our dimensional destination along with Gaia. Once we are fully seated into the 5D energies (those that choose to ascend) we will be living in peace, oneness and unity with a very common goal and destiny—that of restoring our beautiful planet and living as the sovereign, divine Beings that we are. The octopus no longer exists and humanity now embraces life in a non-dualic construct. It flows easily and effortlessly however, because it is the same energies and vibration from which we originally came.

All that Is: (See "God")

Architected Reality: Refers to the reality that has been orchestrated and authored by the powers that were over thousands of years, through the manipulation of humanity via their manufactured systems. These systems were carefully designed in a way that would control the masses, create debt slavery to the banking tentacle and ensure that citizens remained asleep within the systems that they are born into. The powers that were's "reality" consists of greed, control, manipulation, violence, and gross misuse of energy—ours, as well as Gaia's resources.

Amalgamated Whole: Since we are all intrinsically intertwined with each other energetically, we automatically create a united "whole." This oneness is comprised of all Beings, not just on planet Earth or even our solar system, but the entire cosmos made of countless civilizations. We are each absolutely affecting those other Beings and they are affecting us as well. Every particle of contribution and experience creates the "Amalgamated Whole" as an aggregate of the singular.

Aspect of You: We are multidimensional and interdimensional Beings. We each have a "Master Soul Self" that manifests aspects (parts) of itself in many timelines, dimensions and on various planets and galaxies purely for the priceless *experience* that each offers to the cumulative soul's knowledge, growth and wisdom. Each aspect affects the others, and often times, one aspects' experience can "bleed" into another's concurrent experience elsewhere. Many people feel an awareness of this and can tell when something important is happening to one of their other aspects. This awareness is similar to when a twin sibling "knows" and feels when their counter-part is experiencing something of significance.

Beingness: Our natural state of consciousness that can be brought forth to "override" the constant linear, mental mind and the often ruling emotional body. When we put our beingness in charge and remember how to live from this state, we operate in a vibration of deep peace, oneness, calmness and neutrality. It is the state of consciousness within us all that resides *outside* and independent of duality. In our non-physical, non-embodied state, beingness is all that we experience. Once we reach the 5D energies, we will all operate from a state of beingness. Regular meditation (whatever that looks like for you) takes us into this automatically, but we can also learn (remember) how to live our daily lives within this state.

Birthrights: We are born as divine Beings and *as* divine energy. As such, we inherently possess "birthrights" as free, sovereign Beings. Some of our very basic birthrights include abundant healthy food (which there is actually plenty of globally, if not for the octopus' systems dirty work), shelter, clothing, necessities, freedom, sovereignty and basic respect. The octopus has taught us just the opposite, but we are remembering that we possess these basic birthrights. As we do, we will create them with and for each other, remembering that what affects every other Being, affects us equally as well.

Co-Create: As aspects of Source energy, we have the full capability to create and manifest anything and everything we can possibly imagine, and we do so with our Source, not only as a "partnership" but as an inseparable composite. It is no different than a daffodil bulb planted in the earth. The bulb will, through its divine make-up and intrinsic intent to be more than it currently is, co-create with the soil, water and sunlight to transform into a beautiful flower. Our relationship with the Universe and that which we call "god" is exactly the same. It is our freewill, consciousness and intent to create that causes the Law of Attraction to kick in and the relationship of co-creation begins.

Whether we label it good or bad depends upon how focused we are upon what we want, versus what we do not want. It is pure alchemy and our potential for creation is unlimited.

Consciousness: The primary ingredient of creative thought and creation. It is the driving force, the "lighter fluid" that ignites manifestation. The non-matter that creates all matter. Our individual and collective consciousness never cease to exists, and is the force that furthers All That Is, through us and all other Beings in the entire cosmos.

Construct: As referenced in this book, a construct is like the playing field upon which we "play" in this and other realms. It is very much like a "set" upon a theatrical stage and is designed (by all of us at our higher levels) to support our collective roles and actions upon our stage. Just as props are constructed for a stage act, so is this 3D matrix a construct to support our roles while embodied upon this Earthly stage. In fact, the entire theatre is a larger construct for the playhouse itself and serves as the medium to create expression, drama, comedy, tragedy and the mundane. Our realities serve as our constructs for soul-level experiences within this chosen time and space continuum.

Core Self: Also known as our "Higher Self." That sacred part of us that is beyond the constrictions of a time-space reality such as the dense 3D reality we have lived in. It is our "Soul-Self" that we inherently connect to through our crown chakra. The more we heal ourselves, our traumas and our false beliefs, the higher our vibration and the stronger our connection to our core Selves.

Cosmic Consciousness: We have existed in a very limited state of consciousness while living in a 3D world. We have been brainwashed to somehow believe that we exist as an island, alone within a vast Universe that is teeming with highly intelligent, highly spiritual life, far more advanced than we are in every way imaginable. Because the third dimension is dualic and has been controlled by a small faction of Beings, we (Earth) have been basically quarantined from the rest of the Universe so as to limit our ability to harm others in the cosmos. As we grow into 5D consciousness, we will remember that these sentient, advanced Beings are our ancestors and part of our lineage. We will realize that we have been massively lied to by the powers that were and that we have never been alone—not for one second. As we go through this process of remembrance, we regain our higher vibrations and consciousness which will allow us to exist outside of duality, effectively returning us to cosmic consciousness. We will regain our ability and "clearance" to fully communicate with our star families who have watched over us for so long.

Creators of the Lies (The Octopus, Global Elite, Cabal, Powers That Were (also known as the Illuminati): Numerous names for the same handful of families across the globe. They consider themselves highly privileged Beings, far above the masses in which they have controlled through tyranny and manufactured reality constructs. Remaining well-hidden behind their puppets who carry out their agendas, they are now being fully exposed for what and who they really are. This is all part of our global mass awakening and it will continue full force until their energies are completely removed. Their energies cannot survive in a 5D world, it is impossible. If you wonder how such a deeply embedded program could be removed from this planet after existing here for eons, this is how. The newly arriving energies will determine their fate—their low vibrations will not be able to co-exist in the 5D frequencies, their bodies cannot withstand it. That's why every time we heal ourselves and let go of the lower vibrations, we "Lighten" up in every way, including physically at a cellular level. This is preparing us to comfortably exist within a much higher vibration and frequency, such as 5D. You can assist and facilitate in the powers that were's removal by waking up to how powerful you really are and asking "what do I want instead and how can we collectively build it?" The power is within us—it always has been.

Divine Nature: We are each comprised of pure divine Light and Love. Every cell in our bodies is nothing but this. Unconditional love is all that truly exists and we are that energy. We are aspects of that which we call God, and as such, our intrinsic nature could be nothing else.

Duality/Dualic World: When both low energies (low vibration and slow frequency) exist side by side with Light energies (high vibratory, fast frequency) it is called duality or dualic energies. In a 3D world both are able to operate within the same realm of existence.

Emissary: An agent sent on a mission to represent another. In the case of 5D energies, we refer to "Emissarial Leadership" models in which our new leaders come forth in true heart-centered service to all of humanity in the energies of oneness, cosmic consciousness and connection to Source Energy.

Followers of The Lie: Those who are still fast asleep within the illusion and the systems within the matrix of this highly dense, 3D experience.

Frequency: For the purposes of this book, energetically, our own frequency signature is determined by how low or high our vibration is at any given time, which is determined by our emotions, thoughts, responses, beliefs and feelings at any given time. The more we live in positive, high-vibratory states, the higher our frequency is.

God/Source Energy/Prime Creator/Allah/Supreme Being/All That Is: The energy and name/title that we connect to our own sense and perspective of whom/what we call our Source.

Grid: Very powerful energetic grids that run across our planet. They are called *ley lines* and they create intersecting points of cosmic and divine energies. Cleansing these grids is very critical to Gaia's ascension.

Higher Consciousness: When we intend to heal our misperceptions about who we really are and heal our traumas and "baggage" from this and all lifetimes, we achieve far higher levels of consciousness. As we journey into the *remembrance* of who we truly are, it is the remembrance itself that causes the higher consciousness to return to us. It is not a "learning" experience, because it has always been within us. We are not gaining something brand new, we are simply returning to what we have always been, underneath the illusion and veil of forgetfulness. This sacred remembering creates literal changes in our DNA and every cell in the body. This "ascension" is vibratory, physical, mental and of course, spiritual. 3D's heavy density is like having a lamp turned on, but having 20 towels over the lampshade, effectively blocking most of the Light. The light became very dim. But as we begin to acknowledge each and every towel, one by one (indicative of our traumas, wounds, misperceptions and karma) the towels become translucent and our Light gets brighter and brighter until we can actually see the shade again. The lamp never forgot that it had always been brightly lit, but the towels had blocked out the Light for so long that it was easy to forget the source of its Light. As we remove the barriers to our all-encompassing Light, we achieve higher and higher states of consciousness, awareness and *remembrance of who we really are*. When all of the towels are gone from the lamp, this is called "Enlightenment."

Higher Self: Also referred to as our Core Self, Soul Self or Highest Self. We each have a Master Soul that is an infinite stream of divine energy. Our Master Soul has many aspects that "branch off" and incarnate into many various timelines, dimensions and experiences. Why? For growth and ever-expanding experience. We each have the ability to contact and connect with our other soul aspects, and we do constantly, whether we are aware of it or not. When we go within and consciously connect with our Higher Self, we open up that infinite connection to who we are outside of this particular experience as just one aspect of our totality.

Hologram/Holographic: There is increasing scientific evidence that we do indeed live in a projected reality that is not "real" in any true sense, except through our very limited perceptions of how the cosmos operates. See "Illusion." As related to this book, this simulation of reality is the perfect playground, hologram or theatrical stage in which to act out our chosen experiences within this particular time-space continuum.

Illusion: Refers to (in the context of this book) the appearance that our reality is "real" when in fact we are living in a octopus-created "structure" that only appears as real or true. From birth, we are indoctrinated into a false reality and then taught that it is real in every way, hence creating the octopus' illusion. Nothing is as you have been taught and led to believe and the 3D systems' house of cards is now crumbling. Those who are still asleep will adamantly argue that there is no illusion, as they cannot yet perceive, and one cannot "see" what they cannot perceive.

Karmic Law: Our Universe and cosmos is ruled by set Laws of the Universe. One such Law is Karmic Law (Law of Cause and Effect), which loosely states that what we think or do is returned back to us, whether it is positive or negative. For example, if we have caused something to happen to someone else (or to any Being, including Gaia) we must then energetically balance it with a "re-action."

Knowingness: A state of beingness in which our innate intuition is coming through. There are many things that we simply know to be truth at a very deep level, beyond our mental or emotional reasoning and cognitive capacity. This level of intuitive truth is called our *knowingness*. Very often when we are in this "knowingness" state there are not adequate words within our limited languages to express "how" we know what we know—we just know it because there is a deep resonation within us that what we are perceiving is truth.

Law of Attraction/Law of "Like Attracts Like": The Law that states that like energies attract each other, whether of high or low vibration.

The teachings of Abraham (through and by Ester and Jerry Hicks/Abraham-Hicks), were the first to make the "Law of Attraction" a common name, now used around the world.

The Lie: The foundation upon which the 3D Octopus has built their manufactured reality and illusion and because of our allowance of it and our agreement from non-physical to participate in their construct.

Lightworker: A Being who has made a soul-level commitment to live in their divine Light and help others remember that they too are infinite, perfect, divine Beings of Love and Light. One who is here to anchor the Light on Earth and feels an internal drive to be in service to all of humanity and to Gaia.

Manifestation: A creation resulting from intention. This is our true power on this plane of existence. Intention is energy committed to your desired outcome. Worry is the prevention of that intention from happening. Using your imagination to actually *feel* as if what you desire has already happened is the fuel for manifestation and the creation of your life by design, not by default.

Mass Consciousness: The collective consciousness on this planet comprised of over 7 billion (current global population) thoughts and beliefs. The composite of individual consciousness.

The Matrix: The so-called reality that the so many people still believes to be actual, true and real. The matrix simply provides the platform in which we experience within this dimension. It is currently undergoing massive reconstruction for the betterment of humanity and the ending of a very long cosmic cycle.

Mirroring: What we witness in the outside world is in fact a mirror of what we think and believe on the inside. The external world reflects our internal world in every way. As we shift internally, our external world mirrors those changes.

Multidimensional: The nature of our soul. We exist within many dimensions, concurrently and simultaneously. There are aspects of our Master Soul that are experiencing in all dimensions, planes of existence and timelines, but this has been extremely hidden from our knowledge by the octopus. We access these other dimensions in our periods of sleep, but we also travel in and out of these dimensions during our waking hours, but most often without our conscious awareness. We all have the ability to extract and utilize our aspects' experiences, skills and talents by intention and they are able to access ours as well. Anyone can do this.

Octopus: The Global Elite, Powers That Were, Illuminati, Cabal. The handful of elite families that have controlled this planet for thousands of years through their lineage, which they fully believe to be far superior and of more value than the rest of the citizens of Earth.

Parallel Reality: We each operate within many dimensions and time-space realities at any given time and all at once. We are multi and interdimensional Beings. Once an energy stream is started and projected forward, it must complete itself. There are many "versions" of your current reality playing out at once in what is referred to as a "parallel reality." It is much like a multiplex movie theatre, all playing a similar version of what you now call your "reality" and life. All of the projected energy of your life's choices is continuing to play out in these various theatres. We can access these parallel lives if we choose to and we are affected by them and vice-versa. They overlap each other, but are separated, much like the membranes that make up a honey-comb. There is one large honey-comb, but many various spaces within it, separated only by a thin membrane.

Soul Families: A group of souls that frequently reincarnate together, playing varying roles in which to fulfill soul-level agreements and contracts with each other over many, many lifetimes.

Sovereignty: Our innate divine part of God/All That Is renders us sovereign Beings of Light. We have basic, inalienable rights to be completely free of rule, unrestricted, acting on our own behalf to carry out what is in our best and highest good as a divine Being. As we remember who we are, we become "internally governed" by our highest principles that are also based upon the highest good of all, and within the vibration and frequency of Love. In 5D, there is no need for judicial systems and laws that are designed to solely benefit the powers that were. In 5D we are all free Beings and our actions and deeds are based upon the honoring of Universal Laws.

Spirituality: A word or label that has been given to describe our true nature—we are divine Light first and foremost as extensions of our Source. Our soul is often referred to as our "spirit" and as such, the word "spirituality" speaks of the true nature of who we really are. It is our eternal essence beyond our physical bodies. Spirituality has nothing to do with organized religious institutions directly, although many believe that they are intertwined.

The Systems: All of the tentacles of the Octopus; the societal outlets taken over by the Octopus to control the 3D matrix. The primary systems include: education, religious institutions, government/politics, science, the military, the media, the food industry, legal system and our ecology.

Tentacles: See "The Systems."

Tribe: See "Soul Family."

Universal Laws: The many laws that govern our Universe by default. Most are not aware of these basic Universal Laws or that their lives are following these laws, regardless of their awareness of them.

Universal Mind: Individuality is experienced through our personas, but in truth, we are all as one, intricately enmeshed and inseparable. As one, we are part of the Universal Mind. We are bound together by our consciousness—not just on this planet, but also the millions of other planets teeming with life as well. All combined, we encompass Source Mind, and Source Mind encompasses all of us in an ever-expanding web that we call life. There is but one consciousness and it is unbound, unlimited and all encompassing. Your mind and the Universal Mind are inherently one.

Universal Truths: Based upon The Universal Laws. The controlling entities upon this planet have greatly suppressed (by intention) how our Universe truly operates and our individual and collective unlimited capacity to manifest through the Universal Laws. This sacred knowledge has been kept from us at any cost to keep us slumbering to who we really are and what we are actually capable of.

Vibration/Vibrational Energy: A vibration is measured as a body or particle in motion, or oscillating. In spiritual terminology, we are energetic Beings, first and foremost. Our own personal vibration is determined by how we choose to think, believe, and what emotions we process and release or hang on to. Our vibration is also determined by how well we care for our physical, mental, emotional and spiritual bodies. This care is critical to our vibration and resulting frequency. When we are experiencing a high vibration, we feel great, free and happy. Our thoughts are positive, light and produce positive manifestations. When our vibration is low it can feel like a dense, heavy energy surrounds us. The key to our reaching 5D is to continually raise our vibration and learn how to maintain it.

ABOUT THE AUTHOR

For additional information about Nathan Z Townley or *The Global Band of Light Project*, please visit www.nathanztownley.com.

Nathan Z Townley is a visionary, author, entrepreneur, speaker and ordained non-sectarian minister. He is co-founder of *The Global Band of Light Project (GBL)*. GBL collaborates with other humanitarian projects to create new 5D societal systems that are currently anchoring into our reality.

The illusion of separation in mind, body and spirit has prevented our cohesion and unity. *The Global Band of Light Project* offers a new platform in which we can truly express our collective intent for a planet foundationally rooted in love, peace, unity, truth and Light.

Our motto: "If it's not good for all, it's not good for one" **and** "If it's not good for one, it's not good for all." This axiom is critical to the newly arriving 5D (fifth dimensional) energies.

Blessings and Love galore,
Nathan Z Townley, Co-founder
The Global Band of Light Project